Erratum

Owing to a printer's error, pp. l and arabic 1 appear in reversed order.

REGENTS CRITICS SERIES

General Editor: Paul A. Olson

EMERSON'S
LITERARY CRITICISM

Other volumes in the Regents Critics Series are:

Emerson's
Literary Criticism

Edited by
Eric W. Carlson

UNIVERSITY OF NEBRASKA PRESS
LINCOLN AND LONDON

PN
37
.E45

UNP

Publishers on the Plains

Copyrighted material used by permission is listed in the
Acknowledgments, p. 243

Library of Congress Cataloging in Publication Data
Emerson, Ralph Waldo, 1803–1882.
    Emerson's literary criticism.

    (Regents critics series)
    Bibliography: p. 237
    Includes index.
    1. Literature—Collected works.   I. Carlson, Eric W.   II. Title.
PN.37.E45   1979   809   75–38053
ISBN   0-8032-1403-0

MANUFACTURED IN THE UNITED STATES OF AMERICA

Regents Critics Series

The Regents Critics Series provides reading texts of significant literary critics in the Western tradition. The series treats criticism as a useful tool: an introduction to the critic's own poetry and prose if he is a poet or novelist, an introduction to other work in his day if he is more judge than creator. Nowhere is criticism regarded as an end in itself but as what it is—a means to the understanding of the language of art as it has existed and been understood in various periods and societies.

Each volume includes a scholarly introduction which describes how the work collected came to be written, and suggests its uses. All texts are edited in the most conservative fashion consonant with the production of a good reading text; and all translated texts observe the dictum that the letter gives life and the spirit kills when a technical or rigorous passage is being put into English. Other types of passages may be more freely treated. Notes and other scholarly paraphernalia are restricted to the essential minimum. Such features as a bibliographical check-list or an index are carried where they are appropriate to the work in hand. If a volume is the first collection of the author's critical writing, this is noted in the bibliographical data.

PAUL A. OLSON

University of Nebraska–Lincoln

04634

Contents

List of Abbreviations

CEC   *The Correspondence of Emerson and Carlyle.* Edited by Joseph
       Slater. New York: Columbia University Press, 1964.

EL   *The Early Lectures of Ralph Waldo Emerson.* Edited by Stephen E.
       Whicher, Robert E. Spiller, and Wallace E. Williams. 3 vols.
       Cambridge, Mass.: Harvard University Press, Belknap Press,
       1959–72.

J   *The Journals of Ralph Waldo Emerson.* Edited by Edward Waldo
       Emerson and Waldo Emerson Forbes. 10 vols. Boston:
       Houghton Mifflin Co., 1909–14.

JMN   *The Journals and Miscellaneous Notebooks of Ralph Waldo Emerson.*
       Edited by W. H. Gilman et al. 14 vols. Cambridge, Mass.:
       Harvard University Press, Belknap Press, 1960–.

L   *The Letters of Ralph Waldo Emerson.* Edited by Ralph L. Rusk. 6
       vols. New York: Columbia University Press, 1939.

W   *The Complete Works of Ralph Waldo Emerson.* Edited by Edward
       W. Emerson. 12 vols. Boston: Houghton Mifflin Co., 1903–4.

Introduction

The Emerson revival of the 1960s and 1970s is undoubtedly attributable, in part, to the recently published Harvard editions of the early lectures and the journals. The journals especially seem to have become the primary source for new answers to the question *What, exactly, is "Emerson"?*[1] The turbulence of excited discovery has produced its own ground swell of Emerson studies which, if not quite comparable to the flood of the early 1950s, are noteworthy for their distinguished authorship and for their depth, diversity, and significance. These evaluations concentrate on Emerson as literary artist, as poet, as fountainhead of American Orphism and the American Sublime, and as the main channel of cultural continuity through "auto-American-biography."[2] Consequently, Emerson's ideas on art, literature, and criticism have assumed an increasing importance in discussions of his epistemology, symbolism, style, artistic transcendentalism, of the Emersonian Sublime, the Jungian psyche, of critical principles, and cultural values. For two reasons, at least, his literary criticism at its best belongs to the main body of his work: it is both intuitive in mode and poetic in expression; and his treatment of art as experience is closely linked to his conceptions of the self, of nature, of America, and to experience as art. It is in the context of these new appreciations of Emerson that this anthology has been compiled and edited.

The need for an anthology such as this was foreseen by the authors of several earlier studies of Emerson's criticism. In his lengthy survey, *American Criticism* (1928), Norman Foerster remarked that, if Emerson's widely scattered critical ideas were brought together, they would present "an imposing bulk," comprehensive, principled, coherent, and unified by a large vision of man and nature. Similarly, in *American Renaissance* (1941), F. O. Matthiessen noted that Emerson's "service to the development of our literature was enormous in that he made the first full examination of its potentialities," and called attention to the "considerable body of Emerson's observations that pose, with a fullness we will not encounter elsewhere, the problems of the artist as they were faced by Emerson and his contemporaries. Many of these observations also possess a continuing validity. In this respect Emerson is comparable to Coleridge." Subsequently, when Alfred Kazin and Daniel Aaron offered readers a more varied range in *Emerson: A Modern Anthology* (1958), they included passages to show Emerson as the "first great theoretician of an American art based on individual vision and technical function." While praising Emerson as a "luminous and inspiring" critic and as "one of the shrewdest critics who ever lived," with an "extraordinarily developed sense of style as a writer's instrument," they also recognized him as "the great pioneer of a 'functional' American aesthetic."[3]

This anthology attempts, then, to give a representative selection from the formidable bulk of relevant material in the forty-odd volumes (new editions and old) of Emerson's works. Parts I and II overlap, since they contain not only Emerson's principal statements on the functions of art, literature, and language, but also the intimate symbolic relation between these and nature. Thus these two parts necessarily touch on his theories of correspondence, perception (epistemology), and reality as organic process; but they also treat of the inseparable connection within a culture of its art and its science, and, finally, the qualities of Emerson's critical thought that stemmed from his faith in the "Universal" or "Sublime," an aspect of his Transcendentalism. In the corresponding sections 1 and 2 of this introduction I have tried to sum up, in the briefest fashion, the major influences on Emerson's thought: American transcendentalism and experience; Plato, Plotinus, and the "Trismegisti"; the oriental classics; Swedenborg, Sampson Reed, and Coleridge; and the new science.

In Part III, "The Art of Rhetoric," Emerson the rhetorician and master stylist is introduced through some of his most acute observations on the technics of poetry and prose. Part IV, "Toward a Modern Critical Perspective," illustrates Emerson's adaptation of organic theory, his application of a Transcendental aesthetic, his post-Christian modernism, and his views of the novel—all of which are also defined in section 4 of this introduction.

Part V, "Writers and Books," introduced by three general essays on literature, presents a wide range of applied criticism. The headnotes not only comment on the selections, but also often describe Emerson's response to the author's other work. For additional passages on these writers, the reader should consult the index.

1. Art as Experience

One of the great integrators of art, philosophy, and religion, Emerson did not conceive of or apply his theory of criticism as a narrow specialty. Thus his challenging question in *Nature* (1836) implies that the role of art as experience is central to any reconstruction of thought and culture. Speaking of his forerunners, he asks, "Why should we not have a poetry and a philosophy of insight and not of tradition, and a religion by revelation to us, and not the history of theirs?" Hamlin Garland and others read this as a challenge Emerson cannot have intended: why should Garland read Shakespeare rather than write something better for his fellow Americans than any writer now dead could have done? Instead, Emerson intended, in part at least, quite another thought: every generation must recreate great works in terms of its own experience and climate of opinion.

The burden of developing such a radical experientialism fell not only to Emerson and his contemporaries, but also to his followers among pragmatists and process philosophers, notably William James, C. S. Peirce, James Mark Baldwin, John Dewey, Alfred North Whitehead, and Suzanne Langer. Thus today his effect is felt not only by his own admiring readers, but also by those responding to the influence of philosophers he inspired and guided. His belief in experience had momentous consequences he could not have foreseen. One instance is William James. In preparing his address for the Emerson Centenary in Concord in 1903, James annotated and carefully cross-referenced the nine volumes of Emerson's essays. After his reading in "the divine Emerson," he characterized him as an "Artist," adding that Emerson himself was "a real seer," one who not only could perceive "the full squalor of the individual fact," but could also see "the transfiguration." In 1929 John Dewey rated

Emerson "the one citizen of the New World fit to have his name uttered in the same breath with that of Plato."[4] But it had been William James, more than Dewey or the others, who recognized not only Emerson's emphasis on "Action" and "the mutual reaction of thought and life," but also Emerson's "modern transcendental idealism," especially the Over-Soul as an active power transmitting itself through man and nature. It seems only right that James, who saw Emerson as poet, pragmatist, and transcendentalist in one, should himself be singled out as "the central figure of what should be called neo-transcendentalism in New England. Quite definitely in the line of descent from Emerson."[5]

This linking of Emerson with American pragmatism and experientialism may have helped in some measure to liberate his reputation from such undefined and often misleading tags as *romantic, idealist, Platonist,* and *transcendentalist* (which Emerson on one occasion took sharp exception to) (*L* 3:18). Platonic idealism and transcendentalism posit a world of absolute "Ideas" or "Forms", existing only in the realm of essence as "antecedent realities" (to use Dewey's term);[6] such a metaphysic tends to assert that the highest power of the mind is to *escape* into that world of pure "Ideas". Emerson's view, on the contrary, posits the kind of experience in which the intellect discovers reality by perceiving possible new dimensions and by finding unsuspected relations between fact and fact, or fact and thought:

> *Eyes and no eyes.* One man sees the fact or object, and another sees the power of it; one the triangle, and the other the cone which is generated by the revolution of a triangle. [*J* 8:42; *JMN* 11:147]

> *Intellect.* I notice that I value nothing so much as the threads that spin from a thought to a fact, and from one fact to another fact, making both experiences valuable and presentable, which were insignificant before, and weaving together into rich webs all solitary observations. [*J* 8:504; *JMN* 13:373–74]

It was also the concept of nature as process (as "fluxions," "flow," "metamorphosis") that enabled Emerson to transcend the old dichotomy between "Idea-ism" and positivist objectivism. After tracing the evolution of Emerson's method as a philosopher, William B. Barton concluded that "Emerson, in fact, was among the first modern philosophers to set forth the outlines of a thorough-going process philosophy of organism founded on evolutionary principles. In its ontological implications it is at least as imposing as Bergson's or Whitehead's, although his orientation is that of poet rather than scientist or philosopher of science."[7] When the spirit manifests itself in day and night, river and stars, beast and bird, those manifestations are said by Emerson to "pre-exist in necessary Ideas in the mind of God," that is, in organic tendencies within the creative or "educated Will" others call God. Emerson's organicism ("pure Theism," "Beautiful Necessity") anticipates Whitehead's process philosophy, American evolutionary process theology,[8] the noögenesis of Pierre Teilhard de Chardin, and the cosmic humanism of Oliver Reiser.

In looking to the past for influences on his thought, we find that Emerson identified the problem of the relation between mind and matter with the Egyptians and Brahmans, Pythagoras and Plato, Bacon, Leibnitz, and Swedenborg. Others distinguished in this lineage of the *prisci theologi* are named in "Intellect" and in "The Poet": Orpheus, Empedocles, Heraclitus, Plato, Proclus, Iamblichus. Elsewhere the "Trismegisti" are listed as Moses, Zoroaster, Pythagoras, Heraclitus, Socrates, Jesus, Confucius, St. Augustine, Giordano Bruno, Spinoza, Swedenborg, Synesius, Plotinus (*J* 4:498). Iamblichus wrote a life of Pythagoras that Emerson read "with joy." The "cyclus" of "orphic words" is found in Bacon, Ralph Cudworth, and Plutarch, as well as in Plato. These prophets and oracles of "the old religion" combine science and art at once—poetry, music, dancing, mathematics—into a worship of something that makes the "sanctities of Christianity look *parvenues* and popular" (*W* 2:346). According to Harold Bloom, however, Emerson developed a peculiarly American Orphism, which owed very little to these ancients.[9]

The strong and constant influence of Plato on Emerson's thought is most evident in "Plato; or, The Philosopher" and "Plato: New Readings," both in *Representative Men*. Except for certain reservations, Emerson describes Plato's philosophic ideas with such sympathy and cogency that his identification with them (as he understands them) is unmistakable. Plato's idea of the soul as pervasive throughout nature leads Emerson to list a series of interpenetrative polarities and to recognize Plato as the "balanced soul" who perceived and absorbed both Eastern and European values. Though Plato adored the super-essential, the Ineffable, he also had the European belief in the knowableness of things through the correspondence of matter to mind. When he tried to conceptualize the world, he failed: "The perfect enigma remains." Nevertheless, his insights are the product of organic expansions. In Plato, "intellect is always moral" and to *Platonize* is to "delight in giving a spiritual, that is, an ethico-intellectual expression to every truth, by exhibiting an ulterior end [ultimate natural consequence] which is yet legitimate [organic] to it." In short, Emerson's use of *Platonic* seems more often related to bipolar organicism than to Plato's mysticism or classical dualism.[10]

In Neo-Platonism Emerson was most attracted by the idea of God as a ceaseless source of energy, of the All-Soul as a light; and by Plotinus's system of "emanations," of endless flux and flow from the divine source—the basis for the Neo-Platonic theory of beauty, with its faith in pure intuition and in nature as symbolic of spiritual values. For Matthiessen and Vivian Hopkins, this theory of the "flowing" is the dominant philosophical strain in Emerson's aesthetics.[11] Dissatisfied with "unprofitable quietists," however, Emerson defined self-reliance as a participative sharing in the Over-Soul, conceiving beauty as "gliding through the sea of form" and as related to the whole, the local as well as the universal. Emerson did not neglect sensory beauty, whereas the Platonists' ecstasy was experienced through the pure intellect, not through the senses.[12]

Both Frederic Ives Carpenter and Arthur Christy concur in the opinion that Platonism and Neo-Platonism prepared Emerson for his reading of the oriental classics then being translated.[13] Although Emerson wrote of these scriptures, "I want not the metaphysics, but only the literature of them" (*J* 10:248), he recorded from them such ideas as the universality of the moral sentiment, the identity of speculative and practical thought, the goodness of man (in Confucius), the "vast-flowing vigor" (Being) in Mencius, the Tao as a source of cosmic unity, and a whole series of Hindu doctrines: belief in Brahma, the Vedic impersonal Supreme Being, the role of maya, the law of Identity, the karma process as retribution, and the eschatology of Atman.

In his theory of correspondence Emerson proclaimed that "the world is emblematic. . . . The whole of nature is a metaphor of the human mind. . . . The axioms of physics translate the laws of ethics."[14] Such passages resemble Jonathan Edwards's *Images; or, Shadows of Divine Things*, entries #8 and #59, the latter concluding with the question, "Why is it not rational to suppose that the corporeal and visible world should be designedly made and constituted in analogy to the more spiritual, noble, and real world?"[15] However, Emerson's theory probably owed much more to Sampson Reed, Swedenborg, and possibly Alexander von Humboldt. Of Swedenborg's writings, Emerson's library contained fifteen titles, including *A Treatise concerning Heaven and Its Wonders, and also concerning Hell* (London, 1823). In chapters 12 and 13 of that work, Swedenborg wrote: "The whole natural world corresponds to the spiritual world, and not merely the natural world in general, but also every particular of it; and as a consequence every thing in the natural world that springs from the spiritual world is called a correspondent."[16] In 1834 Emerson found the views of the Swedenborgians "deeply interesting"; they had "in common with all the Trismegisti, the belief in the Natural World as strictly the symbol or exponent of the Spiritual, and part for part."[17] Citing Burns, Cowper, Wordsworth, Carlyle, Goethe, and Swedenborg as inspired by this idea, he singled out Swedenborg for having "pierced the emblematic or spiritual character of the visible, audible, tangible world" (*W* 1:112–13). Emerson's indebtedness to Humboldt, however, is not so clear. Although he owned Humboldt's *Travels, Cosmos*, and *Aspects of Nature*, and praised the "wonderful Humboldt" and his *Cosmos* in the published version of the brief tribute at the centennial in 1869 of his birth, he significantly fails to mention the famous dictum on nature as the mirror of mind (*W* 11:457).

Emerson was also impressed by Swedenborg's moral insights, visionary powers, and perception theory (man as product of his own thought, affection, will—"As he is, so he sees"). But in "Swedenborg;

or, The Mystic" (*W* 4:93–146), he incisively criticizes and rejects Swedenborg's study of the spiritual world as having been "narrowed and defeated by the exclusively theologic direction" of his inquiries: "His perception of nature is not human and universal, but is mystical and Hebraic. He fastens each natural object to a theologic notion;—a horse signifies carnal understanding; a tree, perception; the moon, faith. . . . The slippery Proteus is not so easily caught. . . . The dictionary of symbols is yet to be written" (*W* 4:121).

Because Emerson repudiated Swedenborg's symbolism where it became a system of static doctrinal meanings imposed on natural facts, there is no reason to think that he would have been greatly impressed or influenced by the emblem writers of the Renaissance. Emerson's symbology was experiential and organic in its function and context (each in the all), whereas the emblem writer chose his conventional symbol for its predetermined, static meaning, in order to arouse a stock response or to illustrate a moral lesson. Only one of the famous emblem anthologies—Francis Quarles's *Emblems* (1635)—is cited by Emerson, and then as an example of the author's "quite cool" use of Fancy, as distinguished from Imagination (*W* 8:28).

In her analysis of Emerson's theory of the symbol, Vivian Hopkins contrasts Emerson's "ideal" and "spiritual" conception with Blake's "structural" view. Blake "differs from Emerson in maintaining that inner perception cannot be grasped without concrete form. . . . While Blake thinks of an integral fusion between matter and spirit, Emerson conceives of spirit as flowing out of the matter which it has vitalized in the moment of creation."[18] The material object is only of temporary value in objectifying the poet's spiritual intuition; as the spirit flows on, it discards the object, seeking novelty and variety of expression. The poet, in Emerson's words, "perceives the independence of the thought on [from] the symbol, the stability of the thought, the accidency and fugacity of the symbol. . . . he stands one step nearer to things, and sees the flowing or metamorphosis; perceives that thought is multiform; that within the form of every creature is a force impelling it to ascend into a higher form" ("The Poet," Part I). Is this overemphasizing spirit at the expense of vehicle? It is, according to

Vivian Hopkins; Emerson's vision is Plotinian: the spiritual and the material are not reconciled or fused. But that is taking the words *accidency* and *fugacity* out of context and applying them to the individual work of art, which has its own unique "meaning." Rather, the context of the passage implies a philosophical justification: "Within the form of every creature is a force impelling it to ascend into a higher form." But "what baulks all language is, the broad, radiating, immensely distributive action of Nature or spirit. If it were linear, if it were successive, step by step, jet after jet, like our small human agency, we could follow it with language; but it mocks us" (*J* 9:114). "In nature, each individual symbol plays innumerable parts, as each particle of matter circulates in turn through every system. The central identity enables any one symbol to express successively all the qualities and shades of real being" (*W* 4:121). Such are but a few of many statements showing that Emerson earned his way experientially to his radical and democratic aesthetic.[19]

Viewing nature as a dictionary of symbolism, Emerson read avidly in the scientific literature of his day. In science "every secret opened goes to authorize our aesthetics" (*J* 10:393). He recognized the necessity of laboratory science—"of nomenclature, of minute physiological research, of the retort, the scalpel, and the scales" (*EL* 1:80). But such were only means: "analytical inspection" and "dissection" had to be complemented by "divination" and "poetry," by a "theory of animated nature" that would "integrate the particulars." Anticipating the holistic science of a later time, e.g., ecology today, Emerson looked for "the love of the Whole" to integrate analysis with "the place and relations of the subject . . . under the sun and in the landscape" (*J* 3:293; *JMN* 4:288; see also the lectures on science in *EL* 1:183; 2:22–40).

The question of evolution was crucial for Emerson, believing, as he did, in reality as process. Before 1841 he derived his general belief in an ascending "scale of being" from secondary evolutionary thinkers such as F. W. J. Schelling, Leibnitz, Charles Bell, Goethe, and Coleridge, and from scientists J. F. W. Herschel, Charles Lyell, Lamarck, Linnaeus, Erasmus Darwin, Humboldt, and others. In *Nature* (1836) he stated that "the laws of physics translate the laws of ethics."

John Hunter's "electric word" of a hundred years earlier, "*arrested and progressive development*," appealed to him (*W* 8:7–8), as did "melioration," favorable mutational responses to demands of "circumstance" (see "Fate"). By the 1850s Emerson had imaginatively reconciled the biological theory of ameliorating evolution and the ancient doctrine of emanation into a unified science of the cosmos. Unlike Coleridge, he did not reject the "bestial theory" of evolution, nor like Louis Agassiz condemn Charles Darwin's view as "materialistic." Yet, in 1873, he quoted Johann Stallo's "Animals are but foetal forms of man" as if he considered that Darwin's *Origin of Species* presented no more than a confirmation of the pre-Darwinian belief in an upward unfolding of Creative Mind from lower to higher forms of life (*J* 10:423). This new theory of evolution seemed to him to add scientific support to his own "poetic" or symbolic vision of the "moral Sublime," "the law of Laws," and his faith that through the universe "a great and beneficent tendency irresistibly streams" (*W* 4:186).

In the "Emersonian sublime" (Hopkins) and "the American Sublime" (Bloom), the touchstone is the closeness of art to greatness of nature, the artist inspired by awareness of "the sublimest laws" playing "through atoms and galaxies." In Emerson's view, as science continues step by step to verify the operation of law and purposefulness in the universe, it reveals at the same time the laws governing man's mind, spirit, and conduct (*W* 8:211, 223; 10:335). Thus, too, in contrast to the fragmentary Greek and Hebrew scriptures and even the "celestial stanzas" chanted by Jesus, the Moral Poem or Epos (the moral sublime) will have "epical integrity." The "new Teacher" will be the interpreter: he "shall see the world to be the mirror of the soul; shall see the identity of the law of gravitation with purity of heart; and shall show that the Ought, that Duty, is one thing with Science, with Beauty, with Joy" (*J* 4:425; *W* 1:151; *JMN* 5:476).

2. The Creative Process

With "solar eyes," Emerson's "centered" and "spheral" man maintains a delicate balance within his world of experience, his magnetic field of polar energies. Frequent metaphorical allusions to flood tides, streams, and currents of energy imply a Spirit that is not only a universal organic process, but also a dynamic nuclear power which, once tapped, will release the intellectual, emotional, and moral forces within the individual psyche. This "*dream*-power" is not to be equated with blind "instinct," romantic impulse, or whim; nor can it be labeled simply "idealism" or "mysticism" without the risk of serious misunderstanding. Many readers have not made it beyond the shoals of Emerson's occasionally abstract and Platonic language, thus failing to discover Melville's "deep-diver" Emerson or that Emerson characterized by the nature essayist Annie Dillard as "wildman."

In *Symbolism and American Literature*, Charles Feidelson rightly maintains that the ultimate aim of Emerson's work was "to force a revision in philosophy that would justify and encourage literature, while at the same time it proposed the poetic outlook as a corrective to traditional metaphysics and epistemology."[20] For Emerson, this poetic method and symbolic vision would not demean the object or the thing known for the sake of solipsistic introspection, but would, as in the dialogues of Plato, uncover "a germ of expansion" in every fact, so that every fact is carried upward to a higher sense. "The mind does not create what it perceives, any more than the eye creates the rose."[21] Mind and object become functions in the organic process of knowing. Out of the perceiver's interaction with the sensuous fact—this chair or this table—beauty and truth emerge in the process of realization. As Matthiessen also noted, Emerson most admired organic wholeness and, "at his most poised, could reconcile the claims of opposites in his view of art as 'an habitual respect to the whole by an eye loving beauty in detail.' "[22] Emerson described "two powers of the imagination, one that of knowing the symbolic character of things and treating them as representative; and the other . . . is practically the tenaciousness of an image, cleaving unto it and letting it not go" (*J* 7:160; *JMN* 9:360). In another journal passage, however, he referred to poetic perception as "the only truth" because realized "from within":

Poetry is the only verity. Wordsworth said of his Ode it was poetry, but he did not know it was the only truth.

Poet sees the stars, because he makes them. Perception makes. We can only see what we make, all our desires are procreant. Perception has a destiny. I notice that all poetry comes, or all becomes poetry, when we look from within and are using all as if the mind made it. [*J* 8:321]

Despite the "mystical emphasis" that Vivian Hopkins found embarrassing, she concluded that Emerson's concept of inspiration avoided "the opium fumes of De Quincey, the egotism of Byron, the sensualism of the young Goethe," and was more responsible than Plato's "divine madness."[23] Although it included the effort to recapture the freshness of a child's Adam-like vision, it had more of the experiential depth and the disciplined control of a mature mind. Emerson's awareness of the stages of control in the creative process is convincingly made clear in "Inspiration" (*W* 8:272–97), where he answers the question "Are these moods in any degree within control?" by discussing nine sources by which inspiration can be induced. To appreciate Emerson's nineteenth-century insights, one need only compare his many comments on creativity with Henri Poincaré's views as developed by Graham Wallas in *The Art of Thought*.[24] Although creativity at moments seems to Emerson ineffable, the process is often described as having natural cause, continuity, and consequence; it is understandable, verifiable, and, to some degree, controllable. In addition to "Inspiration," the key essays are *Nature*, "The American Scholar," "Self-Reliance," "Intellect," "Experience," "The Natural History of the Intellect," and "Poetry and Imagination."

The process begins with sense perception, "joyful perception" (also described as "recipiency"), followed by "pious reception" or "obedience" on the part of the "intellect receptive." As the artist must "first please the eye," so the appreciator must respond participatively through some yielding, an "active passivity," a "going with." The will must be relatively submissive to avoid interference by "the meddling intellect." Next, after the period of incubation, short or long as the case may be, comes the stage of Intimation-Illumination (the Poincaré-Wallas term). The intimation "hovers in gleams, suggestions, tantalizing, unpossessed" until it reaches the Imagination, "the little chamber in the brain where is generated the explosive force which, by gentle shocks, sets in action the intellectual world." This flash of creative insight Emerson variously calls "inner perception," "symbolic sight," and "inspiration." The process of flowing or flooding or "undulation" culminates in "intellect constructive," a new mode of perception, "a very high sort of seeing." To change the metaphor, the raw material of inchoate experience is converted by "metamorphosis" into realization. The trancelike nature of the Illumination led Emerson to speak of "trance," "ecstasy," and "enthusiasm." The essay "Intellect" (reprinted here) presents an amazingly modern grasp of the creative process, especially the interplay of "receptivity" (or incubation) and "revelation" (or intellective insight). Sometimes the Illumination, "this dangerous little minute," brings such elevating excitement that "the wine glass shakes, the wine is spilled." One such instance, without the wine glass, is described in the famous passage in *Nature* that concludes: ". . . all mean egotism vanishes. I become a transparent eyeball; I am nothing; I see all; the currents of the Universal Being circulate through me; I am part and parcel of God" (*W* 1:10). When the lens of the imagination is clear and in harmonic focus, the power of the Spirit will flow freely ("the currents . . . circulate") through the receptive Self.

Six years later Emerson felt such "moments of illumination" to be in "wild contrast" to the life of the understanding, the two showing no dispositon to reconcile themselves (*W* 1:353–54). "We pass from thought to thought easily, but not from realization to realization" (*J* 8:230). Yet poetry requires precisely such "*supervoluntary ends effected by supervoluntary means*" (*W* 12:72).

Many have seized on Emerson's experiencing such "double consciousness" as proof of his essential dualism. Stephen E. Whicher resolves what he calls this "baffling monistic dualism, or dualistic monism" by crossing the polarities of the One and the Many, of Reason and Understanding, of self-reliance and the Over-Soul, within a "polar field."[25] But Emerson himself described these organic interrelations in his essay "Character":

> Everything in nature is bipolar, or has a positive and a negative pole. There is a male and a female, a spirit and a fact, a north and a south. Spirit is the positive, the event is the negative. Will is the north, action the south pole. Character may be ranked as having its natural place in the north. It shares the magnetic currents of the system. The feeble souls are drawn to the south or negative pole. [*W* 3:97]

In "Fate" the "double consciousness" is likened to a circus rider nimbly alternating from one horse, his private nature, to another horse, his public nature, his relation to the Universe. For all that, Emerson ends on a highly monistic note: "Let us build altars to the Blessed Unity," a line repeated, with slight variation (". . . to the Beautiful Necessity"), in each of his concluding paragraphs. Beauty is deified as one of the manifestations of the "indwelling" God of the Universe.

In *Biographia Literaria*, which Emerson considered "the best book of criticism in the English language,"[26] Coleridge laid out the case for an organic theory of knowing. "All knowledge," he wrote, "rests on the co-incidence of an object with a subject," on their "intimate coalition." Knowledge is a process: "*We* can only *know* by the act of *becoming*." In such knowing there are "unconscious thoughts," out of which "master-currents" reveal themselves in moments of illumination. Inner perception depends on an integrative "identity" or knowing "from within," an "interpenetration" that involves the whole man.

Also very influential on the young Emerson was Sampson Reed's "Observations on the Growth of the Mind" (1826). Like Coleridge, Reed conceived the imagination as interpenetrative: "Finding a resting-place in every created object, it will enter it and explore its hidden treasures, the relation in which it stands to mind, and reveal the love it bears to its Creator." In this act of entering into, the perceiver will "respect the smallest blade which grows, and permit it to speak for itself." At the same time, the mind of the perceiver will be catching "a glimpse of itself" and will be speaking the language "which actually belongs to his own mind" in an experiential realization of his feelings and thoughts. His thinking will be integrative and creative. When thought is reflected back through the object, when "the dim glass" of nature serves as an emblem of the soul's inner life, then the process becomes one of self-realization.

According to Coleridge, a sense of the Beautiful is activated by the harmonic response that occurs when the appreciator's "heart" has been "preconfigured" to an intuitive "taste." Emerson's own *heart* metaphor more graphically suggests the organic function of intellect: "The intelligent mind is forever coming into relation with all the objects of nature and time, until from a vital point it becomes a great heart from which the blood rolls to the distant channels of things, and to which, from those distant channels, it returns" (*J* 4:107). The concept of preconfiguration appears in Emerson's "pre-established harmony," "constitution," "angle of vision," "selecting principle," and "character." It is the point of several aphorisms: "Mind makes the senses it sees with"; " 'Tis the good reader that maketh the good book"; "All the thoughts of turtle are turtle"; "What we are, that only can we see." So, too, "All history becomes subjective" when read actively, when understood in terms of individual history, which is to say, the individual's capacity to imagine or rerealize the culture of the past in terms of his own individuated experience and growth. The ambiguous term *subjective* repeatedly had to be defined, as in the essay "Experience," so as to distinguish its positive from its negative connotations.

Several studies of Emerson's poetry, notably those by Hyatt Waggoner, Harold Bloom, and Albert Gelpi, seem agreed not only that "Bacchus" and "Merlin" are two of Emerson's most characteristic and central statements of his Dionysian-Transcendental view of the poet or artist, but also that "together the two poems form the classic American statements in verse of the Romantic poetic ideal that much of our best and most characteristic poetry has sought to exemplify. And they are not only the first such statements, they remain the best."[27] For Harold Bloom, "Bacchus" is Emerson's "greatest and most ecstatic poem, a furiously energetic rhapsody worthy of its title and subject, and one of the most audacious chants of poetic incarnation and self-recognition in the language, a poem worthy of the Coleridge of *Kubla Khan*."[28] In my headnote interpretations of "Merlin" and "Bacchus" (Part II), I hold that these poems, fully understood, celebrate the cosmic and psychic sources of inspiration. To Albert Gelpi, Emerson's organic poetry is so eye-opening, exhilarating, and original that it is difficult to overvalue it. Through the transcendental impulse Emerson radically changed typology to organic process, in which Nature serves as a stabilizing force in achieving harmony of self-reliance with self-transcendence. In contrast to the fallen isolated ego, the poet's integrative eye and his anima ("aboriginal Self") will make possible a new vision, a new "experiential perception"; that vision will activate "the Spirit of

xxvi REGENTS CRITICS SERIES

America" and thus redeem America.[29] Such, indeed, was the creative power and vision of poetry as Emerson conceived it.

3. The Art of Rhetoric

In 1941, when Matthiessen observed, "No American writer before Emerson had devoted such searching attention to his medium,"[30] that fact had already been richly documented by Emerson Grant Sutcliffe in "Emerson's Theories of Literary Expressions" in 1923. Sutcliffe demonstrated how Emerson derived his views of diction, style, and symbol from his conceptions of the Each and All, self-reliance, and the creative process. Today, Emerson's insights into the rhetoric of prose and verse are seen to have greatly extended the range of expression open to Thoreau, Melville, Whitman, and Emily Dickinson.

A speaker of great eloquence, Emerson would have liked to teach rhetoric. "Why," he asked in his 1862 *Journal*, "has never the poorest country college offered me a professorship of rhetoric?" His ideal was a "natural rhetoric," which he distinguished from disproportion and the use of ornamental details (*J* 4:335–37; *JMN* 5:409). Emerson reflected deeply and often on the nature of *elocutio*, the art of communication; among his major statements are the essays "Eloquence" and "Quotation and Originality" (*W* 8). His basic premises— "Thought exists to be expressed" and "The man is only half himself, the other half his expression"—imply that the writer must seek words to give form, life, and power to his ideas. In declaring that "in good writing, words become one with things," he echoed Coleridge's assertion, "I would endeavor to destroy the old antithesis of Words and Things: elevating Words into Things and living things too."

From 1818, when Emerson first encountered Hugh Blair's *Lectures on Rhetoric and Belles Lettres* (1783), to his own Bowdoin Prize essay of 1821 ("The Present State"), through his early sermons, he followed the dictates of Blair and Lord Kames on correctness in vocabulary, metaphor, hyperbole, periodic sentences, paragraph coherence and organization, point of view, and essay structure. But by 1835 he had thoroughly abandoned the neo-classical rhetoric of the Scottish common-sense school, as had Carlyle. Then, in 1836, after several hundred sermons, he gave up pulpit oratory. Beginning in the late 1820s, his view had shifted to an interest in colloquial, idiomatic, and concrete language as more expressive of feelings and perceptions and closer to the actual life lived than the abstract and ornamental style of the past. The power of images formed by a process of spontaneous "crystallization" led to his view of language as indirection, in which "the aim of the author is not to tell the truth—that he cannot do, but to suggest it" (*J* 3:491; *JMN* 5:51). As Sheldon Liebman, Lawrence Buell, and others have demonstrated, from the middle to late 1830s Emerson's style became rich and flexible with the resources of a new rhetoric—in diction, metaphor, parable, aphorism, proverb, example, and maxim, in sentence style and in essay structure and form. Explicit transitions, logical order, and polemics gave way to indirection, organic context, and compression. "Art and Criticism" is rich with examples of the American vernacular as well as tributes to the flexible idiom and style of Carlyle, Shakespeare, Herrick, Goethe, Bacon, and others. Here, as both advocate and practitioner, Emerson took his place in the long development of an American style, the "plain style," from the Puritans to Twain, Hemingway, and beyond.

In his poetics, Emerson was less an analyst of technique than a theorist of poetic principle and function. Among his writings there is nothing comparable to Poe's "The Philosophy of Composition" or "The Rationale of Verse." The functional test, however, applied to the craft of poetry. As the form takes shape from within, all depends on the thought, the spirit, the "inward music," and the pervading tone behind the images, rhyme, and rhythm. Despite his free-verse experiments, Emerson surrendered to conventional metrics in his final drafts. Whitman's *Leaves of Grass* came too late to serve Emerson as a guide or challenge in his own poetic practice. "Merlin" pronounced that "The kingly bard / Must smite the chords rudely and hard." To Emerson, Tennyson's early poems were weakened by their superfine lyricism. Yet if contemporary poetry suffered from an overemphasis on technique, a lack of craftsmanship could be fatal, as in some of the poems of Ellery Channing and Thoreau, or his own "Ode to Beauty." Emerson felt himself to be only a "a husky singer." His alleged general neglect of architectonic form, however, may be due less to his "mysticism" than to his Transcendentalism, given his belief that ideal intuition can only indirectly be suggested in words, and his pragmatic awareness that meddling with a poem does not always improve it. Emerson's attitude toward art, as expressed in "The Snow-Storm," impressed Matthiessen as "integral to the determination of the American writers of his day to speak out of a direct relationship to experience," and to express that relationship through art as natural growth.[31]

4. Toward a Modern Critical Perspective

To appreciate Emerson's achievement as the Coleridge of American criticism, it is necessary to understand not only his philosophy of art as experience and his psychology of the creative process, but also his organic and transcendental concepts of artistic form. Paralleling Horatio Greenough in his theory of organic architecture, Emerson pioneered the theory of organic poetic form in America. Emerson did so "by way of his general philosophical theories of nature, and Greenough by way of his more specific studies of form in relation to natural function," both arriving at theories considered "modern" today.[32]

In *The Mirror and the Lamp*, M. H. Abrams attributes the major shift that distinguished the Age of Wordsworth from the Age of Johnson to the poet's moving into the center of the critical system.[33] This change from neo-classical to romantic theories took the following development: from *mimetic*, Aristotelian theories of art as a mirroring of life, leading to criticism as judgment derived from rational principles and rules; to *pragmatic* theories of effect, the aim being to teach, please, or move the audience; and to the *expressive* theories of English romantic criticism, in which the feeling and the mind of the poet (imagination, spontaneity, insight, creative process) are expressed. When Plato's trans-empirical Ideas or Forms were transferred to post- or Neo-Platonic ideas in the mind of the artist—the Divine Idea beamed into the soul's mirror—psychological criticism began. A fourth orientation, the *objective* theory, saw the poem as "a heterocosm, a world of its own," as in Poe's view of the "poem *per se* . . . written solely for the poem's sake." Just emerging in the early nineteenth century, this theory developed out of Aristotle's analysis of tragedy as a self-determining whole, with all parts organized around the tragic plot. The development of these theories of art was accompanied by changes in the methods of criticism: from "judicial" analysis and moral judgment to aesthetic and organic concerns.

"Judicial criticism" was a mode that Emerson outgrew. Linked with the Newtonian system of changeless, universal laws, with teleology, social hierarchy, and the neo-classical tradition, it derived from the mimetic theory of a work of art as a rationally constructed composition. Such criticism tended to be negative, weeding out the worthless and pointing out defects. At its best, it concerned itself with unity of logical structure, clarity, verisimilitude, and appropriate style. Emerson's critical approach or method was not textual or analytical; he felt that a great work should be appreciated not by "minute analysis" but by integrative realization.

The shift in Emerson's artistic perspective and method consisted also of a turning from Moralism to Beauty (cf. *JMN* 2:220 and 7:134–35), especially under the guidance and influence of Goethe between 1833 and 1840. Others who stressed this needed emancipation of criticism included Irving, Poe, Lowell, Longfellow, Hawthorne, and Melville. In *Nature* Emerson reconciled any possibly rival claims of morality and beauty with the Platonic view that "truth, and goodness, and beauty, are but different faces of the same All." Out of this principle, Harry Hayden Clark observes, Emerson developed an organic theory that saved him from the traps of "escapism, irresponsible hedonism, a minimizing of moral beauty as merely 'didactic,' or a mechanistic separation of 'instruction' and 'delight.' "[34]

These shifts in critical thinking and method current in Emerson's time clearly point toward organic criticism.[35] Coleridge became "the first important channel for the flow of organicism into the hitherto clear, if perhaps not very deep, stream of English aesthetics."[36] Like Coleridge, Emerson turned away from the " 'Reasoning Machines,' such as Locke and [Samuel] Clarke and Hume" (*J* 1:361; *JMN* 2:238), and created a functional aesthetic based on five kinds of relationship:

1) *The organic relation of the writer and his work:* "The great American vogue of Milton, as part of our early Puritan heritage, encouraged acceptance of his well-known idea that whoever would write a

great poem must first make his own life a true poem and achieve virtue, a theory of the organic relation of literary creation and creator which encouraged biographical criticism."[37] For Emerson, too, a writer must have character, not talent only; the man and the writer must be one. The critic must go beyond the words of the poet to look at "the order of his thoughts and the essential quality of his mind." Here echoing Coleridge, Emerson in his turn was very likely the source for Whitman's expressive theory that "all beauty comes from beautiful blood and a beautiful brain."

2) *Organic form as process:* "Coleridge's theory that the organic form is innate in the germ of the author's material, and that it shapes itself as it develops from within" is represented by Emerson's view of the poem as a "metre-making argument," of the truly "fluxional" symbol as one that catches the flow of reality in the process of becoming, and of rhetoric and eloquence as determined from within (see Part III).[38]

3) *Organic form as structure:* The various elements and aspects of the art object must be interrelated and consonant with the whole, as the branches and roots of a tree with its organic life. To Emerson, unity and depth of tone reflect unity of inner structure. (Bacon's essays lack such unity.) The "low" style and the "mean" symbol are more powerfully suggestive because more organic in origin.

4) *Sentence style and diction:* "The style of individual sentences should draw vitality and muscularity from the writer's own reports of his five senses."[39] Emerson frequently praised the sentences of Thoreau, Montaigne, and Carlyle for these expressive qualities (see Part III).

5) *Historical criticism or literary nationalism:* "The organic mutual relation [exists] between literature and its author's time, place, and race."[40] The shift from mechanism to vitalism in botany and zoology led Crèvecoeur to write that "men are like plants; the goodness and flavor of the fruit proceeds from the peculiar soil and exposition in which they grow."[41] Criticism should see literature in the context of cultural history—its spirit of place, its zeitgeist, and its cultural roots. Milton, for instance, is best appreciated as a product of his English, classical, and Hebraic-Puritan intellectual heritage. This belief that the physical and the social environments

can affect men and, with changed cultural soil and institutions, bring about a distinctively American character was set forth in Crèvecoeur's "What Is an American?", Jefferson's *Notes on Virginia* and his First Inaugural Address, Emerson's "The American Scholar," Whitman's Preface to the 1855 *Leaves of Grass*, and more or less prominently in the works of Poe, Cooper, Thoreau, Hawthorne, and Melville.

Yet a sixth relationship permeates Emerson's thinking about literature: the epic Universal or Sublime in human experience. Emerson, of course, was not alone in believing that the highest values and truths transcend time, history, nationality, and race. Richard Hildreth in 1829 expressed the view that great literature embodies "those great, universal and invariable principles of truth and beauty, which strike and please alike at all times and in all places."[42] Yet Emerson's transcendental test is more than a *consensus gentium*, the consent of all nations through time. With Goethe, Emerson defined the "classic" and the "antique" as independent of time—"there is anything but time in my idea of the antique." Through and beyond the differences of culture and history, "criticism must be transcendental." In the realization of great art, as in the realization of history, truth and beauty are experienced as timeless, universal, of "one age." In "Thoughts on Modern Literature" this insight is identified as a "deep realism," already evident in law, education, and philosophy, as well as in literature. It is "the Feeling of the Infinite," the deep intuitive response to "metaphysical Nature, to the invisible awful facts, to moral abstractions, which are not less Nature than is a river, or a coal-mine,—nay, they are far more Nature,—but its essence and soul."

Emerson's transcendental aesthetic, first formulated in *Nature*, developed out of the correspondence theory into a dynamic psychology of perception (see Parts I and II). Beauty is realized contextually as a function of the organic whole, or gestalt. It is the beauty of the iridescent shell washed by the shining waves of the shore in the poem "Each and All." It is also a realization of the organic universal, as in the fine passage on "Give me insight into to-day" in "The American Scholar." This "universal relation" Emerson called a "creative vortex" because it expressed the life force, or spirit, as in Greek tragedy, which he regarded as more truly epic (in the modern sense) than the popular epic (in the traditional sense) and the pseudo-epic "modern antiques." In "Thoughts" Emerson applied this conception of organic identity as a critical yardstick to Byron, Shelley, Wordsworth, Landor, and Goethe, and as a cultural test to "our graduate and petrified social scale of ranks and employments." In *English Traits* he found it largely lacking in nineteenth-century literary England, but present in "the English transcendental genius" of Coleridge, Carlyle, Wordsworth, Milton, Shakespeare, and Bacon.

In "Art and Criticism" (1850) Emerson included a Goethean contrast of *classic* as organic, healthy, unfolding the "necessity within itself," and *romantic* or *modern* as sick, the product of caprice or chance. At the same time (1849 or 1850), Emerson abandoned the earlier terminology—*Classic*, *Romantic*, and *Reflective or Philosophical*—used in "The American Scholar," in favor of the following three major historic "eras" or climates of opinion:[43]

> 1. *The Greek:* when men deified Nature, Jove was in the air, Neptune in the sea, Pluto in the earth, Naiads in the fountains, Dryads in the woods, Oreads on the mountains; happy beautiful beatitude of Nature;
> 2. *The Christian:* when the soul became pronounced, and craved a heaven out of Nature and above it,—looking on Nature now as evil,—the world was a mere stage and school, a snare, and the powers that ruled here were devils, hostile to the soul; and now, lastly,—
> 3. *The Modern:* when the too idealistic tendencies of the Christian period running into the diseases of cant, monachism, and a church, demonstrating the impossibility of Christianity, have forced men to retrace their steps, and rally again on Nature; but now the tendency is to marry mind to Nature, and to put Nature under the mind, convert the world into the instrument of Right Reason. Man goes forth to the dominion of the world by commerce, by science, and by philosophy. [*J* 8:78; *JMN* 11:201]

Two pages farther on, Emerson added a note that later became this paragraph in "The Powers and Laws of Thought":

> The height of culture, the highest behavior, consists in the identification of the Ego with the universe; so that when a man says I hope, I find, I think, he might properly say, The human race thinks or finds or hopes. And meantime he shall be able continually to keep sight of his

biographical Ego,—I have a desk, I have an office, I am hungry, I had an ague,—as rhetoric or offset to his grand spiritual Ego, without impertinence, or ever confounding them. [*W* 12:62]

To judge from these passages, Emerson's post-Christian Modernism seems solidly based on a psychology of self-transcendence that is experiential and transactional.

Given his own definition of "the modern mind"—"to lop off all superfluity & tradition & fall back on the nature of things" (*JMN* 5:200–201)—it is little wonder that Emerson often deplored the superfluities and trite conventions of the standard English novel: romantic plot, shallow characters, episodic looseness, overreliance on scenery and costume, and the lack of verisimilitude, realistic dialogue, and natural style. In "Books" he cited three novels by George Sand as "great steps" forward from the novel of twenty years earlier. "Yet how far off from life and manners and motives the novel still is! . . . But the novel will find the way to our interiors one day" (*W* 7:214).

A lifelong though not systematic reader of novels, Emerson contributed germinal insights and sound reflections on the nature and range of the novel, and his aesthetic of fiction represents a significant integration of function-theory and technique (plot, style, realism, wit, character). The transcendental function he held to be best served by "the novel of character": a coherent plot as an organic outgrowth of character, indirection and symbolism (rather than didactic moralizing) being of the essence. He wanted to find in the novel "the analogons of our own thoughts" so expressed as to stimulate the reader to realize the universal truth of his own experience and the spirit of the age. However, even in the fiction he classed below the level of "the novel of character," he recognized certain legitimate values. Although weak and conventional in plot and character development, the "novel of fashion" might provide needed escape from boredom or misery; and the "novels of circumstance" might exert an influence for dignity, courtesy, and brilliancy in young men, and greater generosity and "clear, firm conduct" among common folk (*W* 7:215). The *Journals* too contain discriminating judgments of the novel.[44] "You do us great wrong, Henry Thoreau, in railing at the novel reading," he objected in 1847; "the novel is that allowance and frolic their [the common readers'] imagination gets. Everything else pins it" (*JMN* 10:48; *W* 7:213).

5. Writers and Books

When Emerson exchanged the pulpit for the podium, he presented his early lectures in series, ranging widely into literature, art, science, history, "the philosophy of history," "human culture," "human life," and "the present age."

Of the ten early lectures on English literature (*EL* 1:205–385), several of which have been drawn upon elsewhere in this volume, the first is entitled "English Literature: Introductory." Disclaiming full knowledge of English literary history, Emerson in this essay sets forth a transcendental theory of literature that gives highest value to "the majestic ideas of God, of Justice, of Freedom, of Necessity, of War, and of intellectual Beauty" and of Virtue and Love. As spiritual "laws" these "ideas" are not static essences, but dynamic powers organic to man's very being. Again in "Ethical Writers" Emerson asserts that "the law which Ethics treats is that we mean by the nature of things," whether that law be known as Necessity, Spirit, or Power. But his concern for the ethical and transcendental as they appear in English literature is not Emerson's only concern. In "Permanent Traits of the English National Genius" Emerson applies another standard, the cultural, in a portrayal of the English national character through its early literature. At one point he enumerates seven traits of the Anglo-Saxons: gravity and melancholy of spirit; a sense of humor; the love of home and domestic habits; economy or love of utility; accuracy of perception, strong love of truth, passion for justice; a respect for birth; a respect for women (*EL* 1:249). This feeling for the simple virtues is reflected further in "Europe and European Books," where Wordsworth is admired as a critic and conscience of his time, and Goethe, Tennyson, and Leigh Hunt are also highly valued.

English Traits (1856) has been described by Mark Van Doren as "powerful and delightful . . . brilliant . . . the wittiest work of America's wittiest writer."[45] The chapter on literature again puts the

English "transcendental genius" to the test: only Bacon, Shakespeare, and Milton dared generalize to universal truths from insight and analogy; Coleridge, Carlyle, and Wordsworth are the only other noteworthy exceptions to the prevailing "mental materialism" and its fear of ideas, poetry, and religion. Dickens, Scott, Bulwer-Lytton, Thackeray, Macaulay, and Tennyson are among those in need of an "Oriental largeness" as a remedy for self-conceit.

Emerson's views of poetry are tempered and conservative in his late Preface to *Parnassus* (1874), an anthology of his favorite British— chiefly English—and American poems. The brief appraisals of English poets are largely the judgments of earlier years. Poe, Whitman, Shelley, and Emerson are omitted from the anthology; Bryant, Whittier, Longfellow, Holmes, Lowell, and a number of minor American poets are included.

The indebtedness of Emerson to the English "metaphysical" poets of the seventeenth century is widely recognized, as is his appreciation of Jonson and Herrick; Bacon, Milton, Browne, and Newton; devotional writers Cudworth, Henry More, and Jeremy Taylor; historical and biographical authors. Through them, before he discovered Coleridge and Carlyle, he developed his ideas on literature, language, miracles, the religious sentiment, and the relation of man to nature and of the writer to his work. In one of his 1835 lectures on English literature he discussed Jonson, Herrick, Herbert, and Sir Henry Wotton (*EL* 1:337–55). Jonson's poetry he found of great merit; but the plays he found dull, heavy, pedantic, Jonson being "the worst dramatist of any reputation in English," especially when compared to Shakespeare. Herrick's lyrics were delightful in "the light and grace" with which they treated objects of common life; and his elegant, manly style was praised for its "noble idiomatic use of English, a perfect plain style from which he can at any time soar to a fine lyric delicacy or descend to the coarsest sarcasms without losing his firm footing." The poetic power of Herbert's exalted thought is such as to "melt and bend," to "fuse" the words, so flexible is his style. Later Emerson found moral beauty even in Herrick's drinking songs (*J* 7:188; *JMN* 9:406). But this early lecture closed with a characteristic remark to the effect that a "curious reader" of old English plays (Elizabethan and Jacobean) will be struck by "the barbarity of manners and the depravation of morals . . . scenes of profanity and indecency" that should cause us to feel grateful for the "prodigious advancement in purity of conversation and honesty of life."

Of the metaphysicals, Herbert seemed favored over Donne, Cowley, Crashaw, and Marvell; but all were valued for their introspective quality, fresh imagery, and symbolism ("analogy-loving"). Of religious writers writing in, or respected in, the seventeenth century, Emerson valued most highly John Bunyan and Henry Scougal; the Quakers George Fox and James Naylor; the Anglicans Thomas Cranmer, Donne, Herbert, Hooker, and Taylor; the mystics Swedenborg and Jakob Böhme; and the Catholics Saint Augustine, Saint Bernard, Saint Jerome, Fénelon, and Thomas à Kempis. His favorite nonreligious writings of the period included those of John Evelyn and Pepys, histories by Gilbert Burnet, William Camden, and the Earl of Clarendon, and biographies of Donne, Milton, John Hampden, John Pym, and Penn in various collections.

Bacon was another favorite. In Chaucer and Bacon, Emerson distinguished two strains of the English character: Chaucer as representative of the good sense, sincerity, humor, vitality, and social sympathy which made him the superlative man of his age; Bacon as the shrewd moralist and "Platonic" aphorist. In his journals, lectures, and sermons Emerson showed his lifelong interest in Bacon by at least two hundred references to his works. From him Emerson learned to shape his journal notes into essays, beginning with proverbs and aphorisms, though he came to recognize that Bacon's method of collecting *sententiae* was not wholly organic. Montaigne's essays provided Emerson with another example of language extraordinarily earthy, vigorous, and vital. "Cut these words," he wrote, "and they would bleed; they are vascular and alive." Of Emerson's representative men, Montaigne embodied skepticism at its best—a sincere and open-minded search for the truth in the commonplaces of everyday experience. The influence of Bacon and Montaigne on Emerson's intellectual and stylistic development was deep and lasting.

Shakespeare was such an "exceptional genius" that Emerson found it "difficult not to be intemperate" in speaking of him (*J* 10:27, 35). In 1864 he called for a Shakespeare Professorship, there being none at Oxford or Harvard (*J* 10:30). A play like *Hamlet* or *Lear* could have been written, he thought, only "by a multitude of trials and a thousand rejections." And yet Emerson attempted no analysis comparable to Coleridge's or Hazlitt's on *Hamlet*. When the characters seem to defy analysis, he is inclined simply to say that Shakespeare "leaves his children with God" (*J* 2:482; *JMN* 4:19). More often his comments on Hamlet, Lear, Cleopatra, Henry V, Falstaff, Brutus, and Antony are cogent, sometimes rhapsodic, in the tradition of romantic criticism associated with Coleridge. Although intensely interested in knowledge and opinions about Shakespeare, Emerson became impatient with biographical conjectures as "mere fables." The origin of Shakespeare's genius, he felt, is to be found in his works, whose meaning remains to be revealed by a "more cunning reading of the Book itself" (*J* 10:279–80). The highest criticism also depends on historical research into the intellectual and cultural milieu.

Near the end of his 1848 lecture on Shakespeare, Emerson made a rather startling qualification, which must have ruffled the feathers of his London audience: because Shakespeare failed to explore the moral symbolism as well as the beauty of the visible world, he did not reap "a second and final harvest of the mind." This lack of moral feeling, attributed to "an obscure and profane life," kept him from seeing the higher spiritual truth. Yet, because of his great intellect, he represents the archetypal Knower in the moral evolution of Universal Man, according to William M. Wynkoop in *Three Children of the Universe*. After that first stage, classical unity, came the "split universe" and the romantic Fall into the "divided consciousness" as represented by Bacon the Doer, the man of understanding and will. Though Bacon is valued for his philosophy and vision, he is censured by Emerson for his fall from the moral sentiment into servility and intrigue. In the third, modern era of spiritual development, the archetypal Sayer (Milton) redeems man by his power to inspire the moral sentiment and to express the Beautiful.[46] Indeed, Milton is exalted more for his moral perfection and for being the highest representative of "the idea of Man" than for his literary significance. In him truth and love are reunited.

Emerson recognized also the high quality of Milton's writings. "Areopagitica" he judged to be "the most splendid" of the prose works. "Comus" seemed to him "a beautiful poem" which "makes

one holy to read it." "Lycidas," with its "marble beauty," was organically "a copy from the poet's mind . . . as clear and wild as it had
shone at first in the sky of his own thought." *Paradise Lost*, despite
its dated theology and "vicious . . . royal imagery" and conventional
epic form, deserved high regard for its "stately" quality, its craftsmanship and architectonics, its genuine and vital invocation to the
eternal Spirit, and its representation of Eve's "omnipotent" humility.
Milton's character, too, is reflected in *Paradise Lost*: his life being his
greatest poem, the works become parts and expressions of that life.
Though Emerson had misgivings about Milton's being "too learned"
and "the most literary," he did not alter his early view that Milton
was "marked by nature for the great Epic Poet."[47]

The Romantics and Victorians, nearer in time to his own age,
Emerson grew to appreciate—variously and with reservations. He was
two generations younger than Burns and Blake, one generation (more
or less) younger than Coleridge, Scott, and Wordsworth, and almost
contemporary with Byron, Keats, Shelley, Carlyle, Dickens, and
Tennyson. Nurtured in college on the writings and standards of Pope,
Dryden, Swift, Addison, and Johnson, he only gradually overcame
the prejudices of the neo-classical literary reviews against the Lake
Poets. Sheldon W. Liebman has in great detail traced Emerson's
discovery of the English Romantics between 1818 and 1836.[48]
Whereas Blake and Keats made no strong impression, Burns and
Byron did—Burns as a native genius, a poet of nature and of the
common folk; Byron as a born lyricist of feeling and power, though
finally judged to be "no poet" because of his morbid and immoral
view of life. By contrast with Byron, Shelley was praised for his
aspiration, heroic character, and poetic mind, but, because of his
uninspired language, "never a poet." Tennyson, too, until 1843
seemed mainly the superb technician lacking "rude truth." In 1859,
however, Emerson's excitement over *Idylls of the King* knew no
bounds: that poetic work completed the great English "Arthur Epic"
begun by Chaucer. By comparison with the praise lavished on Coleridge's critical and metaphysical works, his poems were all but
ignored. Wordsworth was at first not so much ignored as criticized for
being a poet of "pigmies" and "pismires," then in 1836 was ranked as
"the great philosophical poet of the present day," and shortly there-

after was recognized as the critic and conscience of his time and country.

Emerson left many interesting journal references to Coleridge's keenness as a thinker and critic; yet he produced no lecture or essay other than the segment reprinted in Part V. The incisiveness of those pages testifies to the depth of Emerson's absorption of Coleridge's ideas and to the unique greatness of Coleridge as a critical mind.[49] "Every opinion he expresses is a canon of criticism that should be writ in steel, & his italics are italics of the mind" (*JMN* 5:252; *J* 4:153). Coleridge, the main source for Emerson of the basic distinction between Understanding and Reason, passed the transcendental test of Reason in a way that Carlyle did not, for Carlyle was "not a philosopher." But Carlyle wielded the most powerful rhetoric, especially the vernacular, of his day. Emerson's rhapsodic appreciation of *The French Revolution* is strong testimony to the impact of Carlyle's new historiography.

In her 1948 analysis, Vivian Hopkins concludes that Goethe's was the greatest single influence on Emerson's aesthetic theory: "Heightening Emerson's aesthetic consciousness, helping Emerson to shape his theory of organic form, stimulating his reflections about the creative and the receptive mind, Goethe laid the foundation for Emerson's theory of art and literature."[50] In 1833 Goethe's *Travels in Italy* served as Emerson's guide to the arts in Italy, leading to rewarding aesthetic discoveries in painting, architecture, and sculpture (Michelangelo, above all). In developing his theory of organic form, Emerson drew on Goethe's theory of the *Ur-Pflanze* (recognition of the leaf form throughout nature), as described in *W* 10:338. Emerson's idea of "Each-in-All," in which "the totality of nature" is the context and standard of beauty, found its parallel in Goethe, helping Emerson to modify his earlier leanings toward a Puritan moral judgment of art. Some of his critical terminology he also owed to Goethe: *healthy* vs. *sick*, *antique* vs. *modern*, *classic* vs. *romantic* (see section 4 above, "Art and Criticism" below; *W* 12:303–4; *J* 4:144–45 or *JMN* 5:243–45).

In "Goethe; or, The Writer" (1846) in *Representative Men*, Emerson credits Goethe with defining the function and scope of art and lauded him (with qualifications) for creating *Faust II*, *Wilhelm Meister*, and his

Autobiography. But, like most New Englanders of the time, the young Emerson had disliked Goethe's paganism and Continental worldliness—his "velvet life," "bad morals," and "love-of-ease." However, after returning from his 1834 visit with Carlyle, a Goethe enthusiast, Emerson acquired all, and proceeded to read almost all, of the fifty-five volumes of the *Werke* (Stuttgart, 1828–33). Part I of *Faust* he disliked as grotesque; later it seemed to him "a little too modern and intelligible" (1851), and typical of the age of analysis, introversion, and skepticism (1867). The second part of *Faust* he considered to be "the grandest enterprise of literature" since *Paradise Lost*, and in 1850 he praised it for its range of modern wisdom: reflective and critical, archetypal and mythological.

In the generous portion devoted to Goethe in "Thoughts on Modern Literature" (Part IV), Goethe is seen as a representative of the age in his love of fact, truth, and Nature, and in his subjectiveness and "deep realism." Yet, Emerson concludes, even though *Wilhelm Meister* achieved a new expression of the realism of the Actual, it failed in a higher sense to be creative, to catch the moral sentiment, and to transform present class prejudices into the "new heroic life of man." In "Europe and European Books" (Part V), *Wilhelm Meister* is cited as a significant novel of character, and in "Goethe" as the most thought-provoking book of the century. In England, America, and especially France, Emerson maintains, "men of talent write from talent," whereas the German intellect demands a probity and sincerity that will declare the truth. Goethe was impelled by a devotion to experiential truth: "His is not even the devotion to pure truth; but to truth for the sake of culture. He has no aims less large than the conquest of universal nature, of universal truth, to be his portion."

Despite the academic neglect of the novel at Harvard and the limited quality and number of American novels before 1821, Emerson not only read many of them with pleasure and enthusiasm, but in his occasional comments conceived of the novel in literary rather than moralistic terms. The reading lists in the journals, according to John T. Flanagan, "include references to almost every important novelist (with the omission of the Russians) from Cervantes to Charles Reade."[51] Of course, some writers were ignored, slighted, or disliked: Jane Austen, Thackeray, Bulwer-Lytton, Hawthorne, Melville. His favorite novels included *Jane Eyre*, Disraeli's *Vivian Grey*,

Sand's *Consuelo* and *Lucrezia Floriani*, Manzoni's *I Promessi Sposi*, Cooper's *The Spy* and *The Pioneers*, Longfellow's *Kavanagh*, Stowe's *Uncle Tom's Cabin*, and those by Maria Edgeworth. Dickens largely disappointed Emerson because of his lack of good dialogue and dramatic talent and because of his dependence on caricature, melodrama, and the sordid, as in *Oliver Twist*. Although Emerson enjoyed Scott's novels during his early years, in the 1830s he approved only of *Old Mortality*, *Quentin Durward*, and *The Bride of Lammermoor*. He deplored Scott's "artificial and pedantic" dialogue and his preoccupation with costume and scenery. The Scott centenary address of 1871, based on wide knowledge of the Waverley novels, extolled Scott as a man of sterling character, a writer distinguished for his common sense, his sympathy for the common people, and his popular ballads. But it did not call him a great novelist.

Except for Whitman, American poets were like most English poets—of the "contemporary," not the "eternal" class. Much as Emerson enjoyed Longfellow's "Hiawatha" and Bryant's nature poems (*J* 10:76–77, 80–82), neither poet fulfilled his expectations. To Whittier he referred only in passing. He considered Lowell's "admirable Ode" to be nothing less than a "national poem," and found in "The Cathedral" manly thoughts, although the expression was "not always flowing." *The Biglow Papers* entirely justified his faith in the cultural soil of America. Popular and technically skilled as they were, these poets were too conventional in their ideas and verse to provide "the heavenly bread" or "the grand design" of the highest poetry. Of the younger writers, William Ellery Channing and Jones Very fell under the critical category of "portfolio" poets—poets of sincerity and insight, but of limited range and poetic quality. Thoreau, too, on occasion capable of "rude strength" and "genuine poetry" (as in "Sympathy"), generally fell short of original ideas and poetic finish. Thoreau is said to have been so upset by such criticism from Emerson that he burned many of his early poems. The prevailing lack of critical standards and self-criticism led Emerson to see the urgent need for "a genuine intellectual tribunal" of writer-critics, who might exert a restraining influence on premature publication of mediocre, unfinished work such as that by "Doctor Channing" and others.[52]

All four of the American authors represented significantly here as subjects of Emerson's criticism were close friends of his. Three of them had been introduced by Emerson to the Boston Atheneum, that literary sanctuary of the Boston Brahmins—Thoreau in 1841, Whitman in 1860, Hawthorne in 1861. Although Emerson's many friendly conversations with them must have provided a wealth of insights into their writings as well as their personalities, the record of such insights is disappointingly meager. In a journal portrait of Margaret Fuller, a character sketch of high quality, Emerson describes her remarkable mind and conversation, but not her writing or ideas. A comparably fine eloquence marks Emerson's intimate portrait of Hawthorne, as if the man were indeed greater than his works. From the sketches of Hawthorne the man and the fragmentary comments in the journals, one cannot tell whether Emerson read Hawthorne with any genuine sympathy or understanding. To have accepted the popular view that Zenobia (in Hawthorne's *The Blithedale Romance*) depicted the real-life Margaret Fuller suggests in Emerson a serious lack of aesthetic distance. For him to have remembered Hawthorne chiefly for his "painful solitude," reserve, and humility seems entirely too incomplete a portrait, given Julian Hawthorne's memories of his father.

If, to Emerson, Hawthorne the man was greater than his works, Thoreau the man became one with the writer. Yet Emerson's enthusiasm for the *Week*, *Walden*, and the journals is hardly evident in the famous 1862 funeral address, which eulogized Thoreau as a great nonconformist and individualist, and only secondarily as a poet and prose stylist.[53] In this evaluation Emerson again walks too close to his friend and follower to do justice to his unique qualities as Transcendental artist and thinker. By contrast, Whitman always represented the "Appalachian" range and "buffalo strength" of the American land, experience, and potential, with a power of expression equal to the epic magnitude of the *Leaves*. For the lack of a full statement, however, the record here too is disappointingly incomplete.

In "A Letter" as editor of the *Dial* in 1843, Emerson reported inquiries for "that great absentee American Literature. What can have become of it? The least said is best," he replied, for the time being (*W* 12:404). In his Editor's Address of 1847, he expressed a strong conviction that the new, American freedom would, in the future, find pure expression in "a Columbia of thought and art, which is the last and endless end of Columbus's adventure" (*W* 11:

387). The great promise suggested by the 1855 *Leaves* seems to have been only partially fulfilled, to judge by Emerson's subsequent critical statements on Whitman and his fellow American authors. "I look in vain for the poet I describe," he wrote in 1870. Brief appreciative comments may be found in the journals and letters, but no sustained inquiry or evaluation other than those identified above, and no essay like the chapter "Literature" in *English Traits*.

The realization of an artistic and intellectual Columbia would require a widening commitment to democratic values in American life. In "The Young American" (1844), Emerson complained that "our books are European. . . . We are sent to feudal school to learn democracy." In 1852 Emerson engaged in and recorded pungent conversations with Horatio Greenough, whose "Form follows function" was to have a major impact on American architecture through Louis Sullivan. Greenough, as well as Emerson, Thoreau, and Whitman, sensed that organic functionalism held great promise for American art and literature. In concluding that "Emerson's theory of expression was that on which Thoreau built, to which Whitman gave extension, and to which Hawthorne and Melville were indebted by being forced to react against its philosophical assumptions," Matthiessen might also have noted that Hawthorne and Melville were directly indebted to Emerson's aesthetic as such.[54] In his 1855 Preface Walt Whitman poetically restated Emerson's program for literature in the emerging American democracy.

In his lectures of the 1860s Emerson further applied his cultural and transcendental criticism, but broadly to American society rather than to literature alone. As Bercovitch cogently concludes, Emerson "expressed himself by expressing the myth of America." But, in my view, his was less an abstract or millennial vision than a faith in empiric progress, cultural evolution, social democracy, and "the religious sentiment" in the service of the mission manifest: "the Emersonian-American Self," or American civilization as a way of life. In such an experiential-historic context, Emerson could refer to abolition as "a continuation of Puritanism" (*J* 6:53; *JMN* 8:53) and could speak of Boston as continuing the "holy errand into the wilderness," New England leading the way to a United States of the "the truly Human."[55]

In "Boston" (1861) he surveyed the effects on New England of "the

Jonathanization of John," and restated his hope of fourteen years earlier that American literature would ascend in "spiral form" to a "Columbia" of art and thought (*W* 12:200–201). The lectures on "American Civilization" (1862) and "The Fortune of the Republic" (1863, 1878) reaffirmed his American beliefs in practical idealism, practical democracy, the liberal religious tradition, the need for great individuals, "the complemental man," with a characteristic stress on civilization and the human race, not nationality alone. "Culture, to be sure, is in some sort the very enemy of nationality and makes us citizens of the world; and yet it is essential that it should have the flavor of the soil in which it grew, and combine this with universal sympathies. Thus in this country are new traits and distinctions not known to former history." The "immense difference from Europe" is that "we wish to treat man as man, without regard to rank, wealth, race, color, or caste,—simply as human souls" (*W* 11:644–46). Finally, in 1867, lecturing on "Life and Letters in New England," Emerson laid claim to a simple but satisfying conviction that the rich cultural resources of this continent had nurtured an "excellent and increasing circle of masters in arts and in song and in science, who cheer the intellect of our cities and this country to-day,—whose genius is not a lucky accident, but normal, and with broad foundation of culture, and so inspires the hope of steady strength advancing on itself, and a day without a night" (*W* 10:369–70).

A Note on the Selections and the Text

Wherever possible, within the limits of this volume, selections are reprinted complete. Omitted passages are identified in the original text by three asterisks (*   *   *).

Part V is offered as a convenient grouping of Emerson's views of major writers and books. Many of the commentaries are drawn from the journals, with cross-references in the headnotes and source notes to other passages. Some writers omitted from the table of contents— Ben Jonson, Herrick, Herbert, Goethe, and Swedenborg, in particular—are represented by scattered opinions that can be located through the index. Others—Plato and Plutarch, along with Goethe and Swedenborg—are the subjects of lectures or essays both well known and readily available but containing few passages of strictly literary criticism; hence their omission here. The absence of comment on Jonathan Edwards, Browning, Holmes, Whittier, Melville, Poe, Cooper, Twain, and Dickinson is due to the total, or nearly total, lack of mention in the published work. For example, the only reference to Poe, as "the jingle man," occurred in a conversation with Howells in 1860. Although Emerson ranked the bibles of the world as "the best" of books and the English Bible as preeminent among them, calling it "a wonderful specimen of the strength and music of the English language" (*W* 4:199), it was apparently so deeply and unconsciously a part of his intellectual inheritance that he felt no need to discuss it or judge it as literature, often as he drew upon it for quotations, paraphrases, and allusions.[56]

When this volume was first planned, the new Harvard University Press edition of Emerson was only partially published. With the first volume of *The Collected Works of Ralph Waldo Emerson* in 1971, it became clear that the Centenary Edition (*The Complete Works of Ralph Waldo Emerson*, 1903–1904) is entirely reliable as a basic text for the essays and poems. Alfred R. Ferguson, textual editor of the Belknap edition, assured me that none of the essays except "Character" exist in manuscript. Meanwhile, *The Early Lectures* have appeared. The new *Journals and Miscellaneous Notebooks* reached volume 14 in 1978. Compared with the latter, the *Journals* (1909–14), free of textual variants and symbols, are in that respect more readable and are, as a rule, wholly dependable in content. Where a significant difference appears, that fact has been noted. In any event, the reader will find that the *JMN* reference follows the *J* source for his convenience in consulting the later edition through *JMN* 14. Other basic texts used are *The Letters of Ralph Waldo Emerson*; *The Correspondence of Emerson and Carlyle*; and *Uncollected Writings: Essays, Addresses, Poems, Reviews and Letters by Ralph Waldo Emerson*, edited by Charles C. Bigelow (New York: Lamb Publishing Company, 1912).

More descriptive or more suitable titles have been supplied by me for certain of the selections and excerpts; the source notes to each indicate the original ones. The source notes indicate also, *seriatim*, the text used here, the original publication, the original source, and, in brackets, the date of composition where germane. Where desirable,

Journal dates have been silently supplied and regularized. This edition preserves bracketed material of Emerson's earlier editors, which supplements my own. Where their annotations are used in the Notes, that fact is noted by identification of the source.

ERIC W. CARLSON

University of Connecticut

NOTES

1. Jonathan Bishop, *Emerson on the Soul*, p. 1.

2. *Artist:* ibid. *Poet:* Hyatt Waggoner, *Emerson as Poet*; *American Poets: From the Puritans to the Present*. *Fountainhead:* Harold Bloom, "American Poetic Stances: Emerson to Stevens," in *Wallace Stevens: The Poems of Our Climate*, pp. 1–26; "The Central Man: Emerson, Whitman, Wallace Stevens," *Massachusetts Review* 7 (1966): 23–42; "Emerson and Whitman: The American Sublime," in *Poetry and Repression: Revisionism from Blake to Stevens*, pp. 235–66; "Emerson: The Glory and the Sorrows of American Romanticism," *Virginia Quarterly Review* 47 (1971): 546–63; "The Native Strain: American Orphism," in *Figures of Capable Imagination*, pp. 67–88. See also Waggoner, *Emerson as Poet*, p. 113; and Albert Gelpi, *The Tenth Muse: The Psyche of the American Poet*, pp. 82–83, for views of Emerson as the central defining influence on American poets from Whitman through Olson and Ammons. *Channel:* Sacvan Bercovitch, *The Puritan Origins of the American Self*, pp. 148–186.

3. Norman Foerster, *American Criticism: A Study in Literary Theory from Poe to the Present*, p. 53. F. O. Matthiessen, *American Renaissance: Art and Expression in the Age of Emerson and Whitman*, p. xii, 26–27. Alfred Kazin and Daniel Aaron, *Emerson: A Modern Anthology* (New York: Dell Publishing Co., 1958), p. 230.

4. William James, *Memories and Studies*, pp. 18–34. John Dewey, "Ralph Waldo Emerson," in *Characters and Events*, ed. Joseph Ratner, 1:76. Reprinted in *Emerson: A Collection of Critical Essays*, ed. Milton Konvitz and Stephen E. Whicher, p. 29.

5. Harvey G. Townsend, *Philosophical Ideas in the United States* (New York: American Book Co., 1934), p. 133. For an excellent analysis of the larger philosophic views shared by Emerson and James—especially pluralism (vs. transcendental Absolutism), theory of Will, "Representative" Great Men, self-reliance (actual and potential), the will to believe, and the Over-

Soul—see Frederick Ives Carpenter, "Points of Comparison between Emerson and William James," *New England Quarterly* 2 (1929): 458–74. See also Frederick Ives Carpenter, "William James and Emerson," *American Literature* 11 (1939): 39–57.

6. John Dewey, *The Quest for Certainty* (New York: Minton, Balch, and Co., 1929), chaps. 1–2.

7. William B. Barton, "Emerson's Method as a Philosopher," in *Emerson's Relevance Today*, ed. Eric W. Carlson and J. Lasley Dameron, p. 22.

8. As represented by such followers of Whitehead, Peirce, and Dewey as Charles Hartshorne, John B. Cobb, Jr., Bernard E. Meland, Schubert M. Ogden, Daniel Day Williams, and Henry Nelson Wieman. See William L. Reese and Eugene Freeman, eds., *Process and Divinity: The Hartshorne Festschrift* (Lasalle, Ill.: Open Court Publishing Co., 1964).

9. Harold Bloom, "The Native Strain: American Orphism," in *Figures of Capable Imagination*, pp. 67–88. See John S. Harrison, *The Teachers of Emerson*, for Emerson's borrowings from some of these writers. His allusion to Christianity is echoed in his journal of May, 1865, where he states a strong preference for Plato and Plutarch over St. Paul and St. John. See *J* 10:101–2.

10. Scholars have tended to see Emerson's philosophical Plato as a product of his early reading of Plato in the original Greek. The mystical Plato, by contrast, is attributed to Emerson's imagination as influenced by Thomas Taylor's inaccurate translations and interpretations that confused Plato with Neo-Platonism. But these two Platos can also be traced to the monism of the early Plato and the dualism of his *Timaeus* and later writings, and to Emerson's preference for monistic dualism or bipolar unity. See Frederick Ives Carpenter, *Emerson Handbook*, pp. 213–16; Harrison, *Teachers of Emerson*; Ray Benoit, "Emerson on Plato: The Fire's Center," *American Literature* 34 (1963): 487–98.

11. Matthiessen, *American Renaissance*, pp. 64–70; Vivian Hopkins, *Spires of Form: A Study of Emerson's Aesthetic Theory*, pp. 32–34, 121–27, passim.

12. See Harrison, *Teachers of Emerson*, chaps. 4–5.

13. See Frederick Ives Carpenter, *Emerson and Asia*, pp. 98–100; Arthur Christy, *The Orient in American Transcendentalism: A Study of Emerson, Thoreau, and Alcott*, p. 50.

14. See "Language" (from *Nature*) in Part I.

15. Jonathan Edwards, *Images; or, Shadows of Divine Things*, ed. Perry Miller (New Haven: Yale University Press, 1948 [first publication]). Suggested by Sherman Paul, *Emerson's Angle of Vision: Man and Nature in American Experience*, p. 3.

16. These and other passages from Swedenborg, Sampson Reed, and the *New Jerusalem Magazine* are conveniently reprinted in Kenneth W. Cameron,

Emerson the Essayist: An Outline of His Philosophical Development through 1836, 1:228–94; 2:9–36.

17. *CEC*, p. 109; Cameron, *Emerson the Essayist*, 1:250.

18. Hopkins, *Spires of Form*, pp. 130–34. William J. Scheick, *The Slender Human Word: Emerson's Artistry in Prose*, holds that, like the emblem writers of the Renaissance, Emerson did not distinguish hieroglyph from emblem (p. 13); yet he defines Emerson's hieroglyph as elusive, subliminal, organic, intuitive, mysterious, and glimpsed only momentarily (pp. 19–25). For Emerson's interest in hieroglyphics, see pp. 10–16. Sacvan Bercovitch, *Puritan Origins*, pp. 148–186, contrasts the figuralism of the Renaissance emblem writers to Emerson's recasting of colonial typology into modern symbolism as part of Emerson's reaffirmation of the American vision and mission through "auto-American-biography," itself contrasted to the European Romantic ideal of Self as God.

19. See, for example, *J* 2:446; 4:99–100, 283–84; 5:76, 450, 470–71; 9:207; *W* 12:5–6. Emerson Grant Sutcliffe, "Emerson's Theories of Literary Expressions," *University of Illinois Studies in Language and Literature* 8 (1923): 9–152, is still the most detailed, documented study of Emerson's symbology, with special attention to the interrelatedness of the Each and All, self-reliance, the creative process, language, symbol, and style.

20. Charles Feidelson, *Symbolism and American Literature*, p. 121.

21. Quoted in ibid., p. 121, from *W* 4:82.

22. Matthiessen, *American Renaissance*, p. 28.

23. Hopkins, *Spires of Form*, pp. 61, 198–214, on mystical illumination and the sublime. On mysticism and Transcendentalism, see also Patrick F. Quinn, "Emerson and Mysticism," *American Literature* 21 (1950): 397–414.

24. Graham Wallas, *The Art of Thought* (New York: Harcourt, Brace, and Co., 1926). See especially chapter 4.

25. Stephen E. Whicher, *Freedom and Fate: An Inner Life of Ralph Waldo Emerson*, pp. 31, 55–58.

26. James E. Cabot, *A Memoir of Ralph Waldo Emerson*, 2 vols. (Boston, 1887), 2:723.

27. Waggoner, *Emerson as Poet*, pp. 138–39; Gelpi, *The Tenth Muse*, pp. 87–89, 93–94. Harold Bloom considers these "Emerson's two supreme poems" in *The Ringers in the Tower: Studies in Romantic Tradition*, p. 296.

28. Harold Bloom, "The Central Man: Emerson, Whitman, Wallace Stevens," *Massachusetts Review* 7 (1966): 32.

29. Gelpi, *The Tenth Muse*, pp. 62, 69. See also pp. 105–10 for a discussion of the epistemological shift in Emerson from the typology of *Nature* (1836) to organic theory.

30. Matthiessen, *American Renaissance*, p. 30.

31. Ibid., p. 140.

32. Charles R. Metzger, *Emerson and Greenough: Transcendental Pioneers of an American Esthetic*, p. 136.

33. M. H. Abrams, *The Mirror and the Lamp: Romantic Theory and the Critical Tradition*. For a detailed treatment of this shift and the four theories of art, see chaps. 1–4 and pp. 272–85.

34. Harry Hayden Clark, "Changing Attitudes in Early American Literary Criticism, 1800–1840," in *The Development of American Literary Criticism*, ed. Floyd Stovall, p. 42.

35. See ibid., pp. 71–72; Hopkins, *Spires of Form*, pp. 63–146; Abrams, *The Mirror and the Lamp*, pp. 167–77, 218–25.

36. Abrams, *The Mirror and the Lamp*, p. 168.

37. See Clark, "Changing Attitudes," p. 72, for this definition.

38. Ibid.

39. Ibid.

40. Ibid.

41. Quoted in ibid., p. 63.

42. Quoted in ibid., p. 54.

43. According to Joseph Warren Beach, "Emerson and Evolution," *University of Toronto Quarterly* 3 (1934): 494, this outline of eras owes something to Johann Stallo's *General Principles of the Philosophy of Nature* (Boston, 1848).

44. For some key passages, see *J* 1:128–29; *J* 2:371–74; *JMN* 3:150, 247–48; *JMN* 2:278; *J* 5:514–16; *JMN* 7:418, 468–69; *JMN* 10:361.

45. Mark Van Doren, ed., *The Portable Emerson* (New York: Viking Press, 1946), pp. 2, 14.

46. William M. Wynkoop, *Three Children of the Universe: Emerson's Views of Shakespeare, Bacon, and Milton*, argues that Emerson's trinity of "Knower, Doer, and Sayer" (cf. "The Poet" in Part II) was developed from Ralph Cudworth's *The True Intellectual System of the Universe* (1678) (London, 1820, 1845). Although Vivian Hopkins finds "no close parallel" between Emerson's and the Platonic trinities, she documents his apparent indebtedness to Cudworth for the Jupiter-Pluto-Neptune trinity and for the Edenic myth of preexistence, the "fall" from unity with Nature and Spirit, and the way to reintegration ("Emerson and Cudworth: Plastic Nature and Transcendental Art," *American Literature* 23 [1951]: 94–96).

47. "Areopagitica," *W* 12:251; "Comus," *J* 2:462, *W* 7:402; "Lycidas," *J* 3:571, *JMN* 5:109; *Paradise Lost*, *J* 3:329, *JMN* 4:312–13, *W* 11:413; "too learned," *J* 3:328, *JMN* 4:312; "the most literary," *J* 6:369, *JMN* 8:371; "great epic Poet," *J* 1:71, *JMN* 1:41.

I
ART AS EXPERIENCE

48. Sheldon W. Liebman, "Emerson's Discovery of the English Romantics, 1818–1836," *American Transcendental Quarterly* 21 (1974): 36–44.

49. In 1830 Emerson read *The Friend* "with great interest" and *Aids to Reflection* "with yet deeper" (*L* 1:291).

50. Vivian Hopkins, "The Influence of Goethe on Emerson's Aesthetic Theory," *Philological Quarterly* 27 (1948): 342. On the influence of German writers and philosophers, including Kant, see Ralph L. Rusk, *L* 1:xlix–liii; and Henry A. Pochmann, *German Culture in America: Philosophical and Literary Influences, 1600–1900*, pp. 168–207.

51. John T. Flanagan, "Emerson as Critic of Fiction," *Philological Quarterly* 15 (1936): 31.

52. *J* 6:105–6; *JMN* 8:121–22, 7:468–69; *L* 3:197–98, n. 331, 1:xxxix–xlii.

53. However, in a letter to his brother Charles in July 1846, Emerson wrote that on a summer afternoon "under an oak" Thoreau had read to him some of the manuscript of the *Week*, a work that was "pastoral as Isaak Walton, spicy as flagroot, broad & deep as Menu" (*L* 3:338).

54. Matthiessen, *American Renaissance*, p. xii. See also Bishop, *Emerson on the Soul*, p. 9: "Emerson is a true ancestor." The tradition of art and prophecy that descends from *Nature*, "our primal book," leads through Alcott, Thoreau, Dickinson, and Frost, "but most strongly through the vital center of Melville, Whitman, William James, Henry Adams, and Wallace Stevens . . . our greatest, our one indispensable tradition."

55. See Bercovitch, *Puritan Origins*, pp. 165–67.

56. See Harriet R. Zink, *Emerson's Use of the Bible*, University of Nebraska Studies in Language, Literature, and Criticism, no. 14 (Lincoln, Nebr., 1935).

Beauty (1836)

This essay distinguishes three major kinds of beauty as modes of perception. First is sensory beauty in all its immediacy of visual form, impressionistic tone, and integrated pattern; then there is the moral beauty of heroic act or will; and, finally, the intellectual realization of the object's "identity" with the organic whole, or gestalt. In all three modes, beauty is a function of the perceiver's sensibility, perspective, and insight. But its true and ultimate end is to express the harmony that is organically present within all life forms. Thus, implicit in this early work is the essence of Emerson's transcendental aesthetic: through the Eye and the "I" an Object becomes beautiful when seen (realized) contextually as a symbol of Nature, the organic whole, the universe, "the mind of God."

A nobler want of man is served by nature, namely, the love of Beauty.

The ancient Greeks called the world κόσμος [cosmos: order], beauty. Such is the constitution of all things, or such the plastic power of the human eye, that the primary forms, as the sky, the mountain, the tree, the animal, give us a delight *in and for themselves*; a pleasure arising from outline, color, motion, and grouping. This seems partly owing to the eye itself. The eye is the best of artists. By the mutual action of its structure and of the laws of light, perspective is produced, which integrates every mass of objects, of what character soever, into a well colored and shaded globe, so that where the particular objects are mean and unaffecting, the landscape which they compose is round and symmetrical. And as the eye is the best composer, so light is the first of painters. There is no object so foul that intense light will not make beautiful. And the stimulus it affords to the sense, and a sort of infinitude which it hath, like space and time, make all matter gay. Even the corpse has its own beauty. But besides this general grace diffused over nature, almost all the individual forms are agreeable to the eye, as is proved by our endless imitations of some of them, as the acorn, the grape, the pine-cone, the wheat-ear, the egg, the wings and forms of most birds, the lion's claw, the serpent, the butterfly, sea-shells, flames, clouds, buds, leaves, and the forms of many trees, as the palm.

For better consideration, we may distribute the aspects of Beauty in a threefold manner.

1. First, the simple perception of natural forms is a delight. The influence of the forms and actions in nature is so needful to man, that, in its lowest functions, it seems to lie on the confines of commodity and beauty. To the body and mind which have been cramped by noxious work or company, nature is medicinal and restores their tone. The tradesman, the attorney comes out of the din and craft of the street and sees the sky and the woods, and is a man again. In their eternal calm, he finds himself. The health of the eye seems to demand a horizon. We are never tired, so long as we can see far enough.

But in other hours, Nature satisfies by its loveliness, and without any mixture of corporeal benefit. I see the spectacle of morning from the hilltop over against my house, from daybreak to sunrise, with emotions which an angel might share. The long slender bars of cloud float like fishes in the sea of crimson light. From the earth, as a shore, I look out into that silent sea. I seem to partake its rapid transformations; the active enchantment reaches my dust, and I dilate and conspire [breathe in unison] with the morning wind. How does Nature deify us with a few and cheap elements! Give me health and a day, and I will make the pomp of emperors ridiculous. The dawn is my Assyria [power]; the sunset and moonrise my Paphos [myth], and unimaginable realms of faerie; broad noon shall be my England of the senses and the understanding; the night shall be my Germany of mystic philosophy and dreams.

Not less excellent, except for our less susceptibility in the afternoon, was the charm, last evening, of a January sunset. The western clouds divided and subdivided themselves into pink flakes modulated with tints of unspeakable softness, and the air had so much life and sweetness that it was a pain to come within doors. What was it that nature would say? Was there no meaning in the live repose of the valley behind the mill, and which Homer or Shakspeare could not re-form for me in words? The leafless trees become spires of flame in the sunset, with the blue east for their background, and the stars of

the dead calices of flowers, and every withered stem and stubble
rimed with frost, contribute something to the mute music.

The inhabitants of cities suppose that the country landscape is
pleasant only half the year. I please myself with the graces of the
winter scenery, and believe that we are as much touched by it as by
the genial influences of summer. To the attentive eye, each moment
of the year has its own beauty, and in the same field, it beholds, every
hour, a picture which was never seen before, and which shall never be
seen again. The heavens change every moment, and reflect their glory
or gloom on the plains beneath. The state of the crop in the surrounding farms alters the expression of the earth from week to week.
The succession of native plants in the pastures and roadsides, which
makes the silent clock by which time tells the summer hours, will
make even the divisions of the day sensible to a keen observer. The
tribes of birds and insects, like the plants punctual to their time,
follow each other, and the year has room for all. By water-courses,
the variety is greater. In July, the blue pontederia or pickerel-weed
blooms in large beds in the shallow parts of our pleasant river, and
swarms with yellow butterflies in continual motion. Art cannot rival
this pomp of purple and gold. Indeed the river is a perpetual gala,
and boasts each month a new ornament.

But this beauty of Nature which is seen and felt as beauty, is the
least part. The shows of day, the dewy morning, the rainbow, mountains, orchards in blossom, stars, moonlight, shadows in still water,
and the like, if too eagerly hunted, become shows merely, and mock us
with their unreality. Go out of the house to see the moon, and 't is mere
tinsel; it will not please as when its light shines upon your necessary
journey. The beauty that shimmers in the yellow afternoons of October, who ever could clutch it? Go forth to find it, and it is gone;
't is only a mirage as you look from the windows of diligence.

2. The presence of a higher, namely, of the spiritual element is
essential to its perfection. The high and divine beauty which can be
loved without effeminacy, is that which is found in combination with
the human will. Beauty is the mark God sets upon virtue. Every
natural action is graceful. Every heroic act is also decent [fitting or
seemly], and causes the place and the bystanders to shine. We are
taught by great actions that the universe is the property of every

individual in it. Every rational creature has all nature for his dowry and estate. It is his, if he will. He may divest himself of it; he may creep into a corner, and abdicate his kingdom, as most men do, but he is entitled to the world by his constitution. In proportion to the energy of his thought and will, he takes up the world into himself. "All those things for which men plough, build, or sail, obey virtue;" said Sallust.[1] "The winds and waves," said Gibbon, "are always on the side of the ablest navigators."[2] So are the sun and moon and all the stars of heaven. When a noble act is done,—perchance in a scene of great natural beauty; when Leonidas[3] and his three hundred martyrs consume one day in dying, and the sun and moon come each and look at them once in the steep defile of Thermopylae; when Arnold Winkelried, in the high Alps, under the shadow of the avalanche, gathers in his side a sheaf of Austrian spears to break the line for his comrades;[4] are not these heroes entitled to add the beauty of the scene to the beauty of the deed? When the bark of Columbus nears the shore of America;—before it the beach lined with savages, fleeing out of all their huts of cane; the sea behind; and the purple mountains of the Indian Archipelago around, can we separate the man from the living picture? Does not the New World clothe his form with her palm-groves and savannahs as fit drapery? Ever does natural beauty steal in like air, and envelope great actions. When Sir Harry Vane[5] was dragged up the Tower-hill, sitting on a sled, to suffer death as the champion of the English laws, one of the multitude cried out to him, "You never sate on so glorious a seat!" Charles II., to intimidate the citizens of London, caused the patriot Lord Russell[6] to be drawn in an open coach through the principal streets of the city on his way to the scaffold. "But," his biographer says, "the multitude imagined they saw liberty and virtue sitting by his side." In private places, among sordid objects, an act of truth or heroism seems at once to draw to itself the sky as its temple, the sun as its candle. Nature stretches out her arms to embrace man, only let his thoughts be of equal greatness. Willingly does she follow his steps with the rose and the violet, and bend her lines of grandeur and grace to the decoration of her darling child. Only let his thoughts be of equal scope, and the frame will suit the picture. A virtuous man is in unison with her works, and makes the central figure of the visible sphere. Homer,

Pindar, Socrates, Phocion,[7] associate themselves fitly in our memory with the geography and climate of Greece. The visible heavens and earth sympathize with Jesus. And in common life whosoever has seen a person of powerful character and happy genius, will have remarked how easily he took all things along with him,—the persons, the opinions, and the day, and nature became ancillary to a man.

3. There is still another aspect under which the beauty of the world may be viewed, namely, as it becomes an object of the intellect. Beside the relation of things to virtue, they have a relation to thought. The intellect searches out the absolute order of things as they stand in the mind of God, and without the colors of affection. The intellectual and the active powers seem to succeed each other, and the exclusive activity of the one generates the exclusive activity of the other. There is something unfriendly in each to the other, but they are like the alternate periods of feeding and working in animals; each prepares and will be followed by the other. Therefore does beauty, which, in relation to actions, as we have seen, comes unsought, and comes because it is unsought, remain for the apprehension and pursuit of the intellect; and then again, in its turn, of the active power. Nothing divine dies. All good is eternally reproductive. The beauty of nature re-forms itself in the mind, and not for barren contemplation, but for new creation.

All men are in some degree impressed by the face of the world; some men even to delight. This love of beauty is Taste. Others have the same love in such excess, that, not content with admiring, they seek to embody it in new forms. The creation of beauty is Art.

The production of a work of art throws a light upon the mystery of humanity. A work of art is an abstract or epitome of the world. It is the result or expression of nature, in miniature. For although the works of nature are innumerable and all different, the result or the expression of them all is similar and single. Nature is a sea of forms radically alike and even unique. A leaf, a sunbeam, a landscape, the ocean, make an analogous impression on the mind. What is common to them all,—that perfectness and harmony, is beauty. The standard of beauty is the entire circuit of natural forms,—the totality of nature; which the Italians expressed by defining beauty "il più nell' uno [many in one]." Nothing is quite beautiful alone; nothing but is beautiful in the whole. A single object is only so far beautiful as it suggests this universal grace. The poet, the painter, the sculptor, the musician, the architect, seek each to concentrate this radiance of the world on one point, and each in his several work to satisfy the love of beauty which stimulates him to produce. Thus is Art a nature passed through the alembic of man. Thus in art does Nature work through the will of a man filled with the beauty of her first works.

The world thus exists to the soul to satisfy the desire of beauty. This element I call an ultimate end. No reason can be asked or given why the soul seeks beauty. Beauty, in its largest and profoundest sense, is one expression for the universe. God is the all-fair. Truth, and goodness, and beauty, are but different faces of the same All. But beauty in nature is not ultimate. It is the herald of inward and eternal beauty, and is not alone a solid and satisfactory good. It must stand as a part, and not as yet the last or highest expression of the final cause of Nature.

Nature, Addresses, and Lectures, W 1:15–24; first published as chapter 3 in *Nature* (1836).

Language

This essay, Emerson's earliest and best statement of the correspondence theory of language and symbolism, has become the locus classicus *of American Transcendentalism and its symbolic mode of thinking. For the reader who can see through the Platonic terminology (e.g., "necessary Ideas in the mind of God") and the seeming dualism of nature and spirit, it will be a primary source for understanding Emerson's organic view of reality-as-process and the relation of mind and matter, of moral law and natural law. Emerson here identifies this view with the hermetic tradition (the Egyptians, the Brahmans, Pythagoras, and Plato), and with Bacon, Leibnitz, and Swedenborg. His later lecture "The Poet" (1844), reprinted below, developed and refined his ideas on nature (the "not-Me") as the basic analogical medium of creative insight.*

Language is a third use which Nature subserves to man. Nature is the vehicle of thought, and in a simple, double, and three-fold degree.

1. Words are signs of natural facts.
2. Particular natural facts are symbols of particular spiritual facts.
3. Nature is the symbol of spirit.

1. Words are signs of natural facts. The use of natural history is to give us aid in supernatural history; the use of the outer creation, to give us language for the beings and changes of the inward creation. Every word which is used to express a moral or intellectual fact, if traced to its root, is found to be borrowed from some material appearance. *Right* means *straight*; *wrong* means *twisted*. *Spirit* primarily means *wind*; *transgression*, the crossing of a *line*; *supercilious*, the *raising of the eyebrow*. We say the *heart* to express emotion, the *head* to denote thought; and *thought* and *emotion* are words borrowed from sensible things, and now appropriated to spiritual nature. Most of the process by which this transformation is made, is hidden from us in the remote time when language was framed; but the same tendency may be daily observed in children. Children and savages use only nouns or names of things, which they convert into verbs, and apply to analogous mental acts.

2. But this origin of all words that convey a spiritual import,—so conspicuous a fact in the history of language,—is our least debt to nature. It is not words only that are emblematic; it is things which are emblematic. Every natural fact is a symbol of some spiritual fact. Every appearance in nature corresponds to some state of the mind,[8] and that state of the mind can only be described by presenting that natural appearance as its picture. An enraged man is a lion, a cunning man is a fox, a firm man is a rock, a learned man is a torch. A lamb is innocence; a snake is subtle spite; flowers express to us the delicate affections. Light and darkness are our familiar expression for knowledge and ignorance; and heat for love. Visible distance behind and before us, is respectively our image of memory and hope.

Who looks upon a river in a meditative hour and is not reminded of the flux of all things? Throw a stone into the stream, and the circles that propagate themselves are the beautiful type of all influence. Man is conscious of a universal soul within or behind his individual life, wherein, as in a firmament, the natures of Justice, Truth, Love,

Freedom, arise and shine. This universal soul he calls Reason:[9] it is not mine, or thine, or his, but we are its; we are its property and men. And the blue sky in which the private earth is buried, the sky with its eternal calm, and full of everlasting orbs, is the type of Reason. That which intellectually considered we call Reason, considered in relation to nature, we call Spirit. Spirit is the Creator. Spirit hath life in itself. And man in all ages and countries embodies it in his language as the FATHER.

It is easily seen that there is nothing lucky or capricious in these analogies, but that they are constant, and pervade nature. These are not the dreams of a few poets, here and there, but man is an analogist, and studies relations in all objects. He is placed in the centre of beings, and a ray of relation passes from every other being to him. And neither can man be understood without these objects, nor these objects without man. All the facts in natural history taken by themselves, have no value, but are barren, like a single sex. But marry it to human history, and it is full of life. Whole floras, all Linnaeus' and Buffon's volumes, are dry catalogues of facts; but the most trivial of these facts, the habit of a plant, the organs, or work or noise of an insect, applied to the illustration of a fact in intellectual philosophy, or in any way associated to human nature, affects us in the most lively and agreeable manner. The seed of a plant,—to what affecting analogies in the nature of man is that little fruit made use of, in all discourse, up to the voice of Paul, who calls the human corpse a seed,—"It is sown a natural body; it is raised a spiritual body [1 Cor. 15:44]." The motion of the earth round its axis and round the sun, makes the day and the year. These are certain amounts of brute light and heat. But is there no intent of an analogy between man's life and the seasons? And do the seasons gain no grandeur or pathos from that analogy? The instincts of the ant are very unimportant considered as the ant's; but the moment a ray of relation is seen to extend from it to man, and the little drudge is seen to be a monitor, a little body with a mighty heart, then all its habits, even that said to be recently observed, that it never sleeps, become sublime.

Because of this radical correspondence between visible things and human thoughts, savages, who have only what is necessary, converse in figures. As we go back in history, language becomes more picturesque, until its infancy, when it is all poetry; or all spiritual facts are represented by natural symbols. The same symbols are found to make the original elements of all languages. It has moreover been observed, that the idioms of all languages approach each other in passages of the greatest eloquence and power. And as this is the first language, so is it the last. This immediate dependence of language upon nature, this conversion of an outward phenomenon into a type of somewhat in human life, never loses its power to affect us. It is this which gives that piquancy to the conversation of a strong-natured farmer or backwoodsman, which all men relish.

A man's power to connect his thought with its proper symbol, and so to utter it, depends on the simplicity of his character, that is, upon his love of truth and his desire to communicate it without loss. The corruption of man is followed by the corruption of language. When simplicity of character and the sovereignty of ideas is broken up by the prevalence of secondary desires,—the desire of riches, of pleasure, of power, and of praise,—and duplicity and falsehood take place of simplicity and truth, the power over nature as an interpreter of the will is in a degree lost; new imagery ceases to be created, and old words are perverted to stand for things which are not; a paper currency is employed, when there is no bullion in the vaults. In due time the fraud is manifest, and words lose all power to stimulate the understanding or the affections. Hundreds of writers may be found in every long-civilized nation who for a short time believe and make others believe that they see and utter truths, who do not of themselves clothe one thought in its natural garment, but who feed unconsciously on the language created by the primary writers of the country, those, namely, who hold primarily on nature.

But wise men pierce this rotten diction and fasten words again to visible things; so that picturesque language is at once a commanding certificate that he who employs it is a man in alliance with truth and God. The moment our discourse rises above the ground line of familiar facts and is inflamed with passion or exalted by thought, it clothes itself in images. A man conversing in earnest, if he watch his intellectual processes, will find that a material image more or less luminous arises in his mind, contemporaneous with every thought, which furnishes the vestment of the thought. Hence, good writing and brilliant discourse are perpetual allegories. This imagery is spontaneous. It is the blending of experience with the present action of the mind. It is proper creation. It is the working of the Original Cause through the instruments he has already made.

These facts may suggest the advantage which the country-life possesses, for a powerful mind, over the artificial and curtailed life of cities. We know more from nature than we can at will communicate. Its light flows into the mind evermore, and we forget its presence. The poet, the orator, bred in the woods, whose senses have been nourished by their fair and appeasing changes, year after year, without design and without heed,—shall not lose their lesson altogether, in the roar of cities or the broil of politics. Long hereafter, amidst agitation and terror in national councils,—in the hour of revolution,—these solemn images shall reappear in their morning lustre, as fit symbols and words of the thoughts which the passing events shall awaken. At the call of a noble sentiment, again the woods wave, the pines murmur, the river rolls and shines, and the cattle low upon the mountains, as he saw and heard them in his infancy. And with these forms, the spells of persuasion, the keys of power are put into his hands.

3. We are thus assisted by natural objects in the expression of particular meanings. But how great a language to convey such pep-per-corn informations! Did it need such noble races of creatures, this profusion of forms, this host of orbs in heaven, to furnish man with the dictionary and grammar of his municipal speech? Whilst we use this grand cipher to expedite the affairs of our pot and kettle, we feel that we have not yet put it to its use, neither are able. We are like travellers using the cinders of a volcano to roast their eggs. Whilst we see that it always stands ready to clothe what we would say, we cannot avoid the question whether the characters are not significant of themselves. Have mountains, and waves, and skies, no significance but what we consciously give them when we employ them as em-blems of our thoughts? The world is emblematic. Parts of speech are metaphors, because the whole of nature is a metaphor of the human mind. The laws of moral nature answer to those of matter as face to face in a glass. "The visible world and the relation of its parts, is the dial plate of the invisible."[10] The axioms of physics translate the laws of ethics.[11] Thus, "the whole is greater than its part;" "reaction is

equal to action;" "the smallest weight may be made to lift the great-est, the difference of weight being compensated by time;" and many the like propositions, which have an ethical as well as physical sense. These propositions have a much more extensive and universal sense when applied to human life, than when confined to technical use.

In like manner, the memorable words of history and the proverbs of nations consist usually of a natural fact, selected as a picture or parable of a moral truth. Thus; A rolling stone gathers no moss; A bird in the hand is worth two in the bush; A cripple in the right way will beat a racer in the wrong; Make hay while the sun shines; 'T is hard to carry a full cup even; Vinegar is the son of wine; The last ounce broke the camel's back; Long-lived trees make roots first;—and the like. In their primary sense these are trivial facts, but we repeat them for the value of their analogical import. What is true of prov-erbs, is true of all fables, parables, and allegories.

This relation between the mind and matter is not fancied by some poet, but stands in the will of God, and so is free to be known by all men. It appears to men, or it does not appear.[12] When in fortunate hours we ponder this miracle, the wise man doubts if at all other times he is not blind and deaf;

> "Can such things be,
> And overcome us like a summer's cloud,
> Without our special wonder?"
>
> [*Macbeth* 3.4.110–12]

for the universe becomes transparent, and the light of higher laws than its own shines through it. It is the standing problem which has exercised the wonder and the study of every fine genius since the world began; from the era of the Egyptians and the Brahmins to that of Pythagoras, of Plato, of Bacon, of Leibnitz, of Swedenborg.[13] There sits the Sphinx at the road-side, and from age to age, as each prophet comes by, he tries his fortune at reading her riddle.[14] There seems to be a necessity in spirit to manifest itself in material forms; and day and night, river and storm, beast and bird, acid and alkali, preëxist in necessary Ideas in the mind of God, and are what they are by virtue of preceding affections in the world of spirit. A Fact is the end or last issue of spirit. The visible creation is the terminus or the circumference of the invisible world. "Material objects," said a French philosopher, "are necessarily kinds of *scoriae* [dross] of the substantial thoughts of the Creator, which must always preserve an exact relation to their first origin; in other words, visible nature must have a spiritual and moral side."[15]

This doctrine is abstruse, and though the images of "garment," "scoriae," "mirror," etc., may stimulate the fancy, we must summon the aid of subtler and more vital expositors to make it plain. "Every scripture is to be interpreted by the same spirit which gave it forth,"[16]—is the fundamental law of criticism. A life in harmony with Nature, the love of truth and of virtue, will purge the eyes to understand her text. By degrees we may come to know the primitive sense of the permanent objects of nature, so that the world shall be to us an open book, and every form significant of its hidden life and final cause.

A new interest surprises us, whilst, under the view now suggested, we contemplate the fearful extent and multitude of objects; since "every object rightly seen, unlocks a new faculty of the soul."[17] That which was unconscious truth, becomes, when interpreted and defined in an object, a part of the domain of knowledge,—a new weapon in the magazine of power.

Nature, Addresses, and Lectures, W 1:25–35; first published as chapter 4 in *Nature* (1836).

Art

The importance of art in Emerson's pantheon of values is suggested not only by the prominent placement of this essay at its first publication, but also by its early origin. Reacting to the exhibitionist and escapist nature of contemporary art, Emerson sets forth the essentials of a truly functional aesthetics. Creative art, whether in painting, sculpture, or literature, must not only offer a sensory experience—"the gloom of gloom and the sunshine of sunshine"—but also use the symbols of its time and place. Art must transmute experience, however plain or commonplace, into universal truth and stimulate the appreciator to a sense of the "universal relation," the dynamic flow of life. Art and science should integrate beauty with use through "love." Indeed, the art of living itself is as truly a high art as the lyric or the epic.

> Give to barrows, trays and pans
> Grace and glimmer of romance,
> Bring the moonlight into noon
> Hid in gleaming piles of stone;
> On the city's pavéd street
> Plant gardens lined with lilac sweet,
> Let spouting fountains cool the air,
> Singing in the sun-baked square.
> Let statue, picture, park and hall,
> Ballad, flag and festival,
> The past restore, the day adorn
> And make each morrow a new morn.
> So shall the drudge in dusty frock
> Spy behind the city clock
> Retinues of airy kings,
> Skirts of angels, starry wings,
> His fathers shining in bright fables,
> His children fed at heavenly tables.
> 'T is the privilege of Art
> Thus to play its cheerful part,
> Man in Earth to acclimate
> And bend the exile to his fate,
> And, moulded of one element
> With the days and firmament,
> Teach him on these as stairs to climb
> And live on even terms with Time;
> Whilst upper life the slender rill
> Of human sense doth overfill.[18]

Because the soul is progressive, it never quite repeats itself, but in every act attempts the production of a new and fairer whole. This appears in works both of the useful and fine arts, if we employ the popular distinction of works according to their aim either at use or beauty. Thus in our fine arts, not imitation but creation is the aim. In landscapes the painter should give the suggestion of a fairer creation than we know. The details, the prose of nature he should omit and give us only the spirit and splendor. He should know that the landscape has beauty for his eye because it expresses a thought which is to him good; and this because the same power which sees through his eyes is seen in that spectacle; and he will come to value the expression of nature and not nature itself, and so exalt in his copy the features that please him. He will give the gloom of gloom and the sunshine of sunshine. In a portrait he must inscribe the character and not the features, and must esteem the man who sits to him as himself only an imperfect picture or likeness of the aspiring original within.

What is that abridgment and selection we observe in all spiritual activity, but itself the creative impulse? for it is the inlet of that higher illumination which teaches to convey a larger sense by simpler symbols. What is a man but nature's finer success in self-explication? What is a man but a finer and compacter landscape than the horizon figures,—nature's eclecticism? and what is his speech, his love of painting, love of nature, but a still finer success,—all the weary miles and tons of space and bulk left out, and the spirit or moral of it contracted into a musical word, or the most cunning stroke of the pencil?

But the artist must employ the symbols in use in his day and nation to convey his enlarged sense to his fellow-men. Thus the new in art is always formed out of the old. The Genius of the Hour sets his ineffaceable seal on the work and gives it an inexpressible charm for the imagination. As far as the spiritual character of the period overpowers the artist and finds expression in his work, so far it will retain a certain grandeur, and will represent to future beholders the Unknown, the Inevitable, the Divine. No man can quite exclude this element of Necessity from his labor. No man can quite emancipate himself from his age and country, or produce a model in which the education, the religion, the politics, usages and arts of his times shall have no share. Though he were never so original, never so wilful and fantastic, he cannot wipe out of his work every trace of the thoughts amidst which it grew. The very avoidance betrays the usage he avoids. Above his will and out of his sight he is necessitated by the air he breathes and the idea on which he and his contemporaries live and toil, to share the manner of his times, without knowing what that manner is. Now that which is inevitable in the work has a higher charm than individual talent can ever give, inasmuch as the artist's pen or chisel seems to have been held and guided by a gigantic hand to inscribe a line in the history of the human race. This circumstance gives a value to the Egyptian hieroglyphics, to the Indian, Chinese and Mexican idols, however gross and shapeless. They denote the height of the human soul in that hour, and were not fantastic, but sprung from a necessity as deep as the world. Shall I now add that the whole extant product of the plastic arts has herein its highest value, *as history*; as a stroke drawn in the portrait of that fate, perfect and beautiful, according to whose ordinations all beings advance to their beatitude?

Thus, historically viewed, it has been the office of art to educate the perception of beauty. We are immersed in beauty, but our eyes have no clear vision. It needs, by the exhibition of single traits, to assist and lead the dormant taste. We carve and paint, or we behold what is carved and painted, as students of the mystery of Form. The virtue of art lies in detachment, in sequestering one object from the embarrassing variety. Until one thing comes out from the connection of things, there can be enjoyment, contemplation, but no thought. Our happiness and unhappiness are unproductive. The infant lies in a pleasing trance, but his individual character and his practical power depend on his daily progress in the separation of things, and dealing with one at a time. Love and all the passions concentrate all existence around a single form. It is the habit of certain minds to give an all-excluding fulness to the object, the thought, the word they alight upon, and to make that for the time the deputy of the world. These are the artists, the orators, the leaders of society. The power to detach and to magnify by detaching is the essence of rhetoric in the hands of the orator and the poet. This rhetoric, or power to fix the momentary eminency of an object,—so remarkable in Burke, in Byron, in Carlyle,—the painter and sculptor exhibit in color and in stone. The power depends on the depth of the artist's insight of that object he contemplates. For every object has its roots in central nature, and may of course be so exhibited to us as to represent the world. Therefore each work of genius is the tyrant of the hour and concentrates attention on itself. For the time, it is the only thing worth naming to do that,—be it a sonnet, an opera, a landscape, a statue, an oration, the plan of a temple, of a campaign, or of a voyage of discovery. Presently we pass to some other object, which rounds itself into a whole as did the first; for example a well-laid garden; and nothing seems worth doing but the laying out of gardens. I should think fire the best thing in the world, if I were not acquainted with air, and water, and earth. For it is the right and property of all natural objects, of all genuine talents, of all native properties whatsoever, to be for their moment the top of the world. A squirrel leaping from bough to bough and making the wood but one wide tree for his pleasure, fills the eye not less than a lion,—is beautiful, self-sufficing, and stands then and there for nature. A good ballad draws my ear and heart whilst I listen, as much as an epic has done before. A dog, drawn by a master, or a litter of pigs, satisfies and is a reality not less than the frescoes of Angelo [Michelangelo]. From this succession of excellent objects we learn at last the immensity of the world, the opulence of human nature, which can run out to infinitude in any direction. But I also learn that what astonished and fascinated me in the first work, astonished me in the second work also; that excellence of all things is one.

The office of painting and sculpture seems to be merely initial. The best pictures can easily tell us their last secret. The best pictures are rude draughts of a few of the miraculous dots and lines and dyes which make up the ever-changing "landscape with figures" amidst which we dwell. Painting seems to be to the eye what dancing is to the limbs. When that has educated the frame to self-possession, to nimbleness, to grace, the steps of the dancing-master are better forgotten; so painting teaches me the splendor of color and the expression of form, and as I see many pictures and higher genius in the art, I see the boundless opulence of the pencil, the indifferency in which the artist stands free to choose out of the possible forms. If he can draw every thing, why draw any thing? and then is my eye opened to the eternal picture which nature paints in the street, with moving men and children, beggars and fine ladies, draped in red and green and blue and gray; long-haired, grizzled, white-faced, black-faced, wrinkled, giant, dwarf, expanded, elfish,—capped and based by heaven, earth and sea.

A gallery of sculpture teaches more austerely the same lesson. As picture teaches the coloring, so sculpture the anatomy of form. When I have seen fine statues and afterwards enter a public assembly, I understand well what he meant who said, "When I have been reading Homer, all men look like giants." I too see that painting and sculpture are gymnastics of the eye, its training to the niceties and curiosities of its function. There is no statue like this living man, with his infinite advantage over all ideal sculpture, of perpetual variety. What a gallery of art have I here! No mannerist made these varied groups and diverse original single figures.[19] Here is the artist himself improvising, grim and glad, at his block. Now one thought strikes him, now another, and with each moment he alters the whole air, attitude and expression of his clay. Away with your nonsense of oil and easels, of marble and chisels; except to open your eyes to the masteries of eternal art, they are hypocritical rubbish.

The reference of all production at last to an aboriginal Power explains the traits common to all works of the highest art,—that they are universally intelligible; that they restore to us the simplest states of mind, and are religious. Since what skill is therein shown is the reappearance of the original soul, a jet of pure light, it should produce a similar impression to that made by natural objects. In happy hours, nature appears to us one with art; art perfected,—the work of genius. And the individual in whom simple tastes and susceptibility to all the great human influences overpower the accidents of a local and special culture, is the best critic of art. Though we travel the world over to find the beautiful, we must carry it with us, or we find it not. The best of beauty is a finer charm than skill in surfaces, in outlines, or rules of art can ever teach, namely a radiation from the work of art, of human character,—a wonderful expression through stone, or canvas, or musical sound, of the deepest and simplest attributes of our nature, and therefore most intelligible at last to those souls which have these attributes. In the sculptures of the Greeks, in the masonry of the Romans, and in the pictures of the Tuscan and Venetian masters, the highest charm is the universal language they speak. A confession of moral nature, of purity, love, and hope, breathes from them all. That which we carry to them, the same we bring back more fairly illustrated in the memory. The traveller who visits the Vatican and passes from chamber to chamber through galleries of statues, vases, sarcophagi and candelabra, through all forms of beauty cut in the richest materials, is in danger of forgetting the simplicity of the principles out of which they all sprung, and that they had their origin from thoughts and laws in his own breast. He studies the technical rules on these wonderful remains, but forgets that these works were not always thus constellated; that they are the contributions of many ages and many countries; that each came out of the solitary workshop of one artist, who toiled perhaps in ignorance of the existence of other sculpture, created his work without other model save life, household life, and the sweet and smart of personal relations, of beating hearts, and meeting eyes; of poverty and necessity and hope and fear. These were his inspirations, and these are the effects he carries home to your heart and mind. In proportion to his force, the artist will find in his work an outlet for his proper character. He must not be in any manner pinched or hindered by his material, but through his necessity of imparting himself the adamant will be wax in his hands, and will allow an adequate communication of himself, in his full stature and proportion. He need not cumber himself with a conventional nature and culture, nor ask what is the mode in Rome or in Paris, but that house and weather and manner of living which poverty and the fate of birth have made at once so odious and so dear, in the gray unpainted wood cabin, on the corner of a New Hampshire farm, or in the log-hut of the backwoods, or in the narrow lodging where he has endured the constraints and seeming of a city poverty, will serve as well as any other condition as the symbol of a thought which pours itself indifferently through all.

I remember when in my younger days I had heard of the wonders of Italian painting, I fancied the great pictures would be great strangers; some surprising combination of color and form; a foreign wonder, barbaric pearl and gold, like the spontoons and standards of the militia, which play such pranks in the eyes and imaginations of school-boys. I was to see and acquire I knew not what. When I came at last to Rome and saw with eyes the pictures, I found that genius left to novices the gay and fantastic and ostentatious, and itself pierced directly to the simple and true; that it was familiar and sincere; that it was the old, eternal fact I had met already in so many forms,—unto which I lived; that it was the plain *you and me* I knew so well,—had left at home in so many conversations. I had had the same experience already in a church at Naples. There I saw that nothing was changed with me but the place, and said to myself— 'Thou foolish child, hast thou come out hither, over four thousand miles of salt water, to find that which was perfect to thee there at home?' That fact I saw again in the Academmia at Naples, in the chambers of sculpture, and yet again when I came to Rome and to the paintings of Raphael, Angelo, Sacchi,[20] Titian, and Leonardo da Vinci. "What, old mole! workest thou in the earth so fast?" It had travelled by my side; that which I fancied I had left in Boston was here in the Vatican, and again at Milan and at Paris, and made all travelling ridiculous as a treadmill. I now require this of all pictures, that they domesticate me, not that they dazzle me. Pictures must not be too picturesque. Nothing astonishes men so much as common-sense and plain dealing. All great actions have been simple, and all great pictures are.

The Transfiguration, by Raphael, is an eminent example of this peculiar merit. A calm benignant beauty shines over all this picture, and goes directly to the heart. It seems almost to call you by name. The sweet and sublime face of Jesus is beyond praise, yet how it disappoints all florid expectations! This familiar, simple, home-speaking countenance is as if one should meet a friend. The knowledge of picture dealers has its value, but listen not to their criticism when your heart is touched by genius. It was not painted for them, it was painted for you; for such as had eyes capable of being touched by simplicity and lofty emotions.

Yet when we have said all our fine things about the arts, we must end with a frank confession that the arts, as we know them, are but initial. Our best praise is given to what they aimed and promised, not to the actual result. He has conceived meanly of the resources of man, who believes that the best age of production is past. The real value of the Iliad or the Transfiguration is as signs of power; billows or ripples they are of the stream of tendency; tokens of the everlasting effort to produce,[21] which even in its worst estate the soul betrays. Art has not yet come to its maturity if it do not put itself abreast with the most potent influences of the world, if it is not practical and moral, if it do not stand in connection with the conscience, if it do not make the poor and uncultivated feel that it addresses them with a voice of lofty cheer. There is higher work for Art than the arts. They are abortive births of an imperfect or vitiated instinct. Art is the need to create; but in its essence, immense and universal, it is impatient of working with lame or tied hands, and of making cripples and monsters, such as all pictures and statues are. Nothing less than the creation of man and nature is its end. A man should find in it an outlet for his whole energy. He may paint and carve only as long as he can do that. Art should exhilarate, and throw down the walls of circumstance on every side, awakening in the beholder the same sense of universal relation and power which the work evinced in the artist, and its highest effect is to make new artists.

*   *   *

Picture and sculpture are the celebrations and festivities of form. But true art is never fixed, but always flowing. The sweetest music is not in the oratorio, but in the human voice when it speaks from its instant life tones of tenderness, truth, or courage. The oratorio has already lost its relation to the morning, to the sun, and the earth, but that persuading voice is in tune with these. All works of art should not be detached, but extempore performances. A great man is a new statue in every attitude and action. A beautiful woman is a picture which drives all beholders nobly mad. Life may be lyric or epic, as well as a poem or a romance.

*   *   *

The art that thus separates is itself first separated. Art must not be a superficial talent, but must begin farther back in man. Now men do not see nature to be beautiful, and they go to make a statue which shall be. They abhor men as tasteless, dull, and inconvertible, and console themselves with color-bags and blocks of marble. They reject life as prosaic, and create a death which they call poetic. They despatch the day's weary chores, and fly to voluptuous reveries. They eat and drink, that they may afterwards execute the ideal. Thus is art vilified; the name conveys to the mind its secondary and bad senses; it stands in the imagination as somewhat contrary to nature, and struck with death from the first. Would it not be better to begin higher up,—to serve the ideal before they eat and drink; to serve the ideal in eating and drinking, in drawing the breath, and in the functions of life? Beauty must come back to the useful arts, and the distinction between the fine and the useful arts be forgotten. If history were truly told, if life were nobly spent, it would be no longer easy or possible to distinguish the one from the other. In nature, all is useful, all is beautiful. It is therefore beautiful because it is alive, moving, reproductive; it is therefore useful because it is symmetrical and fair. Beauty will not come at the call of a legislature, nor will it repeat in England or America its history in Greece. It will come, as always, unannounced, and spring up between the feet of brave and earnest men. It is in vain that we look for genius to reiterate its miracles in the old arts; it is its instinct to find beauty and holiness in new and necessary facts, in the field and road-side, in the shop and mill. Proceeding from a religious heart it will raise to a divine use the railroad, the insurance office, the joint-stock company; our law, our primary assemblies, our commerce, the galvanic battery, the electric jar, the prism, and the chemist's retort; in which we seek now only an economical use. Is not the selfish and even cruel aspect which belongs to our great mechanical works, to mills, railways, and machinery, the effect of the mercenary impulses which these works obey? When its errands are noble and adequate, a steamboat bridging the Atlantic between Old and New England and arriving at its ports with the punctuality of a planet, is a step of man into harmony with nature. The boat at St. Petersburg, which plies along the Lena[22] by magnetism, needs little to make it sublime. When science is learned in love, and its powers are wielded by love, they will appear the supplements and continuations of the material creation.

Essays: First Series, *W* 2:349–56, 358–63, 365, 367–69; first published as final chapter in *Essays: First Series* (1841); origin in "Art," *EL* 2:41–54, lecture (1836) in course "Philosophy of History."

The Poet

This essay is Emerson's major statement on art as experience, organic form and symbolism, and the contribution of art to democratic culture and to the collective development of man. Rich with insights, it prepares the way for Whitman's great Preface of 1855. Imagine the impact on Whitman of such words as these: "Stand there, balked and dumb, stuttering and stammering, hissed and hooted, stand and strive, until at last rage draw out of thee that dream-*power which every night shows thee is thine own; a power transcending all limit and privacy, and by virtue of which a man is the conductor of the whole river of electricity. Nothing walks, or creeps, or grows, or exists, which must not in turn arise and walk before him as exponent of his meaning." Although there is no explicit evidence of Emerson's indebtedness to the medieval allegorists or the emblem writers of the Renaissance, he does acknowledge his debt to the Neo-Platonists (Proclus, Iamblichus) and to "the highest minds of the world" (Orpheus, Plato, Empedocles, Heraclitus, Plutarch, Swedenborg). On the other hand, he anticipates the modern functional aesthetics of John Dewey's* Art as Experience: *the organic principle that "it is not metres, but a metre-making argument that makes a poem"; that "all symbols are fluxional," not static and conventional; that realistic symbols ("small and mean things") and natural symbols of the life process (sex, gestation, birth, growth) are the most powerful. The inspired American poet, who "speaks somewhat wildly," his "intellect inebriated by nectar" drawn from common influences and experiences, has not yet arrived; "yet America is a poem in our eyes," waiting to be realized by the genius and reconciler to come.*

> A moody child and wildly wise
> Pursued the game with joyful eyes,
> Which chose, like meteors, their way,
> And rived the dark with private ray:
> They overleapt the horizon's edge,
> Searched with Apollo's privilege;
> Through man, and woman, and sea, and star
> Saw the dance of nature forward far;
> Through worlds, and races, and terms, and times
> Saw musical order, and pairing rhymes.[23]

> Olympian bards who sung
> Divine ideas below,
> Which always find us young,
> And always keep us so.[24]

Those who are esteemed umpires of taste are often persons who have acquired some knowledge of admired pictures or sculptures, and have an inclination for whatever is elegant; but if you inquire whether they are beautiful souls, and whether their own acts are like fair pictures, you learn that they are selfish and sensual. Their cultivation is local, as if you should rub a log of dry wood in one spot to produce fire, all the rest remaining cold. Their knowledge of the fine arts is some study of rules and particulars, or some limited judgment of color or form, which is exercised for amusement or for show. It is a proof of the shallowness of the doctrine of beauty as it lies in the minds of our amateurs [connoisseurs], that men seem to have lost the perception of the instant dependence of form upon soul. There is no doctrine of forms in our philosophy. We were put into our bodies, as fire is put into a pan to be carried about; but there is no accurate adjustment between the spirit and the organ, much less is the latter the germination of the former. So in regard to other forms, the intellectual men do not believe in any essential dependence of the material world on thought and volition. Theologians think it a pretty air-castle to talk of the spiritual meaning of a ship or a cloud, of a city or a contract, but they prefer to come again to the solid ground of historical evidence; and even the poets are contented with a civil and conformed manner of living, and to write poems from the fancy, at a safe distance from their own experience. But the highest minds of the world have never ceased to explore the double meaning, or shall I say the quadruple or the centuple or much more manifold meaning, of every sensuous fact; Orpheus, Empedocles, Heraclitus, Plato, Plutarch, Dante, Swedenborg, and the masters of sculpture, picture and poetry. For we are not pans and barrows, nor even porters of the fire and torch-bearers, but children of the fire, made of it, and only the same divinity transmuted and at two or three removes, when we know least about it.[25] And this hidden truth, that the fountains whence all this river of Time and its creatures floweth are intrinsically ideal and beautiful, draws us to the consideration of the nature and functions of the Poet, or the man of Beauty; to the means and materials he uses, and to the general aspect of the art in the present time.

The breadth of the problem is great, for the poet is representative. He stands among partial men for the complete man, and apprises us not of his wealth, but of the common wealth. The young man reveres men of genius, because, to speak truly, they are more himself than he is. They receive of the soul as he also receives, but they more. Nature enhances her beauty, to the eye of loving men, from their belief that the poet is beholding her shows at the same time. He is isolated among his contemporaries by truth and by his art, but with this consolation in his pursuits, that they will draw all men sooner or later. For all men live by truth and stand in need of expression. In love, in art, in avarice, in politics, in labor, in games, we study to utter our painful secret. The man is only half himself, the other half is his expression.

Notwithstanding this necessity to be published, adequate expression is rare. I know not how it is that we need an interpreter, but the great majority of men seem to be minors, who have not yet come into possession of their own, or mutes, who cannot report the conversation they have had with nature. There is no man who does not anticipate a supersensual utility in the sun and stars, earth and water. These stand and wait to render him a peculiar service. But there is some obstruction or some excess of phlegm in our constitution, which does not suffer them to yield the due effect.[26] Too feeble fall the impressions of nature on us to make us artists. Every touch should thrill. Every man should be so much an artist that he could report in conversation what had befallen him. Yet, in our experience, the rays or appulses have sufficient force to arrive at the senses, but not enough to reach the quick and compel the reproduction of themselves in speech.[27] The poet is the person in whom these powers are in balance, the man without impediment, who sees and handles that which others dream of, traverses the whole scale of experience, and is representative of man, in virtue of being the largest power to receive and to impart.

For the Universe has three children, born at one time, which reappear under different names in every system of thought, whether they be called cause, operation and effect; or, more poetically, Jove,

Pluto, Neptune; or, theologically, the Father, the Spirit and the Son; but which we will call here the Knower, the Doer and the Sayer. These stand respectively for the love of truth, for the love of good, and for the love of beauty. These three are equal. Each is that which he is, essentially, so that he cannot be surmounted or analyzed, and each of these three has the power of the others latent in him and his own, patent.

The poet is the sayer, the namer, and represents beauty. He is a sovereign, and stands on the centre. For the world is not painted or adorned, but is from the beginning beautiful and God has not made some beautiful things, but Beauty is the creator of the universe. Therefore the poet is not any permissive potentate, but is emperor in his own right. Criticism is infested with a cant of materialism, which assumes that manual skill and activity is the first merit of all men, and disparages such as say and do not, overlooking the fact that some men, namely poets, are natural sayers, sent into the world to the end of expression, and confounds them with those whose province is action but who quit it to imitate the sayers. But Homer's words are as costly and admirable to Homer as Agamemnon's victories are to Agamemnon. The poet does not wait for the hero or the sage, but, as they act and think primarily, so he writes primarily what will and must be spoken, reckoning the others, though primaries also, yet, in respect to him, secondaries and servants; as sitters or models in the studio of a painter, or as assistants who bring building-materials to an architect.

For poetry was all written before time was, and whenever we are so finely organized that we can penetrate into that region where the air is music, we hear those primal warblings and attempt to write them down, but we lose ever and anon a word or a verse and substitute something of our own, and thus miswrite the poem. The men of more delicate ear write down these cadences more faithfully, and these transcripts, though imperfect, become the songs of the nations. For nature is as truly beautiful as it is good, or as it is reasonable, and must as much appear as it must be done, or be known. Words and deeds are quite indifferent modes of the divine energy. Words are also actions, and actions are a kind of words.

The sign and credentials of the poet are that he announces that which no man foretold. He is the true and only doctor [learned man]; he knows and tells; he is the only teller of news, for he was present and privy to the appearance which he describes. He is a beholder of ideas and an utterer of the necessary and causal. For we do not speak now of men of poetical talents, or of industry and skill in metre, but of the true poet. I took part in a conversation the other day concerning a recent writer of lyrics, a man of subtle mind, whose head appeared to be a music-box of delicate tunes and rhythms, and whose skill and command of language we could not sufficiently praise.[28] But when the question arose whether he was not only a lyrist but a poet, we were obliged to confess that he is plainly a contemporary, not an eternal man. He does not stand out of our low limitations, like a Chimborazo under the line,[29] running up from a torrid base through all the climates of the globe, with belts of the herbage of every latitude on its high and mottled sides; but this genius is the landscape-garden of a modern house, adorned with fountains and statues, with well-bred men and women standing and sitting in the walks and terraces. We hear, through all the varied music, the groundtone of conventional life. Our poets are men of talents who sing, and not the children of music. The argument is secondary, the finish of the verses is primary.

For it is not metres, but a metre-making argument that makes a poem,—a thought so passionate and alive that like the spirit of a plant or an animal it has an architecture of its own, and adorns nature with a new thing. The thought and the form are equal in the order of time, but in the order of genesis the thought is prior to the form. The poet has a new thought; he has a whole new experience to unfold; he will tell us how it was with him, and all men will be the richer in his fortune. For the experience of each new age requires a new confession, and the world seems always waiting for its poet. I remember when I was young how much I was moved one morning by tidings that genius had appeared in a youth who sat near me at table. He had left his work and gone rambling none knew whither, and had written hundreds of lines, but could not tell whether that which was in him was therein told; he could tell nothing but that all was changed,— man, beast, heaven, earth and sea. How gladly we listened! how credulous! Society seemed to be compromised. We sat in the aurora of a sunrise which was to put out all the stars. Boston seemed to be at twice the distance it had the night before, or was much farther than that. Rome,—what was Rome? Plutarch and Shakspeare were in the yellow leaf, and Homer no more should be heard of.[30] It is much to know that poetry has been written this very day, under this very roof, by your side. What! that wonderful spirit has not expired! These stony moments are still sparkling and animated! I had fancied that the oracles were all silent, and nature had spent her fires; and behold! all night, from every pore, these fine auroras have been streaming. Every one has some interest in the advent of the poet, and no one knows how much it may concern him. We know that the secret of the world is profound, but who or what shall be our interpreter, we know not. A mountain ramble, a new style of face, a new person, may put the key into our hands. Of course the value of genius to us is in the veracity of its report. Talent may frolic and juggle; genius realizes and adds. Mankind in good earnest have availed so far in understanding themselves and their work, that the foremost watchman on the peak announces his news. It is the truest word ever spoken, and the phrase will be the fittest, most musical, and the unerring voice of the world for that time.

All that we call sacred history attests that the birth of a poet is the principal event in chronology. Man, never so often deceived, still watches for the arrival of a brother who can hold him steady to a truth until he has made it his own. With what joy I begin to read a poem which I confide in as an inspiration! And now my chains are to be broken; I shall mount above these clouds and opaque airs in which I live,—opaque, though they seem transparent,—and from the heaven of truth I shall see and comprehend my relations. That will reconcile me to life and renovate nature, to see trifles animated by a tendency, and to know what I am doing. Life will no more be a noise; now I shall see men and women, and know the signs by which they may be discerned from fools and satans. This day shall be better than my birthday: then I became an animal; now I am invited into the science [knowledge] of the real. Such is the hope, but the fruition is postponed. Oftener it falls that this winged man, who will carry me into the heaven, whirls me into mists, then leaps and frisks about with me as it were from cloud to cloud, still affirming that he is bound heavenward; and I, being myself a novice, am slow in perceiving that he does not know the way into the heavens, and is merely bent that I should admire his skill to rise like a fowl or a flying fish, a little way from the ground or the water; but the all-piercing, all-feeding and ocular [all-seeing] air of heaven that man shall never inhabit. I tumble down again soon into my old nooks, and lead the life of exaggerations as before, and have lost my faith in the possibility of any guide who can lead me thither where I would be.

But, leaving these victims of vanity, let us, with new hope, observe how nature, by worthier impulses, has insured the poet's fidelity to his office of announcement and affirming, namely by the beauty of things, which becomes a new and higher beauty when expressed. Nature offers all her creatures to him as a picture-language. Being used as a type, a second wonderful value appears in the object, far better than its old value; as the carpenter's stretched cord, if you hold your ear close enough, is musical in the breeze. "Things more excellent than every image," says Jamblichus, "are expressed through images."[31] Things admit of being used as symbols because nature is a symbol, in the whole, and in every part. Every line we can draw in the sand has expression; and there is no body without its spirit or genius. All form is an effect of character; all condition, of the quality of the life; all harmony, of health; and for this reason a perception of beauty should be sympathetic, or proper only to the good. The beautiful rests on the foundations of the necessary. The soul makes the body, as the wise Spenser teaches:—

> "So every spirit, as it is more pure,
> And hath in it the more of heavenly light,
> So it the fairer body doth procure
> To habit in, and it more fairly dight,
> With cheerful grace and amiable sight.
> For, of the soul, the body form doth take,
> For soul is form, and doth the body make."[32]

Here we find ourselves suddenly not in a critical speculation but in a holy place, and should go very warily and reverently. We stand before the secret of the world, there where Being passes into Appearance and Unity into Variety.

The Universe is the externization of the soul. Wherever the life is, that bursts into appearance around it. Our science is sensual, and therefore superficial.[33] The earth and the heavenly bodies, physics and chemistry, we sensually treat, as if they were self-existent; but these are the retinue of that Being we have. "The mighty heaven," said Proclus, "exhibits, in its transfigurations, clear images of the splendor of intellectual perceptions; being moved in conjunction with the unapparent periods of intellectual natures."[34] Therefore science always goes abreast with the just elevation of the man, keeping step with religion and metaphysics; or the state of science is an index of our self-knowledge. Since every thing in nature answers to a moral power, if any phenomenon remains brute and dark it is because the corresponding faculty in the observer is not yet active.

No wonder then, if these waters be so deep, that we hover over them with a religious regard. The beauty of the fable proves the importance of the sense; to the poet, and to all others; or, if you please, every man is so far a poet as to be susceptible of these enchantments of nature; for all men have the thoughts whereof the universe is the celebration. I find that the fascination resides in the symbol. Who loves nature? Who does not? Is it only poets, and men of leisure and cultivation, who live with her? No; but also hunters, farmers, grooms and butchers, though they express their affection in their choice of life and not in their choice of words. The writer wonders what the coachman or the hunter values in riding, in horses and dogs. It is not superficial qualities. When you talk with him he holds these at as slight a rate as you. His worship is sympathetic; he has no definitions, but he is commanded in nature by the living power which he feels to be there present. No imitation or playing of these things would content him; he loves the earnest of the north wind, of rain, of stone and wood and iron. A beauty not explicable is dearer than a beauty which we can see to the end of. It is nature the symbol, nature certifying the supernatural, body overflowed by life which he worships with coarse but sincere rites.

The inwardness and mystery of this attachment drive men of every class to the use of emblems. The schools of poets and philosophers are not more intoxicated with their symbols than the populace with theirs. In our political parties, compute the power of badges and emblems. See the great ball which they roll from Baltimore to Bunker Hill![35] In the political processions, Lowell goes in a loom, and Lynn in a shoe, and Salem in a ship.[36] Witness the cider-barrel, the log-cabin, the hickory-stick, the palmetto, and all the cognizances of party.[37] See the power of national emblems. Some stars, lilies, leopards, a crescent, a lion,[38] an eagle, or other figure which came into credit God knows how, on an old rag of bunting, blowing in the wind on a fort at the ends of the earth, shall make the blood tingle under the rudest or the most conventional exterior. The people fancy they hate poetry, and they are all poets and mystics!

Beyond this universality of the symbolic language, we are apprised of the divineness of this superior use of things, whereby the world is a temple whose walls are covered with emblems, pictures and commandments of the Deity,—in this, that there is no fact in nature which does not carry the whole sense of nature; and the distinctions which we make in events and in affairs, of low and high, honest and base, disappear when nature is used as a symbol. Thought makes everything fit for use. The vocabulary of an omniscient man would embrace words and images excluded from polite conversation. What would be base, or even obscene, to the obscene, becomes illustrious, spoken in a new connection of thought. The piety of the Hebrew prophets purges their grossness. The circumcision is an example of the power of poetry to raise the low and offensive. Small and mean things serve as well as great symbols. The meaner the type by which a law is expressed, the more pungent it is, and the more lasting in the memories of men; just as we choose the smallest box or case in which any needful utensil can be carried. Bare lists of words are found suggestive to an imaginative and excited mind; as it is related of Lord Chatham that he was accustomed to read in Bailey's Dictionary when he was preparing to speak in Parliament.[39] The poorest experience is rich enough for all the purposes of expressing thought. Why covet a knowledge of new facts? Day and night, house and garden, a few books, a few actions, serve us as well as would all trades and all spectacles. We are far from having exhausted the significance of the few symbols we use. We can come to use them yet with a terrible simplicity. It does not need that a poem should be long. Every word was once a poem. Every new relation is a new word. Also we use defects and deformities to a sacred purpose, so expressing our sense that the evils of the world are such only to the evil eye.[40] In the old mythology, mythologists observe, defects are ascribed to divine natures, as lameness to Vulcan, blindness to Cupid, and the like,—to signify exuberances.[41]

For as it is dislocation and detachment from the life of God that makes things ugly, the poet, who re-attaches things to nature and the Whole,—re-attaching even artificial things and violation of nature, to nature, by a deeper insight,—disposes very easily of the most disagreeable facts. Readers of poetry see the factory-village and the railway, and fancy that the poetry of the landscape is broken up by these; for these works of art are not yet consecrated in their reading; but the poet sees them fall within the great Order not less than the beehive or the spider's geometrical web. Nature adopts them very fast into her vital circles, and the gliding train of cars she loves like her own. Besides, in a centred mind, it signifies nothing how many mechanical inventions you exhibit. Though you add millions, and never so surprising, the fact of mechanics has not gained a grain's weight. The spiritual fact remains unalterable, by many or by few particulars; as no mountain is of any appreciable height to break the curve of the sphere. A shrewd country-boy goes to the city for the first time, and the complacent citizen is not satisfied with his little wonder. It is not that he does not see all the fine houses and know that he never saw such before, but he disposes of them as easily as the poet finds place for the railway. The chief value of the new fact is to enhance the great and constant fact of Life, which can dwarf any and every circumstance, and to which the belt of wampum and the commerce of America are alike.

The world being thus put under the mind for verb and noun, the poet is he who can articulate it. For though life is great, and fascinates and absorbs; and though all men are intelligent of the symbols through which it is named; yet they cannot originally use them. We are symbols and inhabit symbols; workmen, work, and tools, words and things, birth and death, all are emblems; but we sympathize with the symbols, and being infatuated with the economical uses of things, we do not know that they are thoughts. The poet, by an ulterior intellectual perception, gives them a power which makes their old use forgotten, and puts eyes and a tongue into every dumb and inanimate object. He perceives the independence of the thought on the symbol, the stability of the thought, the accidency and fugacity of the symbol.[42] As the eyes of Lyncaeus[43] were said to see through the earth, so the poet turns the world to glass, and shows us all things in their right series and procession. For through that better perception he stands one step nearer to things, and sees the flowing or metamorphosis; perceives that thought is multiform; that within the form of every creature is a force impelling it to ascend into a higher form; and following with his eyes the life, uses the forms which express that life, and so his speech flows with the flowing of nature. All the facts of the animal economy, sex, nutriment, gestation, birth, growth, are symbols of the passage of the world into the soul of man, to suffer there a change and reappear a new and higher fact. He uses forms according to the life, and not according to the form. This is true science. The poet alone knows astronomy, chemistry, vegetation and animation, for he does not stop at these facts, but employs them as signs. He knows why the plain or meadow of space was strown with these flowers we call suns and moons and stars; why the great deep is adorned with animals, with men and gods; for in every word he speaks he rides on them as the horses of thought.

By virtue of this science the poet is the Namer or Language-maker, naming things sometimes after their appearance, sometimes after their essence, and giving to every one its own name and not another's, thereby rejoicing the intellect, which delights in detachment or boundary. The poets made all the words, and therefore language is the archives of history, and, if we must say it, a sort of tomb of the muses. For though the origin of most of our words is forgotten, each word was at first a stroke of genius, and obtained currency because for the moment it symbolized the world to the first speaker and to the hearer. The etymologist finds the deadest word to have been once a brilliant picture. Language is fossil poetry. As the limestone of the continent consists of infinite masses of the shells of animalcules,[44] so language is made up of images or tropes, which now, in their second-ary use, have long ceased to remind us of their poetic origin. But the poet names the thing because he sees it, or comes one step nearer to it than any other. This expression or naming is not art, but a second nature, grown out of the first, as a leaf out of a tree. What we call nature is a certain self-regulated motion or change; and nature does all things by her own hands, and does not leave another to baptize her but baptizes herself; and this through the metamorphosis again. I remember that a certain poet described it to me thus:—[45]

Genius is the activity which repairs the decays of things, whether wholly or partly of a material and finite kind. Nature, through all her kingdoms, insures herself. Nobody cares for planting the poor fungus; so she shakes down from the gills of one agaric[46] countless spores, any one of which, being preserved, transmits new billions of spores to-morrow or next day. The new agaric of this hour has a chance which the old one had not. This atom of seed is thrown into a new place, not subject to the accidents which destroyed its parent two rods off. She makes a man; and having brought him to ripe age, she will no longer run the risk of losing this wonder at a blow, but she detaches from him a new self, that the kind may be safe from accidents to which the individual is exposed. So when the soul of the poet has come to ripeness of thought, she detaches and sends away from it its poems or songs,—a fearless, sleepless, deathless progeny, which is not exposed to the accidents of the weary kingdom of time; a fearless, vivacious offspring, clad with wings (such was the virtue of the soul out of which they came) which carry them fast and far, and infix them irrecover-ably into the hearts of men. These wings are the beauty of the poet's soul. The songs, thus flying immortal from their mortal parent, are pursued by clamorous flights of censures, which swarm in far greater numbers and threaten to devour them; but these last are not winged. At the end of a very short leap they fall plump down and rot, having received from the souls out of which they came no beautiful wings. But the melodies of the poet ascend and leap and pierce into the deeps of infinite time.

So far the bard taught me, using his freer speech. But nature has a higher end, in the production of new individuals, than security, namely *ascension*, or the passage of the soul into higher forms. I knew in my younger days the sculptor who made the statue of the youth which stands in the public garden. He was, as I remember, unable to tell directly what made him happy or unhappy, but by wonderful indirections he could tell. He rose one day, according to his habit, before the dawn, and saw the morning break, grand as the eternity out of which it came, and for many days after, he strove to express this tranquillity, and lo! his chisel had fashioned out of marble the form of a beautiful youth, Phosphorus,[47] whose aspect is such that it is said all persons who look on it become silent. The poet also resigns himself to his mood, and that thought which agitated him is expressed, but *alter idem* [similar, but different], in a manner totally new. The expression

is organic, or the new type which things themselves take when liberated. As, in the sun, objects paint their images on the retina of the eye,
so they, sharing the aspiration of the whole universe, tend to paint a
far more delicate copy of their essence in his mind. Like the metamorphosis of things into higher organic forms is their change into
melodies. Over everything stands its daemon or soul, and, as the form
of the thing is reflected by the eye, so the soul of the thing is reflected
by a melody. The sea, the mountain-ridge, Niagara, and every
flower-bed, pre-exist, or super-exist, in pre-cantations,[48] which sail
like odors in the air, and when any man goes by with an ear sufficiently fine, he overhears them and endeavors to write down the notes
without diluting or depraving them. And herein is the legitimation of
criticism, in the mind's faith that the poems are a corrupt version of
some text in nature with which they ought to be made to tally. A
rhyme in one of our sonnets should not be less pleasing than the
iterated nodes of a seashell, or the resembling difference of a group of
flowers. The pairing of the birds is an idyl, not tedious as our idyls are;
a tempest is a rough ode, without falsehood or rant; a summer, with
its harvest sown, reaped and stored, is an epic song, subordinating
how many admirable executed parts. Why should not the symmetry
and truth that modulate these, glide into our spirits, and we participate the invention of nature?

This insight, which expresses itself by what is called Imagination, is
a very high sort of seeing, which does not come by study, but by the
intellect being where and what it sees; by sharing the path or circuit
of things through forms, and so making them translucid to others.
The path of things is silent. Will they suffer a speaker to go with
them? A spy they will not suffer; a lover, a poet, is the transcendency
of their own nature,—him they will suffer. The condition of true
naming, on the poet's part, is his resigning himself to the divine *aura*
which breathes through forms, and accompanying that.

It is a secret which every intellectual man quickly learns, that
beyond the energy of his possessed and conscious intellect he is capable of a new energy (as of an intellect doubled on itself), by
abandonment to the nature of things; that beside his privacy of
power as an individual man, there is a great public power on which
he can draw, by unlocking, at all risks, his human doors, and suffering

the ethereal tides to roll and circulate through him; then he is caught up into the life of the Universe, his speech is thunder, his thought is law, and his words are universally intelligible as the plants and animals. The poet knows that he speaks adequately then only when he speaks somewhat wildly, or "with the flower of the mind," not with the intellect used as an organ, but with the intellect released from all service and suffered to take its direction from its celestial life; or as the ancients were wont to express themselves, not with intellect alone but with the intellect inebriated by nectar. As the traveller who has lost his way throws his reins on his horse's neck and trusts to the instinct of the animal to find his road, so must we do with the divine animal who carries us through this world. For if in any manner we can stimulate this instinct, new passages are opened for us into nature; the mind flows into and through things hardest and highest, and the metamorphosis is possible.

This is the reason why bards love wine, mead, narcotics, coffee, tea, opium, the fumes of sandalwood and tobacco, or whatever other procurers of animal exhilaration. All men avail themselves of such means as they can, to add this extraordinary power to their normal powers; and to this end they prize conversation, music, pictures, sculpture, dancing, theatres, travelling, war, mobs, fires, gaming, politics, or love, or science, or animal intoxication,—which are several coarser or finer *quasi*-mechanical substitutes for the true nectar, which is the ravishment of the intellect by coming nearer to the fact. These are auxiliaries to the centrifugal tendency of a man, to his passage out into free space, and they help him to escape the custody of that body in which he is pent up, and of that jail-yard of individual relations in which he is enclosed. Hence a great number of such as were professionally expressers of Beauty, as painters, poets, musicians and actors, have been more than others wont to lead a life of pleasure and indulgence; all but the few who received the true nectar; and, as it was a spurious mode of attaining freedom, as it was an emancipation not into the heavens but into the freedom of baser places, they were punished for that advantage they won, by a dissipation and deterioration. But never can any advantage be taken of nature by a trick. The spirit of the world, the great calm presence of the Creator, comes not forth to the sorceries of opium or of wine. The sublime vision

comes to the pure and simple soul in a clean and chaste body. That is
not an inspiration, which we owe to narcotics, but some counterfeit
excitement and fury. Milton says that the lyric poet may drink wine
and live generously, but the epic poet, he who shall sing of the gods
and their descent unto men, must drink water out of a wooden bowl.
For poetry is not 'Devil's wine,' but God's wine.[49] It is with this as it is
with toys. We fill the hands and nurseries of our children with all
manner of dolls, drums and horses; withdrawing their eyes from the
plain face and sufficing objects of nature, the sun and moon, the animals, the water and stones, which should be their toys. So the poet's
habit of living should be set on a key so low that the common influences should delight him. His cheerfulness should be the gift of the
sunlight; the air should suffice for his inspiration, and he should be
tipsy with water. That spirit which suffices quiet hearts, which seems
to come forth to such from every dry knoll of sere grass, from every
pine stump and half-imbedded stone on which the dull March sun
shines, comes forth to the poor and hungry, and such as are of simple
taste. If thou fill thy brain with Boston and New York, with fashion
and covetousness, and wilt stimulate thy jaded senses with wine and
French coffee, thou shalt find no radiance of wisdom in the lonely
waste of the pine woods.

If the imagination intoxicates the poet, it is not inactive in other
men. The metamorphosis excites in the beholder an emotion of joy.
The use of symbols has a certain power of emancipation and exhilaration for all men. We seem to be touched by a wand which makes
us dance and run about happily, like children. We are like persons
who come out of a cave or cellar into the open air. This is the effect on
us of tropes, fables, oracles and all poetic forms. Poets are thus
liberating gods. Men have really got a new sense, and found within
their world another world, or nest of worlds; for, the metamorphosis
once seen, we divine that it does not stop. I will not now consider
how much this makes the charm of algebra and the mathematics,
which also have their tropes, but it is felt in every definition; as when
Aristotle defines *space* to be an immovable vessel in which things are
contained;[50]–or when Plato defines a *line* to be a flowing point; or
figure to be a bound of solid; and many the like. What a joyful sense of
freedom we have when Vitruvius[51] announces the old opinion of

artists that no architect can build any house well who does not know
something of anatomy. When Socrates, in Charmides, tells us that the
soul is cured of its maladies by certain incantations, and that these
incantations are beautiful reasons, from which temperance is generated in souls; when Plato calls the world an animal, and [in] Timaeus affirms that the plants also are animals; or affirms a man to be
a heavenly tree, growing with his root, which is his head, upward; and,
as George Chapman, following him, writes,

> "So in our tree of man, whose nervie root
> "Springs in his top;"[52]

when Orpheus speaks of hoariness as "that white flower which marks
extreme old age;" when Proclus calls the universe the statue of the
intellect; when Chaucer, in his praise of 'Gentilesse,' compares good
blood in mean condition to fire, which, though carried to the darkest
house betwixt this and the mount of Caucasus, will yet hold its
natural office and burn as bright as if twenty thousand men did it
behold;[53] when John saw, in the Apocalypse, the ruin of the world
through evil, and the stars fall from heaven as the fig tree casteth her
untimely fruit;[54] when Aesop reports the whole catalogue of common
daily relations through the masquerade of birds and beasts;—we take
the cheerful hint of the immortality of our essence and its versatile
habit and escapes, as when the gypsies say of themselves "it is in vain
to hang them, they cannot die."

The poets are thus liberating gods. The ancient British bards had
for the title of their order, "Those who are free throughout the
world." They are free, and they make free. An imaginative book
renders us much more service at first, by stimulating us through its
tropes, than afterward when we arrive at the precise sense of the
author. I think nothing is of any value in books excepting the transcendental and extraordinary. If a man is inflamed and carried away
by his thought, to that degree that he forgets the authors and the
public and heeds only this one dream which holds him like an
insanity, let me read his paper, and you may have all the arguments
and histories and criticism. All the value which attaches to Pythagoras, Paracelsus, Cornelius Agrippa, Cardan, Kepler, Swedenborg,
Schelling, Oken,[55] or any other who introduces questionable facts

into his cosmogony, as angels, devils, magic, astrology, palmistry, mesmerism, and so on, is the certificate we have of departure from routine, and that here is a new witness. That also is the best success in conversation, the magic of liberty, which puts the world like a ball in our hands. How cheap even the liberty then seems; how mean to study, when an emotion communicates to the intellect the power to sap and unheave nature; how great the perspective! nations, times, systems, enter and disappear like threads in tapestry of large figure and many colors; dream delivers us to dream, and while the drunkenness lasts we will sell our bed, our philosophy, our religion, in our opulence.

There is good reason why we should prize this liberation. The fate of the poor shepherd, who, blinded and lost in the snow-storm, perishes in a drift within a few feet of his cottage door, is an emblem of the state of man. On the brink of the waters of life and truth, we are miserably dying. The inaccessibleness of every thought but that we are in, is wonderful. What if you come near to it; you are as remote when you are nearest as when you are farthest. Every thought is also a prison; every heaven is also a prison. Therefore we love the poet, the inventor, who in any form, whether in an ode or in an action or in looks and behavior, has yielded us a new thought. He unlocks our chains and admits us to a new scene.

This emancipation is dear to all men, and the power to impart it, as it must come from greater depth and scope of thought, is a measure of intellect. Therefore all books of the imagination endure, all which ascend to that truth that the writer sees nature beneath him, and uses it as his exponent. Every verse or sentence possessing this virtue will take care of its own immortality. The religions of the world are the ejaculations of a few imaginative men.

But the quality of the imagination is to flow, and not to freeze. The poet did not stop at the color or the form, but read their meaning; neither may he rest in this meaning, but he makes the same objects exponents of his new thought. Here is the difference betwixt the poet and the mystic, that the last nails a symbol to one sense, which was a true sense for a moment, but soon becomes old and false. For all symbols are fluxional; all language is vehicular and transitive, and is good, as ferries and horses are, for conveyance, not as farms and houses are, for homestead. Mysticism consists in the mistake of an accidental and individual symbol for an universal one. The morning-redness happens to be the favorite meteor to the eyes of Jacob Behmen,[56] and comes to stand to him for truth and faith; and, he believes, should stand for the same realities to every reader. But the first reader prefers as naturally the symbol of a mother and child, or a gardener and his bulb, or a jeweller polishing a gem. Either of these, or of a myriad more, are equally good to the person to whom they are significant. Only they must be held lightly, and be very willingly translated into the equivalent terms which others use. And the mystic must be steadily told,—All that you say is just as true without the tedious use of that symbol as with it. Let us have a little algebra, instead of this trite rhetoric,—universal signs, instead of these village symbols,—and we shall both be gainers. The history of hierarchies seems to show that all religious error consisted in making the symbol too stark and solid, and was at last nothing but an excess of the organ of language.

Swedenborg, of all men in the recent ages, stands eminently for the translator of nature into thought. I do not know the man in history to whom things stood so uniformly for words. Before him the metamorphosis continually plays. Everything on which his eye rests, obeys the impulses of moral nature. The figs become grapes whilst he eats them. When some of his angels affirmed a truth, the laurel twig which they held blossomed in their hands. The noise which at a distance appeared like gnashing and thumping, on coming nearer was found to be the voice of disputants. The men in one of his visions, seen in heavenly light, appeared like dragons, and seemed in darkness; but to each other they appeared as men, and when the light from heaven shone into their cabin, they complained of the darkness, and were compelled to shut the window that they might see.[57]

There was this perception in him which makes the poet or seer an object of awe and terror, namely that the same man or society of men may wear one aspect to themselves and their companions, and a different aspect to higher intelligences. Certain priests, whom he describes as conversing very learnedly together, appeared to the children who were at some distance, like dead horses; and many the like misappearances. And instantly the mind inquires whether these fishes under the bridge, yonder oxen in the pasture, those dogs in the yard, are immutably fishes, oxen and dogs, or only so appear to me, and perchance to themselves appear upright men; and whether I appear as a man to all eyes. The Brahmins and Pythagoras propounded the same question, and if any poet has witnessed the transformation he doubtless found it in harmony with various experiences. We have all seen changes as considerable in wheat and caterpillars. He is the poet and shall draw us with love and terror, who sees through the flowing vest the firm nature, and can declare it.

I look in vain for the poet whom I describe. We do not with sufficient plainness or sufficient profoundness address ourselves to life, nor dare we chaunt our own times and social circumstance. If we filled the day with bravery, we should not shrink from celebrating it. Time and nature yield us many gifts, but not yet the timely man, the new religion, the reconciler, whom all things await. Dante's praise is that he dared to write his autobiography in colossal cipher, or into universality. We have yet had no genius in America,[58] with tyrannous eye, which knew the value of our incomparable materials, and saw, in the barbarism and materialism of the times, another carnival of the same gods whose picture he so much admires in Homer; then in the Middle Age; then in Calvinism. Banks and tariffs, the newspaper and caucus, Methodism and Unitarianism, are flat and dull to dull people, but rest on the same foundations of wonder as the town of Troy and the temple of Delphi, and are as swiftly passing away. Our log-rolling, our stumps and their politics, our fisheries, our Negroes and Indians, our boasts and our repudiations,[59] the wrath of rogues and the pusillanimity of honest men, the northern trade, the southern planting, the western clearing, Oregon and Texas, are yet unsung. Yet America is a poem in our eyes; its ample geography dazzles the imagination, and it will not wait long for metres. If I have not found that excellent combination of gifts in my countrymen which I seek, neither could I aid myself to fix the idea of the poet by reading now and then in Chalmers's collection[60] of five centuries of English poets. These are wits more than poets, though there have been poets among them. But when we adhere to the ideal of the poet, we have our difficulties even with Milton and Homer. Milton is too literary, and Homer too literal and historical.

But I am not wise enough for a national criticism, and must use the old largeness a little longer, to discharge my errand from the muse to the poet concerning his art.

Art is the path of the creator to his work. The paths or methods are ideal and eternal, though few men ever see them; not the artist himself for years, or for a lifetime, unless he come into the conditions. The painter, the sculptor, the composer, the epic rhapsodist, the orator, all partake one desire, namely to express themselves symmetrically and abundantly, not dwarfishly and fragmentarily. They found or put themselves in certain conditions, as, the painter and sculptor before some impressive human figures; the orator into the assembly of the people; and the others in such scenes as each has found exciting to his intellect; and each presently feels the new desire. He hears a voice, he sees a beckoning. Then he is apprised, with wonder, what herds of daemons hem him in. He can no more rest; he says, with the old painter, "By God it is in me and must go forth of me." He pursues a beauty, half seen, which flies before him. The poet pours out verses in every solitude. Most of the things he says are conventional, no doubt; but by and by he says something which is original and beautiful. That charms him. He would say nothing else but such things. In our way of talking we say 'That is yours, this is mine;' but the poet knows well that it is not his; that it is as strange and beautiful to him as to you; he would fain hear the like eloquence at length. Once having tasted this immortal ichor, he cannot have enough of it, and as an admirable creative power exists in these intellections, it is of the last importance that these things get spoken. What a little of all we know is said! What drops of all the sea of our science are baled up! and by what accident it is that these are exposed, when so many secrets sleep in nature! Hence the necessity of speech and song; hence these throbs and heart-beatings in the orator, at the door of the assembly, to the end namely that thought may be ejaculated as Logos, or Word.

Doubt not, O poet, but persist. Say 'It is in me, and shall out.' Stand there, balked and dumb, stuttering and stammering, hissed and hooted, stand and strive, until at last rage draw out of thee that *dream*-power which every night shows thee is thine own; a power transcending all limit and privacy, and by virtue of which a man is the conductor of the whole river of electricity. Nothing walks, or creeps, or grows, or exists, which must not in turn arise and walk before him as exponent of his meaning. Comes he to that power, his genius is no longer exhaustible. All the creatures by pairs and by tribes pour into his mind as into a Noah's ark, to come forth again to people a new world. This is like the stock of air for our respiration or for the combustion of our fireplace; not a measure of gallons, but the entire atmosphere if wanted. And therefore the rich poets, as Homer, Chaucer, Shakspeare, and Raphael, have obviously no limits to their works except the limits of their lifetime, and resemble a mirror carried through the street, ready to render an image of every created thing.

O poet! a new nobility is conferred in groves and pastures, and not in castles or by the sword-blade any longer. The conditions are hard, but equal. Thou shalt leave the world, and know the muse only. Thou shalt not know any longer the times, customs, graces, politics, or opinions of men, but shalt take all from the muse. For the time of towns is tolled from the world by funereal chimes, but in nature the universal hours are counted by succeeding tribes of animals and plants, and by growth of joy on joy. God wills also that thou abdicate a manifold and duplex life, and that thou be content that others speak for thee. Others shall be thy gentlemen and shall represent all courtesy and worldly life for thee; others shall do the great and resounding actions also. Thou shalt lie close hid with nature, and canst not be afforded to the Capitol or the Exchange. The world is full of renunciations and apprenticeships, and this is thine; thou must pass for a fool and a churl for a long season. This is the screen and sheath in which Pan has protected his well-beloved flower, and thou shalt be known only to thine own, and they shall console thee with tenderest love. And thou shalt not be able to rehearse the names of thy friends in thy verse, for an old shame before the holy ideal. And this is the reward; that the ideal shall be real to thee, and the impressions of the actual world shall fall like summer rain, copious, but not troublesome to thy invulnerable essence. Thou shalt have the whole land for thy park and manor, the sea for thy bath and navigation, without tax and without envy; the woods and the rivers thou shalt own, and thou shalt possess that wherein others are only tenants and boarders. Thou true landlord! sea-lord! air-lord! Wherever snow falls or water flows or birds fly, wherever day and night meet in twilight, wherever the blue heaven is hung by clouds or sown with stars, wherever are forms with transparent boundaries, wherever are outlets into celestial space, wherever is danger, and awe, and love, —there is Beauty, plenteous as rain, shed for thee, and though thou shouldst walk the world over, thou shalt not be able to find a condition inopportune or ignoble.

Essays: Second Series, *W* 3:1–42; first published as first chapter in *Essays: Second Series* (1844).

Beauty (1860)

At a time of increasing specialization and arid research, Emerson called for a humanized science, akin to sociobiology today. Beyond the opening pages on science, omitted here, Emerson extols art as the needed humanizing power by virtue of the functional and dynamic qualities of beauty and the varied kinds or levels of beauty. Characteristically, Emerson moves from the beauty of the human form to that of the moral, intellectual, and transcendental levels. Functional architecture has its paradigm in the organic form of every natural function and process of becoming in man, animal, or plant. Dynamic process, as in the "circulation" of blood, waters, and planets, has a beauty of its own. And yet, beauty is less in the form than in the mind, less in the fact than in the "symbolic character of the fact" as seen by the realizing imagination. Emerson exalts "the human heart" as the catalyst of that insight which enables "the deep man" to believe in miracles, magic, and love. Mythology also embodies this truth: Cupid is drawn with a bandage as if blind "because he does not see what he does not like; but the sharpest-sighted hunter in the universe is Love, for finding what he seeks, and only that . . . and Beauty leads him as a guide." In the poem "Cupido," similarly, "The solid, solid universe / Is pervious to Love; / With bandaged eyes he never errs, / Around, below, above" (W 9:257*).*

Was never form and never face
So sweet to Seyd[61] as only grace

Which did not slumber like a stone
But hovered gleaming and was gone.
Beauty chased he everywhere,
In flame, in storm, in clouds of air.
He smote the lake to feed his eye
With the beryl beam of the broken wave.
He flung in pebbles well to hear
The moment's music which they gave.
Oft pealed for him a lofty tone
From nodding pole and belting zone.
He heard a voice none else could hear
From centred and from errant sphere.
The quaking earth did quake in rhyme,
Seas ebbed and flowed in epic chime.
In dens of passion, and pits of woe,
He saw strong Eros struggling through,
To sun the dark and solve the curse,
And beam to the bounds of the universe.
While thus to live he gave his days
In loyal worship, scorning praise,
How spread their lures for him, in vain,
Thieving Ambition and paltering Gain!
He thought it happier to be dead,
To die for Beauty, than live for bread.[62]

*   *   *

I am warned by the ill fate of many philosophers not to attempt a
definition of Beauty. I will rather enumerate a few of its qualities. We
ascribe beauty to that which is simple; which has no superfluous
parts; which exactly answers its end; which stands related to all
things; which is the mean of many extremes. It is the most enduring
quality, and the most ascending quality. We say love is blind, and the
figure of Cupid is drawn with a bandage round his eyes. Blind: yes,
because he does not see what he does not like; but the sharpest-
sighted hunter in the universe is Love, for finding what he seeks, and
only that; and the mythologists tell us that Vulcan was painted lame
and Cupid blind, to call attention to the fact that one was all limbs,
and the other all eyes. In the true mythology Love is an immortal
child, and Beauty leads him as a guide: nor can we express a deeper
sense than when we say, Beauty is the pilot of the young soul.

Beyond their sensuous delight, the forms and colors of nature have a new charm for us in our perception that not one ornament was added for ornament, but each is a sign of some better health or more excellent action. Elegance of form in bird or beast, or in the human figure, marks some excellence of structure: or, beauty is only an invitation from what belongs to us. 'T is a law of botany that in plants the same virtues follow the same forms. It is a rule of largest application, true in a plant, true in a loaf of bread, that in the construction of any fabric or organism any real increase of fitness to its end is an increase of beauty.

The lesson taught by the study of Greek and of Gothic art, of antique and of Pre-Raphaelite[63] painting, was worth all the research, —namely, that all beauty must be organic; that outside embellishment is deformity. It is the soundness of the bones that ultimates itself in a peach-bloom complexion; health of constitution that makes the sparkle and the power of the eye. 'T is the adjustment of the size and of the joining of the sockets of the skeleton that gives grace of outline and the finer grace of movement. The cat and the deer cannot move or sit inelegantly. The dancing-master can never teach a badly built man to walk well. The tint of the flower proceeds from its root, and the lustres of the seashell begin with its existence. Hence our taste in building rejects paint, and all shifts, and shows the original grain of the wood: refuses pilasters and columns that support nothing, and allows the real supporters of the house honestly to show themselves. Every necessary or organic action pleases the beholder. A man leading a horse to water, a farmer sowing seed, the labors of haymakers in the field, the carpenter building a ship, the smith at his forge, or whatever useful labor, is becoming to the wise eye. But if it is done to be seen, it is mean. How beautiful are ships on the sea! but ships in the theatre,—or ships kept for picturesque effect on Virginia Water by George IV., and men hired to stand in fitting costumes at a penny an hour! What a difference in effect between a battalion of troops marching to action, and one of our independent companies on a holiday! In the midst of a military show and a festal procession gay with banners, I saw a boy seize an old tin pan that lay rusting under a wall, and poising it on the top of a stick, he set it turning and made it describe the most elegant imaginable curves, and drew away attention from the decorated procession by this startling beauty.

Another text from the mythologists. The Greeks fabled that Venus was born of the foam of the sea. Nothing interests us which is stark or bounded, but only what streams with life, what is in act or endeavor to reach somewhat beyond. The pleasure a palace or a temple gives the eye is, that an order and method has been communicated to stones, so that they speak and geometrize, become tender or sublime with expression. Beauty is the moment of transition, as if the form were just ready to flow into other forms. Any fixedness, heaping or concentration on one feature,—a long nose, a sharp chin, a hump-back,—is the reverse of the flowing, and therefore deformed. Beautiful as is the symmetry of any form, if the form can move we seek a more excellent symmetry. The interruption of equilibrium stimulates the eye to desire the restoration of symmetry, and to watch the steps through which it is attained. This is the charm of running water, sea waves, the flight of birds and the locomotion of animals. This is the theory of dancing, to recover continually in changes the lost equilibrium, not by abrupt and angular but by gradual and curving movements. I have been told by persons of experience in matters of taste that the fashions follow a law of gradation, and are never arbitrary. The new mode is always only a step onward in the same direction as the last mode, and a cultivated eye is prepared for and predicts the new fashion. This fact suggests the reason of all mistakes and offence in our own modes. It is necessary in music, when you strike a discord, to let down the ear by an intermediate note or two to the accord again; and many a good experiment, born of good sense and destined to succeed, fails only because it is offensively sudden. I suppose the Parisian milliner who dresses the world from her imperious boudoir will know how to reconcile the Bloomer costume[64] to the eye of mankind, and make it triumphant over Punch himself, by interposing the just gradations. I need not say how wide the same law ranges, and how much it can be hoped to effect. All that is a little harshly claimed by progressive parties may easily come to be conceded without question, if this rule be observed. Thus the circumstances may be easily imagined in which woman may speak, vote, argue causes, legislate and drive a coach, and all the most naturally in the world, if only it come by degrees. To this streaming or flowing belongs the beauty that all circular movement has; as the circulation of waters, the circulation of the blood, the periodical motion of planets, the annual wave of vegetation, the action and reaction of nature; and if we follow it out, this demand in our thought for an ever onward action is the argument for the immortality.

One more text from the mythologists is to the same purpose,— *Beauty rides on a lion.* Beauty rests on necessities. The line of beauty is the result of perfect economy. The cell of the bee is built at that angle which gives the most strength with the least wax; the bone or the quill of the bird gives the most alar [winged] strength with the least weight. "It is the purgation of superfluities," said Michael Angelo. There is not a particle to spare in natural structures. There is a compelling reason in the uses of the plant for every novelty of color or form; and our art saves material by more skilful arrangement, and reaches beauty by taking every superfluous ounce that can be spared from a wall, and keeping all its strength in the poetry of columns. In rhetoric, this art of omission is a chief secret of power, and, in general, it is proof of high culture to say the greatest matters in the simplest way.

Veracity first of all, and forever. *Rien de beau que le vrai.*[65] In all design, art lies in making your object prominent, but there is a prior art in choosing objects that are prominent. The fine arts have nothing casual, but spring from the instincts of the nations that created them.

*   *   *

But the sovereign attribute remains to be noted. Things are pretty, graceful, rich, elegant, handsome, but, until they speak to the imagination, not yet beautiful. This is the reason why beauty is still escaping out of all analysis. It is not yet possessed, it cannot be handled. Proclus[66] says, "It swims on the light of forms." It is properly not in the form, but in the mind. It instantly deserts possession, and flies to an object in the horizon. If I could put my hand on the North Star, would it be as beautiful? The sea is lovely, but when we bathe in it the beauty forsakes all the near water. For the imagination and senses cannot be gratified at the same time. Wordsworth rightly speaks of "a light that never was on sea or land," meaning that it was supplied by the observer; and the Welsh bard[67] warns his countrywomen, that

> "Half of their charms with Cadwallon shall die."

The new virtue which constitutes a thing beautiful is a certain cos-
mical quality, or a power to suggest relation to the whole world, and
so lift the object out of a pitiful individuality. Every natural feature
—sea, sky, rainbow, flowers, musical tone—has in it somewhat which
is not private but universal, speaks of that central benefit which is the
soul of nature, and thereby is beautiful. And in chosen men and
women I find somewhat in form, speech and manners, which is not of
their person and family, but of a humane, catholic and spiritual
character, and we love them as the sky. They have a largeness of
suggestion, and their face and manners carry a certain grandeur, like
time and justice.[68]

The feat of the imagination is in showing the convertibility of every
thing into every other thing. Facts which had never before left their
stark common sense suddenly figure as Eleusinian mysteries.[69] My
boots and chair and candlestick are fairies in disguise, meteors and
constellations. All the facts in nature are nouns of the intellect, and
make the grammar of the eternal language. Every word has a double, treble or centuple use and meaning. What! has my stove and
pepper-pot a false bottom? I cry you mercy, good shoe-box! I did not
know you were a jewel-case. Chaff and dust begin to sparkle, and are
clothed about with immortality. And there is a joy in perceiving the
representative or symbolic character of a fact, which no bare fact or
event can ever give. There are no days in life so memorable as those
which vibrated to some stroke of the imagination.

The poets are quite right in decking their mistresses with the spoils
of the landscape, flower-gardens, gems, rainbows, flushes of morning
and stars of night, since all beauty points at identity; and whatsoever
thing does not express to me the sea and sky, day and night, is
somewhat forbidden and wrong. Into every beautiful object there
enters somewhat immeasurable and divine, and just as much into
form bounded by outlines, like mountains on the horizon, as into
tones of music or depths of space. Polarized light[70] showed the secret
architecture of bodies; and when the *second-sight* of the mind is
opened, now one color or form or gesture, and now another, has a
pungency, as if a more interior ray had been emitted, disclosing its
deep holdings in the frame of things.

The laws of this translation we do not know, or why one feature or gesture enchants, why one word or syllable intoxicates; but the fact is familiar that the fine touch of the eye, or a grace of manners, or a phrase of poetry, plants wings at our shoulders; as if the Divinity, in his approaches, lifts away mountains of obstruction, and deigns to draw a truer line, which the mind knows and owns. This is that haughty force of beauty, "*vis superba formae*,"[71] which the poets praise,—under calm and precise outline the immeasurable and divine; Beauty hiding all wisdom and power in its calm sky.

All high beauty has a moral element in it, and I find the antique sculpture as ethical as Marcus Antoninus;[72] and the beauty ever in proportion to the depth of thought. Gross and obscure natures, however decorated, seem impure shambles; but character gives splendor to youth and awe to wrinkled skin and gray hairs. An adorer of truth we cannot choose but obey, and the woman who has shared with us the moral sentiment,—her locks must appear to us sublime. Thus there is a climbing scale of culture, from the first agreeable sensation which a sparkling gem or a scarlet stain affords the eye, up through fair outlines and details of the landscape, features of the human face and form, signs and tokens of thought and character in manners, up to the ineffable mysteries of the intellect. Wherever we begin, thither our steps tend: an ascent from the joy of a horse in his trappings, up to the perception of Newton that the globe on which we ride is only a larger apple falling from a larger tree; up to the perception of Plato that globe and universe are rude and early expressions of an all-dissolving Unity,—the first stair on the scale to the temple of the Mind.

The Conduct of Life, *W* 6:279, 289–95, 302–6; first published in *The Conduct of Life* (1860).

NOTES

1. C. Sallustius Crispus (86–34 B.C.), Roman historian and politician. The passage quoted may be a paraphrase from memory, though it is in Milton's *Apology for Smectymnuus*.

2. From chapter 68 of *The Decline and Fall of the Roman Empire* by Edward Gibbon.

3. King of Sparta, general of the three hundred Spartans who defended the pass of Thermopylae against Xerxes' army.

4. At the battle of Sempach in 1836, so tradition holds.

5. English Puritan (1613–62), executed for treason under Charles II.

6. William Russell (1639–83), accused of high treason in the Rye House Plot and executed.

7. Athenian general and statesman (402?–317 B.C.).

8. This is the central principle of Swedenborg's correspondence theory; the 1823 edition of *A Treatise concerning Heaven and Its Wonders, and also concerning Hell* was owned by Emerson.

9. Intuition in the transcendental philosophy, as opposed to understanding or common sense.

10. Swedenborg. Cf. *JMN* 4:33; 6:219.

11. Possibly adapted from Mme de Staël: "Almost all the axioms of physics correspond with the maxims of morals." Cf. *JMN* 3:255.

12. Plotinus, quoted in Coleridge's *Biographia Literaria*.

13. Each of these men considered the universe as "transparent," as the word is used by Emerson.

14. According to classical legend, the Theban Sphinx posed a riddle to each traveler who pased by; she killed all, for none before Oedipus could solve the riddle. When at last he unraveled the mystery, she slew herself, and Oedipus became king of Thebes, as the Oracle at Delphi had predicted.

15. G. Oegger's Swedenborgian *The True Messiah* (1842), available to Emerson in manuscript. Cf. *JMN* 5:66–69.

16. George Fox, the Quaker (1624–91).

17. Coleridge, in *Aids to Reflection*.

18. "Art," *Poems*, *W* 9:277–78.

19. *Mannerist:* seventeenth-century school of Italian art which emphasized style and technique rather than subject matter.

20. Andrea Sacchi (1599–1661), Italian artist who treated religious subjects in a classical manner; most of his paintings and frescoes are in Rome.

21. *Billows . . . produce:* The *Works* points out that the evolutionary doctrines of John Hunter (1728–93) and Lamarck are apparent in this passage.

22. Emerson must be referring to the Neva River, which passes through Leningrad (originally Saint Petersburg).

23. Cf. *Poems*, *W* 9:311, ll. 63–72, for a slightly different version of these ten lines.

24. "Ode to Beauty," *Poems*, *W* 9:87–90, ll. 60–63.

25. *Children of the fire:* derived from Heraclitus, Greek philosopher. He proposed the doctrine of the universal mind or pre-immanent spirit, symbolized by fire, as underlying all change or cosmic processes.

26. *Phlegm:* the medieval concept of an internal fluid or humor which predisposed a person to a lethargic response.

27. *Appulses:* impingements, as of rays striking a surface.

28. Probably Tennyson, whose poetry was first published in the United States at Emerson's urging; Tennyson was later more fully appreciated by Emerson.

29. Chimborazo, the highest mountain of Ecuador (20,561 ft.), is in the western range of the Andes quite close to the equator.

30. A literary allusion to Shakespeare's *Macbeth*, 5.3.22–23: "My way of life is fall'n into the sere, the yellow leaf." The image was incorporated by Byron in "On This Day I Complete My Thirty-sixth Year": "My days are in the yellow leaf."

31. Fourth-century Neo-Platonist philosopher, the teacher of Proclus, and author of *Life of Pythagoras*, which Emerson read. [*W*]

32. From Spenser's "An Hymne in Honour of Beautie," stanza 19.

33. *Sensual:* sensory or physical; preoccupied with appearances, not inner spirit. The first sentence of this essay includes another similar use, not uncommon in Emerson's time.

34. Neo-Platonist (A.D. 411–485), one of several whom Emerson read in the translations by Thomas Taylor.

35. A campaign stunt by the Whigs in 1840 just prior to Harrison's election.

36. An allusion to the textile and shoe factories of Lowell and Lynn, respectively, and the shipping commerce of Salem.

37. The cider barrel and the log cabin were associated with Harrison; the hickory stick and the palmetto with Andrew Jackson and South Carolina.

38. *Lilies:* France; *leopards:* Scotland; *crescent:* Turkey; *lion:* England.

39. William Pitt, Earl of Chatham (1708–78), statesman and orator; *The Universal Etymological English Dictionary* (1721) by Nathan Bailey.

40. *The evils of the world are such only to the evil eye:* Taken out of context, and so misunderstood by Melville. This statement refers to so-called "evils" conventionally viewed, whether the factory town and the railroad, as cited here, or the rat in "Limits": "His wicked eye / Is cruel to thy cruelty."

41. See headnote and opening paragraph of next essay, "Beauty," for clarification of the allusions to Vulcan and Cupid.

42. *Accidency:* chance or fortuitous quality; *fugacity:* fleeting quality.

43. *Lyncaeus:* the keenest-eyed lookout among Jason's Argonauts.

44. *Animalcules:* a minute animal imperceptible to the naked eye.

45. *A certain poet:* most likely Emerson paraphrasing Plato.

46. *Agaric:* a gilled or shell-like fungus.

47. From Phosphor, literally the light-bearer in Greek (cf. Lucifer). The

son of Aurora (Eos) and Cephalus, Phosphorus represents the Morning Star, the morning aspect of Venus; torch in hand, he is depicted as a winged god preceding his mother's chariot.

48. *Pre-cantations:* preexisting melodic manifestations of an object's soul or essence.

49. Milton. Cf. "Elegy VI", ll. 55–78.

50. *As . . . contained:* cf. Aristotle, *Physics* 4.212a14–21.

51. Roman architect, author of *De Architectura*.

52. See Dedication to Prince Henry in Chapman's translation of the *Iliad*, ll. 132–33.

53. See "The Wife of Bath's Tale."

54. Rev. 6:13.

55. *Pythagoras:* sixth century B.C., Greek mathematician and philosopher. *Paracelsus:* (1493–1541), Swiss alchemist and physician. *Agrippa:* Heinrich Cornelius Agrippa von Nettesheim (1468–1535), German physicist interested in magic, whose biography by Henry Morley appeared in 1856. *Cardan:* Geronimo Cardano (1501–76), Italian physician, mathematician, and astrologer, a study of whom by Henry Morley was published in 1854. *Kepler:* Johannes Kepler (1571–1630), German astronomer. *Swedenborg:* Emanuel Swedenborg (1688–1782), Swedish scientist, philosopher, and mystic theologian. *Schelling:* F. W. J. von Schelling (1775–1854), German naturalist and transcendental philosopher. *Oken:* Lorenz Oken (1779–1851), German biologist, naturalist, and mystic philosopher.

56. Jakob Böhme (or Boehme), German theosophist and mystic (1575–1624).

57. These examples are from *The Apocalypse* (1836) by Swedenborg.

58. With the publication of Whitman's *Leaves of Grass* eleven years later, Emerson's hope was largely realized.

59. *Repudiations:* the refusals of some states to repay bonded debts, etc.

60. Alexander Chalmers (1759–1834), British biographer and editor of *The Works of the English Poets from Chaucer to Cowper*, whose collection of English poetry drew chiefly from the Restoration and the eighteenth century.

61. *Seyd:* or Saadi, the Persian poet; here, the ideal poet.

62. "Beauty," *Poems, W* 9:275–76.

63. *Pre-Raphaelite:* in the literal sense, Italian painting before Raphael (1438–1520); not to be confused here with the Pre-Raphaelite Brotherhood founded in England in 1848 by Rossetti, Millet, and Hunt.

64. A costume of short skirt and loose trousers gathered at the ankles was introduced about 1850.

65. Cf. this passage in Emerson's lecture "Michael Angelo" (*W* 12:219): "Hence the celebrated French maxim of Rhetoric, *Rien de beau que le vrai:*

'Nothing is beautiful but what is true.' It had much wider application than to Rhetoric; as wide, namely as the terms of the proposition admit. . . . The common eye is satisfied with the surface on which it rests. The wise eye knows that it is surface, and, if beautiful, only the result of interior harmonies."

66. See note 34 above.

67. The hero of Sir Walter Scott's "Dying Bard," from which Emerson quotes.

68. I saw a hand whose beauty seemed to me to express Hope and Purity, and as that hand goes working, grasping, beckoning on, in the daily life of its owner, some of this high virtue, I think, will pass out of it. [W]

69. Ceremonies performed in ancient Greece, originally at Eleusis, in honor of Demeter in which only initiates could participate, who thus acquired an air of mystery and select wisdom.

70. Light affected by special materials in such a way that its rays all travel in the same direction.

71. In a note to an earlier similar passage, Emerson observes: "When that which is so fair and noble passes, I am enlarged, my thoughts grow spacious, the chambers of the brain, the lobes of the heart are bigger. How I am cheered by traits of that *vis superba formae*."

72. Marcus Aurelius Antoninus (A.D. 121–180), Roman emperor (161–180) and Stoic philosopher.

II
THE CREATIVE PROCESS

Intellect

In this key essay, Emerson presents a remarkably modern description of the art of creative thought, of intellective insight, not of intellect as the faculty of logical reasoning. It represents his major definition of experiential realization as an organic process, with a fine sense of the stages of incubation and intimation-illumination, or the interplay of receptivity and revelation. That true self-reliance requires this intuitive mode of perception is the conclusion reached here, as is also evident in the essay "Self-Reliance." A later, three-part essay, "Natural History of the Intellect" (W 12:1–110), develops further implications of this epistemology.

> Go, speed the stars of Thought
> On to their shining goals;—
> The sower scatters broad his seed;
> The wheat thou strew'st be souls.[1]

Every substance is negatively electric to that which stands above it in the chemical tables, positively to that which stands below it. Water dissolves wood and iron and salt; air dissolves water; electric fire dissolves air, but the intellect dissolves fire, gravity, laws, method, and the subtlest unnamed relations of nature in its resistless menstruum. Intellect lies behind genius, which is intellect constructive. Intellect is the simple power anterior to all action or construction. Gladly would I unfold in calm degrees a natural history of the intellect, but what man has yet been able to mark the steps and boundaries of that transparent essence? The first questions are always to be asked, and the wisest doctor is gravelled by the inquisitiveness of a child. How can we speak of the action of the mind under any divisions, as of its knowledge, of its ethics, of its works, and so forth, since it melts will into perception, knowledge into act? Each becomes the other. Itself alone is. Its vision is not like the vision of the eye, but is union with the things known.

Intellect and intellection signify to the common ear consideration

of abstract truth. The considerations of time and place, of you and
me, of profit and hurt, tyrannize over most men's minds. Intellect
separates the fact considered, from *you*, from all local and personal
reference, and discerns it as if it existed for its own sake. Heraclitus
looked upon the affections as dense and colored mists. In the fog of
good and evil affections it is hard for man to walk forward in a straight
line. Intellect is void of affection and sees an object as it stands in the
light of science, cool and disengaged. The intellect goes out of the
individual, floats over its own personality, and regards it as a fact, and
not as *I* and *mine*. He who is immersed in what concerns person or
place cannot see the problem of existence. This the intellect always
ponders. Nature shows all things formed and bound. The intellect
pierces the form, overleaps the wall, detects intrinsic likeness between
remote things and reduces all things into a few principles.

The making a fact the subject of thought raises it. All that mass of
mental and moral phenomena which we do not make objects of
voluntary thought, come within the power of fortune; they constitute
the circumstance of daily life; they are subject to change, to fear and
hope. Every man beholds his human condition with a degree of
melancholy. As a ship aground is battered by the waves, so man,
imprisoned in mortal life, lies open to the mercy of coming events.
But a truth, separated by the intellect, is no longer a subject of destiny.
We behold it as a god upraised above care and fear. And so any fact in
our life, or any record of our fancies or reflections, disentangled from
the web of our unconsciousness, becomes an object impersonal and
immortal. It is the past restored, but embalmed. A better art than
that of Egypt has taken fear and corruption out of it. It is eviscerated
of care. It is offered for science. What is addressed to us for contemplation does not threaten us but makes us intellectual beings.

The growth of the intellect is spontaneous in every expansion. The
mind that grows could not predict the times, the means, the mode of
that spontaneity. God enters by a private door into every individual.[2]
Long prior to the age of reflection is the thinking of the mind. Out of
darkness it came insensibly into the marvellous light of to-day. In the
period of infancy it accepted and disposed of all impressions from the
surrounding creation after its own way. Whatever any mind doth or
saith is after a law, and this native law remains over it after it has

come to reflection or conscious thought. In the most worn, pedantic, introverted self-tormentor's life, the greatest part is incalculable by him, unforeseen, unimaginable, and must be, until he can take himself up by his own ears. What am I? What has my will done to make me that I am? Nothing. I have been floated into this thought, this hour, this connection of events, by secret currents of might and mind, and my ingenuity and wilfulness have not thwarted, have not aided to an appreciable degree.

Our spontaneous action is always the best. You cannot with your best deliberation and heed come so close to any question as your spontaneous glance shall bring you, whilst you rise from your bed, or walk abroad in the morning after meditating the matter before sleep on the previous night. Our thinking is a pious reception. Our truth of thought is therefore vitiated as much by too violent direction given by our will, as by too great negligence. We do not determine what we will think. We only open our senses, clear away as we can all obstruction from the fact, and suffer the intellect to see. We have little control over our thoughts. We are the prisoners of ideas. They catch us up for moments into their heaven and so fully engage us that we take no thought for the morrow, gaze like children, without an effort to make them our own. By and by we fall out of that rapture, bethink us where we have been, what we have seen, and repeat as truly as we can what we have beheld. As far as we can recall these ecstasies we carry away in the ineffaceable memory the result, and all men and all the ages confirm it. It is called truth. But the moment we cease to report and attempt to correct and contrive, it is not truth.

If we consider what persons have stimulated and profited us, we shall perceive the superiority of the spontaneous or intuitive principle over the arithmetical or logical. The first contains the second, but virtual and latent. We want in every man a long logic; we cannot pardon the absence of it, but it must not be spoken. Logic is the procession or proportionate unfolding of the intuition; but its virtue is as silent method; the moment it would appear as propositions and have a separate value, it is worthless.

In every man's mind, some images, words and facts remain, without effort on his part to imprint them, which others forget, and afterwards these illustrate to him important laws. All our progress is an unfolding, like the vegetable bud. You have first an instinct, then an opinion, then a knowledge, as the plant has root, bud and fruit. Trust the instinct to the end, though you can render no reason. It is vain to hurry it. By trusting it to the end, it shall ripen into truth and you shall know why you believe.

Each mind has its own method. A true man never acquires after college rules. What you have aggregated in a natural manner surprises and delights when it is produced. For we cannot oversee each other's secret. And hence the differences between men in natural endowment are insignificant in comparison with their common wealth. Do you think the porter and the cook have no anecdotes, no experiences, no wonders for you? Everybody knows as much as the savant. The walls of rude minds are scrawled all over with facts, with thoughts. They shall one day bring a lantern and read the inscriptions. Every man, in the degree in which he has wit and culture, finds his curiosity inflamed concerning the modes of living and thinking of other men, and especially of those classes whose minds have not been subdued by the drill of school education.

This instinctive action never ceases in a healthy mind, but becomes richer and more frequent in its informations through all states of culture. At last comes the era of reflection, when we not only observe, but take pains to observe; when we of set purpose sit down to consider an abstract truth; when we keep the mind's eye open whilst we converse, whilst we read, whilst we act, intent to learn the secret law of some class of facts.

What is the hardest task in the world? To think. I would put myself in the attitude to look in the eye an abstract truth, and I cannot. I blench and withdraw on this side and on that. I seem to know what he meant who said, No man can see God face to face and live. For example, a man explores the basis of civil government. Let him intend his mind without respite, without rest, in one direction. His best heed long time avails him nothing. Yet thoughts are flitting before him. We all but apprehend, we dimly forbode the truth. We say I will walk abroad, and the truth will take form and clearness to me. We go forth, but cannot find it. It seems as if we needed only the stillness and composed attitude of the library to seize the thought. But we come in, and are as far from it as at first. Then, in a moment, and unannounced, the truth appears. A certain wandering light appears, and is the distinction, the principle, we wanted. But the oracle comes because we had previously laid siege to the shrine. It seems as if the law of the intellect resembled that law of nature by which we now inspire, now expire the breath; by which the heart now draws in, then hurls out the blood,—the law of undulation. So now you must labor with your brains, and now you must forbear your activity and see what the great Soul showeth.

The immortality of man is as legitimately preached from the intellections as from the moral volitions. Every intellection is mainly prospective. Its present value is its least. Inspect what delights you in Plutarch, in Shakspeare, in Cervantes. Each truth that a writer acquires is a lantern which he turns full on what facts and thoughts lay already in his mind, and behold, all the mats and rubbish which had littered his garret become precious. Every trivial fact in his private biography becomes an illustration of this new principle, revisits the day, and delights all men by its piquancy and new charm. Men say, Where did he get this? and think there was something divine in his life. But no; they have myriads of facts just as good, would they only get a lamp to ransack their attics withal.

We are all wise. The difference between persons is not in wisdom but in art. I knew, in an academical club, a person who always deferred to me; who, seeing my whim for writing, fancied that my experiences had somewhat superior; whilst I saw that his experiences were as good as mine. Give them to me and I would make the same use of them. He held the old; he holds the new; I had the habit of tacking together the old and the new which he did not use to exercise. This may hold in the great examples. Perhaps, if we should meet Shakspeare we should not be conscious of any steep inferiority; no, but of a great equality,—only that he possessed a strange skill of using, of classifying his facts, which we lacked. For notwithstanding our utter incapacity to produce anything like Hamlet and Othello, see the perfect reception this wit and immense knowledge of life and liquid eloquence find in us all.

If you gather apples in the sunshine, or make hay, or hoe corn, and then retire within doors and shut your eyes and press them with your hand, you shall still see apples hanging in the bright light with boughs and leaves thereto, or the tasselled grass, or the corn-flags, and this for five or six hours afterwards. There lie the impressions on the retentive organ, though you knew it not. So lies the whole series of natural images with which your life has made you acquainted, in your memory, though you know it not; and a thrill of passion flashes light on their dark chamber, and the active power seizes instantly the fit image, as the word of its momentary thought.

It is long ere we discover how rich we are. Our history, we are sure, is quite tame: we have nothing to write, nothing to infer. But our wiser years still run back to the despised recollections of childhood, and always we are fishing up some wonderful article out of that pond; until by and by we begin to suspect that the biography of the one foolish person we know is, in reality, nothing less than the miniature paraphrase of the hundred volumes of the Universal History.

In the intellect constructive, which we popularly designate by the word Genius, we observe the same balance of two elements as in intellect receptive. The constructive intellect produces thoughts, sentences, poems, plans, designs, systems. It is the generation of the mind, the marriage of thought with nature. To genius must always go two gifts, the thought and the publication. The first is revelation, always a miracle, which no frequency of occurrence or incessant study can ever familiarize, but which must always leave the inquirer stupid with wonder. It is the advent of truth into the world, a form of thought now for the first time bursting into the universe, a child of the old eternal soul, a piece of genuine and immeasurable greatness. It seems, for the time, to inherit all that has yet existed and to dictate to the unborn. It affects every thought of man and goes to fashion every institution. But to make it available it needs a vehicle or art by which it is conveyed to men. To be communicable it must become picture or sensible object. We must learn the language of facts. The most wonderful inspirations die with their subject if he has no hand to paint them to the senses. The ray of light passes invisible through space and only when it falls on an object is it seen. When the spiritual energy is directed on something outward, then it is a thought. The relation between it and you first makes you, the value of you, apparent to me. The rich inventive genius of the painter must be smothered and lost for want of the power of drawing, and in our happy hours we should be inexhaustible poets if once we could break through the silence into adequate rhyme. As all men have some access to primary truth, so all have some art or power of communication in their head, but only in the artist does it descend into the hand. There is an inequality, whose laws we do not yet know, between two men and between two moments of the same man, in respect to this faculty. In common hours we have the same facts as in the uncommon or inspired, but they do not sit for their portrait; they are not detached, but lie in a web. The thought of genius is spontaneous; but the power of picture or expression, in the most enriched and flowing nature, implies a mixture of will, a certain control over the spontaneous states, without which no production is possible. It is a conversion of all nature into the rhetoric of thought, under the eye of judgment, with a strenuous exercise of choice. And yet the imaginative vocabulary seems to be spontaneous also. It does not flow from experience only or mainly, but from a richer source. Not by any conscious imitation of particular forms are the grand strokes of the painter executed, but by repairing to the fountain-head of all forms in his mind. Who is the first drawing-master? Without instruction we know very well the ideal of the human form. A child knows if an arm or a leg be distorted in a picture; if the attitude be natural or grand or mean; though he has never received any instruction in drawing or heard any conversation on the subject, nor can himself draw with correctness a single feature. A good form strikes all eyes pleasantly, long before they have any science on the subject, and a beautiful face sets twenty hearts in palpitation, prior to all consideration of the mechanical proportions of the features and head. We may owe to dreams some light on the fountain of this skill; for as soon as we let our will go and let the unconscious states ensue, see what cunning draughtsmen we are! We entertain ourselves with wonderful forms of men, of women, of animals, of gardens, of woods and of monsters, and the mystic pencil wherewith we then draw has no awkwardness or inexperience, no meagreness or poverty; it can design well and group well; its composition is full of art, its colors are well laid on and the whole canvas which it paints is lifelike and apt to touch us with terror, with tenderness, with desire and with grief. Neither are the artist's copies from experience ever mere copies, but always touched and softened by tints from this ideal domain.

The conditions essential to a constructive mind do not appear to be so often combined but that a good sentence or verse remains fresh and memorable for a long time. Yet when we write with ease and come out into the free air of thought, we seem to be assured that nothing is easier than to continue this communication at pleasure. Up, down, around, the kingdom of thought has no inclosures, but the Muse makes us free of her city. Well, the world has a million writers. One would think then that good thought would be as familiar as air and water, and the gifts of each new hour would exclude the last. Yet we can count all our good books; nay, I remember any beautiful verse for twenty years. It is true that the discerning intellect of the world is always much in advance of the creative, so that there are many competent judges of the best book, and few writers of the best books. But some of the conditions of intellectual construction are of rare occurrence. The intellect is a whole and demands integrity in every work. This is resisted equally by a man's devotion to a single thought and by his ambition to combine too many.

Truth is our element of life, yet if a man fasten his attention on a single aspect of truth and apply himself to that alone for a long time, the truth becomes distorted and not itself but falsehood; herein resembling the air, which is our natural element and the breath of our nostrils, but if a stream of the same be directed on the body for a time, it causes cold, fever, and even death. How wearisome the grammarian, the phrenologist, the political or religious fanatic, or indeed any possessed mortal whose balance is lost by the exaggeration of a single topic. It is incipient insanity. Every thought is a prison also. I cannot see what you see, because I am caught up by a strong wind and blown so far in one direction that I am out of the hoop of your horizon.

Is it any better if the student, to avoid this offence and to liberalize himself, aims to make a mechanical whole of history, or science, or philosophy, by a numerical addition of all the facts that fall within his vision? The world refuses to be analyzed by addition and subtraction. When we are young we spend much time and pains in filling our note-books with all definitions of Religion, Love, Poetry, Politics, Art, in the hope that in the course of a few years we shall have condensed into our encyclopaedia the net value of all the theories at which the world has yet arrived. But year after year our tables get no completeness, and at last we discover that our curve is a parabola, whose arcs will never meet.

Never by detachment, neither by aggregation is the integrity of the intellect transmitted to its works, but by a vigilance which brings the intellect in its greatness and best state to operate every moment. It must have the same wholeness which nature has. Although no diligence can rebuild the universe in a model by the best accumulation or disposition of details, yet does the world reappear in miniature in every event, so that all the laws of nature may be read in the smallest fact. The intellect must have the like perfection in its apprehension and in its works. For this reason, an index or mercury of intellectual proficiency is the perception of identity. We talk with accomplished persons who appear to be strangers in nature. The cloud, the tree, the turf, the bird, are not theirs, have nothing of them; the world is only their lodging and table. But the poet, whose verses are to be spheral and complete, is one whom Nature cannot deceive, whatsoever face of strangeness she may put on. He feels a strict consanguinity, and detects more likeness than variety in all her changes. We are stung by the desire for new thought; but when we receive a new thought it is only the old thought with a new face, and though we make it our own we instantly crave another; we are not really enriched. For the truth was in us before it was reflected to us from natural objects; and the profound genius will cast the likeness of all creatures into every product of his wit.

But if the constructive powers are rare and it is given to few men to be poets, yet every man is a receiver of this descending holy ghost, and may well study the laws of its influx. Exactly parallel is the whole rule of intellectual duty to the rule of moral duty. A self-denial no less austere than the saint's is demanded of the scholar. He must worship truth, and forego all things for that, and choose defeat and pain, so that his treasure in thought is thereby augmented.

God offers to every mind its choice between truth and repose. Take which you please,—you can never have both. Between these, as a pendulum, man oscillates. He in whom the love of repose predominates will accept the first creed, the first philosophy, the first political party he meets,—most likely his father's. He gets rest, commodity and reputation; but he shuts the door of truth. He in whom the love of truth predominates will keep himself aloof from all moorings, and afloat. He will abstain from dogmatism, and recognize all the opposite negations between which, as walls, his being is swung. He submits to the inconvenience of suspense and imperfect opinion, but he is a candidate for truth, as the other is not, and respects the highest law of his being.

The circle of the green earth he must measure with his shoes to find the man who can yield him truth. He shall then know that there is somewhat more blessed and great in hearing than in speaking. Happy is the hearing man; unhappy the speaking man. As long as I hear truth I am bathed by a beautiful element and am not conscious of any limits to my nature. The suggestions are thousand-fold that I hear and see. The waters of the great deep have ingress and egress to the soul. But if I speak, I define, I confine and am less. When Socrates speaks, Lysis and Menexenus[3] are afflicted by no shame that they do not speak. They also are good. He likewise defers to them, loves them, whilst he speaks. Because a true and natural man contains and is the same truth which an eloquent man articulates; but in the eloquent man, because he can articulate it, it seems something the less to reside, and he turns to these silent beautiful with the more inclination and respect. The ancient sentence said, Let us be silent, for so are the gods.[4] Silence is a solvent that destroys personality, and gives us leave to be great and universal. Every man's progress is through a succession of teachers, each of whom seems at the time to have a superlative influence, but it at last gives place to a new. Frankly let him accept it all. Jesus says, Leave father, mother, house and lands, and follow me. Who leaves all, receives more. This is as true intellectually as morally. Each new mind we approach seems to require an abdication of all our past and present possessions. A new doctrine seems at first a subversion of all our opinions, tastes, and manner of living. Such has Swedenborg, such has Kant, such has Coleridge, such has Hegel or his interpreter Cousin seemed to many young men in this country. Take thankfully and heartily all they can give. Exhaust them, wrestle with them, let them not go until their blessing be won, and after a short season the dismay will be overpast, the excess of influence withdrawn, and they will be no longer an alarming meteor, but one more bright star shining serenely in your heaven and blending its light with all your day.

But whilst he gives himself up unreservedly to that which draws him, because that is his own, he is to refuse himself to that which draws him not, whatsoever fame and authority may attend it, because it is not his own. Entire self-reliance belongs to the intellect. One soul is a counterpoise of all souls, as a capillary column of water is a balance for the sea. It must treat things and books and sovereign genius as itself also a sovereign. If Aeschylus be that man he is taken for, he has not yet done his office when he has educated the learned of Europe for a thousand years. He is now to approve himself a master of delight to me also. If he cannot do that, all his fame shall avail him nothing with me. I were a fool not to sacrifice a thousand Aeschyluses to my intellectual integrity. Especially take the same ground in regard to abstract truth, the science of the mind. The Bacon, the Spinoza, the Hume, Schelling, Kant, or whosoever propounds to you a philosophy of the mind, is only a more or less awkward translator of things in your consciousness which you have also your way of seeing, perhaps of denominating. Say then, instead of too timidly poring into his obscure sense, that he has not succeeded in rendering back to you your consciousness. He has not succeeded; now let another try. If Plato cannot, perhaps Spinoza will. If Spinoza cannot, then perhaps Kant. Anyhow, when at last it is done, you will find it is no recondite, but a simple, natural, common state which the writer restores to you.

But let us end these didactics. I will not, though the subject might provoke it, speak to the open question between Truth and Love. I shall not presume to interfere in the old politics of the skies,—"The cherubim know most; the seraphim love most." The gods shall settle their own quarrels. But I cannot recite, even thus rudely, laws of the intellect, without remembering that lofty and sequestered class who have been its prophets and oracles, the high-priesthood of the pure reason, the *Trismegisti*,[5] the expounders of the principles of thought from age to age. When at long intervals we turn over their abstruse pages, wonderful seems the calm and grand air of these few, these great spiritual lords who have walked in the world,—these of the old religion,—dwelling in a worship which makes the sanctities of Christianity look *parvenues* and popular; for "persuasion is in soul, but necessity is in intellect."[6] This band of grandees, Hermes, Heraclitus, Empedocles, Plato, Plotinus, Olympiodorus, Proclus, Synesius and the rest,[7] have somewhat so vast in their logic, so primary in their thinking, that it seems antecedent to all the ordinary distinctions of rhetoric and literature, and to be at once poetry and music and dancing and astronomy and mathematics. I am present at the sowing of the seed of the world. With a geometry of sunbeams the soul lays the foundations of nature. The truth and grandeur of their thought is proved by its scope and applicability, for it commands the entire schedule and inventory of things for its illustration. But what marks its elevation and has even a comic look to us, is the innocent serenity with which these babe-like Jupiters sit in their clouds, and from age to age prattle to each other and to no contemporary. Well assured that their speech is intelligible and the most natural thing in the world, they add thesis to thesis, without a moment's heed of the universal astonishment of the human race below, who do not comprehend their plainest argument; nor do they ever relent so much as to insert a popular or explaining sentence, nor testify the least displeasure or petulance at the dulness of their amazed auditory. The angels are so enamored of the language that is spoken in heaven that they will not distort their lips with the hissing and unmusical dialects of men, but speak their own, whether there be any who understand it or not.

Essays: First Series, W 2:323–47; first published in *Essays: First Series* (1841).

Bacchus

"Bacchus" symbolically expresses Emerson's deep thirst for the wine of creative inspiration. Bacchus is elevated to a god of spiritual ecstasy in a transcendental communion with the epic origins and powers of the universe. It is an inspiration nourished by the springs that run deep under the continents and mountain ranges, by the sun and the oceanic streams, until from these primal energies the poet achieves godhood, both Dionysian and transcendent, in the power of his "remembering" insight. So inspired, he will, in his "dazzling memory" of ages gone, revive our consciousness of the long evolution of Man from primordial Chaos (the Unconscious). The promised evolution of Man depends, then, on the poet's Platonic Identity with the universals of life, with the Over-Soul as the

continuum of life's primal energy. The affirmation is not of resurrection over death but of the epic evolution and power of human creativity, of inspired insight into the destiny of man. This "Wine which Music is,—Music and Wine are one" implies the deep harmonies of organic process, of "cosmic humanism," in Oliver Reiser's sense of the term, which is neither a Christian nor a Platonic typology. For his germinal idea Emerson may, of course, be indebted to Platonic, Neo-Platonic, Renaissance, or Persian sources.[8]

Bring me wine, but wine which never grew
In the belly of the grape,
Or grew on vine whose tap-roots, reaching through
Under the Andes to the Cape,
Suffer no savor of the earth to scape.

Let its grapes the morn salute
From a nocturnal root,
Which feels the acrid juice
Of Styx and Erebus;
And turns the woe of Night,
By its own craft, to a more rich delight.

We buy ashes for bread;
We buy diluted wine;
Give me of the true,—
Whose ample leaves and tendrils curled
Among the silver hills of heaven
Draw everlasting dew;
Wine of wine,
Blood of the world,
Form of forms, and mould of statures,
That I intoxicated,
And by the draught assimilated,
May float at pleasure through all natures;
The bird-language rightly spell,
And that which roses say so well.

Wine that is shed
Like the torrents of the sun

Up the horizon walls,
Or like the Atlantic streams, which run
When the South Sea calls.

Water and bread,
Food which needs no transmuting,
Rainbow-flowering, wisdom-fruiting,
Wine which is already man,
Food which teach and reason can.

Wine which Music is,—
Music and wine are one,—
That I, drinking this,
Shall hear far Chaos talk with me;
Kings unborn shall walk with me;
And the poor grass shall plot and plan
What it will do when it is man.
Quickened so, will I unlock
Every crypt of every rock.

I thank the joyful juice
For all I know;—
Winds of remembering
Of the ancient being blow,
And seeming-solid walls of use
Open and flow.

Pour, Bacchus! the remembering wine;
Retrieve the loss of me and mine!
Vine for vine be antidote,
And the grape requite the lote!
Haste to cure the old despair,—
Reason in Nature's lotus drenched,
The memory of ages quenched;
Give them again to shine;
Let wine repair what this undid;
And where the infection slid,
A dazzling memory revive;
Refresh the faded tints,

Recut the aged prints,
And write my old adventures with the pen
Which on the first day drew,
Upon the tablets blue,
The dancing Pleiads and eternal men.

Poems, W 9:125–27; first published in *Poems* (1846).

Merlin

As in "Bacchus," here the poetic function is conceived in terms of an epic teleology or cosmic humanism (cf. ll. 14–26). "Merlin's mighty line" echoes the primal forces in the universe and in the hearts of men, both primitive and civilized (ll. 14–26). But most of part I is an essay in method, the right use of the poet's medium, gift, or skill in keeping with his high aims (ll. 1–13, 27–58), contrasting genuine creativity with the "meddling wit" that lacks inspiration (ll. 59–77). Merlin the bard represents the Emersonian ideal of the creative poet who mounts by "the stairway of surprise" (unpredictable moments of inspiration) to the highest levels of realization and power. As for its poetic qualities, "Merlin" has been praised as one of Emerson's most noteworthy achievements in organic form. Indeed, within the limits of its mostly end-stopped four-stress lines, it makes very effective functional use of alliteration, assonance, syntax, metrical variation, rhyme pattern, and line variation, with strong suggestions of free verse. As Hyatt Waggoner says, its movement seems inevitable, not arbitrary.[9] Part II develops the theme of polarity, briefly introduced earlier in lines 51–58. The poet's art (insight) enables him to realize the law of polarity as it is manifested throughout balance-loving nature: the complementary nature of colors, tones, tastes, and touching; the androgynous nature of the human psyche; the polar nature of thinking, of imagination, and of justice; animal life; and the Fates or forces that rhythmically sing and spin, build and unbuild, our lives. Merlin's poetic insight must function on all levels of Transcendental Reality.

I

Thy trivial harp will never please
Or fill my craving ear;
Its chords should ring as blows the breeze,
Free, peremptory, clear.
No jingling serenader's art,
Nor tinkle of piano strings,
Can make the wild blood start
In its mystic springs.
The kingly bard
Must smite the chords rudely and hard,
As with hammer or with mace;
That they may render back
Artful thunder, which conveys
Secrets of the solar track,
Sparks of the supersolar blaze.
Merlin's blows are strokes of fate,
Chiming with the forest tone,
When boughs buffet boughs in the wood;
Chiming with the gasp and moan
Of the ice-imprisoned flood;
With the pulse of manly hearts;
With the voice of orators;
With the din of city arts;
With the cannonade of wars;
With the marches of the brave;
And prayers of might from martyrs' cave.

Great is the art,
Great be the manners, of the bard.
He shall not his brain encumber
With the coil of rhythm and number;
But, leaving rule and pale forethought,
He shall aye climb
For his rhyme.
'Pass in, pass in,' the angels say,
'In to the upper doors,

Nor count compartments of the floors,
But mount to paradise
By the stairway of surprise.'

Blameless master of the games,
King of sport that never shames,
He shall daily joy dispense
Hid in song's sweet influence.
Forms more cheerly live and go,
What time the subtle mind
Sings aloud the tune whereto
Their pulses beat,
And march their feet,
And their members are combined.

By Sybarites beguiled,
He shall no task decline;
Merlin's mighty line
Extremes of nature reconciled,—
Bereaved a tyrant of his will,
And made the lion mild.
Songs can the tempest still,
Scattered on the stormy air,
Mould the year to fair increase,
And bring in poetic peace.

He shall not seek to weave,
In weak, unhappy times,
Efficacious rhymes;
Wait his returning strength.
Bird that from the nadir's floor
To the zenith's top can soar,—
The soaring orbit of the muse exceeds that journey's length.
Nor profane affect to hit
Or compass that, by meddling wit,
Which only the propitious mind
Publishes when 't is inclined.
There are open hours
When the God's will sallies free,

And the dull idiot might see
The flowing fortunes of a thousand years;—
Sudden, at unawares,
Self-moved, fly-to the doors,
Nor sword of angels could reveal
What they conceal.

II

The rhyme of the poet
Modulates the king's affairs;
Balance-loving Nature
Made all things in pairs.
To every foot its antipode;
Each color with its counter glowed;
To every tone beat answering tones,
Higher or graver;
Flavor gladly blends with flavor;
Leaf answers leaf upon the bough;
And match the paired cotyledons.[10]
Hands to hands, and feet to feet,
In one body grooms and brides;
Eldest rite, two married sides
In every mortal meet.
Light's far furnace shines,
Smelting balls and bars,
Forging double stars,
Glittering twins and trines.
The animals are sick with love,
Lovesick with rhyme;
Each with all propitious Time
Into chorus wove.

Like the dancers' ordered band,
Thoughts come also hand in hand;
In equal couples mated,
Or else alternated;
Adding by their mutual gage,

One to other, health and age.
Solitary fancies go
Short-lived wandering to and fro,
Most like to bachelors,
Or an ungiven maid,
Not ancestors,
With no posterity to make the lie afraid,
Or keep truth undecayed.
Perfect-paired as eagle's wings,
Justice is the rhyme of things;
Trade and counting use
The self-same tuneful muse;
And Nemesis,
Who with even matches odd,
Who athwart space redresses
The partial wrong,
Fills the just period,
And finishes the song.

Subtle rhymes, with ruin rife,
Murmur in the house of life,
Sung by the Sisters as they spin;
In perfect time and measure they
Build and unbuild our echoing clay
As the two twilights of the day
Fold us music-drunken in.

Poems, *W* 9:120–24; first published in *Poems* (1846).

NOTES

1. This motto was originally penned in one of Emerson's notebooks and reappeared among "Fragments on the Poet," third stanza, in the Appendix to *Poems*, *W* 9.

2. Thoughts come into our minds by avenues which we never left open. [Emerson's note.]

3. *Lysis and Menexenus:* famous orators of ancient Greece.

4. Perhaps an obscure reference to the Egyptian god Horus, whose lips were sealed by his fingers.

5. A group of Neo-Platonists naming themselves after Hermes Trismegistus ("thrice-great"), the Greek name for the mythical Egyptian Thoth, who reputedly wrote forty-two works on magic, astrology, and alchemy.

6. From Plotinus.

7. All mystical and/or Platonic philosophers. Hermes is the Trismegistus of n. 5.

8. On the Persian poet Hafiz as parallel and source, see *J* 7:278–80 or *JMN* 10:67–70; *W* 8:244–54; and J. D. Yohannan, "The Influence of Persian Poetry on Emerson's Work," *American Literature* 15 (1943): 25–41.

9. Hyatt Waggoner, *Emerson as Poet*, p. 142.

10. *Cotyledons:* the first leaf developed by the embryo in seed plants, frequently serving as a storehouse of nourishment for the embryo.

III
THE ART OF RHETORIC

Diction and Style

Out of a typically American distrust of the rhetorical tradition, Emerson developed, in Odell Shepard's words, "the way of a mind with a style." With the salty New England idiom of Aunt Mary Moody ringing in his ears, along with frequent reading of Bacon, Montaigne, Shakespeare, and Carlyle, it is little wonder that he abandoned his conventional, ministerial style for a "natural rhetoric" free of ornamental details. He came to demand "initiative, spermatic, prophesying, man-making words" and sentences to match. Where the neo-classical stylist would have written "Bind thy chariot with filaments of light," Emerson wrote "Hitch your wagon to a star." As every moment was potentially inspired, the self-reliant Man Thinking must seek a distinctive style consonant with his individualized insights. First of all, the writer had to be a man of character or there would be no conviction, no quality, to his writing. Then, his "thought must take the stupendous step of passing into realization" (in words). Avoiding stock or sentimental rhetoric, he would strive for "a noble idiomatic English"—simple but fresh, homely, exact, and concrete. "Speak with the vulgar, think with the wise," is Emerson's credo. The most vital style draws upon the power of Saxon words, as in the vernacular of nicknames, oaths, proverbs, and slang; the names of places, plants, trees, grasses; and the example of Dante and the Bible. A greater richness and range of style was appropriate in Rabelais, Burke, and Clarendon. Otherwise, understatement carries greater force than superlatives, and compression than elaboration. Like Robert Frost, Emerson would test sentences by reading them aloud.

Good Writing Keeps Only What Is Vital

1869

Good writing. All writing should be selection in order to drop every dead word. Why do you not save out of your speech or thinking only the vital things,—the spirited *mot* which amused or warmed you when you spoke it,—because of its luck and newness? I have just been reading, in this careful book of a most intelligent and learned man, any number of flat conventional words and sentences. If a man would learn to read his own manuscript severely,—becoming really a third person, and search only for what interested him, he would blot to purpose,—and how every page would gain! Then all the words will be sprightly, and every sentence a surprise.

Compression Distinguished from Elliptical Style

1839

Compression.—There is a wide difference between compression and an elliptical style. The dense writer has yet ample room and choice of phrase, and even a gamesome mood often, between his noble words. There is no disagreeable contraction in his sentence any more than there is a human face, where in a square space of a few inches is found room for command and love and frolic and wisdom and for the expression even of great amplitude of surface.

Carlyle: Stylist but Not Philosopher

1840

Carlyle shall make a statement of a fact, shall draw a portrait, shall inlay nice shades of meaning, shall play, shall insinuate, shall banter, shall paralyze with sarcasm, shall translate, shall sing a Tyrtaen song,[1] and speak out like the Liturgy, or the old English Pentateuch, all the secrets of manhood. This he shall do and much more, being an upright, plain-dealing, hearty, loving soul of the clearest eye and of infinite wit, and using the language like a protean engine which can cut, thrust, saw, rasp, tickle or pulverize as occasion may require. But he is not a philosopher: his strength does not lie in the statement of abstract truth. His contemplation has no wings.

He exhausts his topic. There is no more to be said when he has ended. He is not suggestive.

Every new history that shall be written will be indebted to him. It will not be stately, but will go now into the street and sitting-room and the ale-house and kitchen.

What he has said shall be proverb; nobody shall be able to say it otherwise.

The Vernacular Gives Power to Style

1840

Montaigne.— The language of the street is always strong. What can describe the folly and emptiness of scolding like the word *jawing*? I feel too the force of the double negative, though clean contrary to our grammar rules. And I confess to some pleasure from the stinging rhetoric of a rattling oath in the mouth of truckmen and teamsters. How laconic and brisk it is by the side of a page of the *North American Review*. Cut these words and they would bleed; they are vascular and alive; they walk and run. Moreover they who speak them have this elegancy, that they do not trip in their speech. It is a shower of bullets, whilst Cambridge men and Yale men correct themselves and begin again at every half sentence.

I know nobody among my contemporaries except Carlyle who writes with any sinew and vivacity comparable to Plutarch and Montaigne. Yet always this profane swearing and bar-room wit has salt and fire in it. I cannot now read Webster's speeches. Fuller and Browne and Milton are quick, but the list is soon ended. Goethe seems to be well alive, no pedant. Luther too.[2]

Dante as a Textbook in Rhetoric

July 1849

In Dante pleases the friendly conversation with Brunetto Latino. —*Inferno* xv, 82.

Education.

> . . . In la mente m' è fitta, ed or m' accuora
> La cara buona imagine paterna
> Di voi, quando nel mondo ad ora ad ora
> M' insegnavate come l' uom s' eterna.[3]

I think, if I were professor of Rhetoric,—teacher of the art of writing well to young men,—I should use Dante for my text-book. Come hither, youth, and learn how the brook that flows at the bottom of your garden, or the farmer who ploughs the adjacent field, your

father and mother, your debts and credits, and your web of habits are
the very best basis of poetry, and the material which you must work
up. Dante knew how to throw the weight of his body into each act,
and is, like Byron, Burke, and Carlyle, the Rhetorician. I find him full
of the *nobil volgare eloquenza*; that he knows "God damn," and can be
rowdy if he please, and he does please. Yet is not Dante reason or
illumination and that essence we were looking for, but only a new
exhibition of the possibilities of genius? Here is an imagination that
rivals in closeness and precision the senses. But we must prize him as
we do a rainbow, we can appropriate nothing of him.

Could we some day admit into our oyster heads the immense figure
which these flagrant points compose when united, the hands of Phidias, the conclusion of Newton, the pantheism of Goethe, the all-wise
music of Shakespeare, the robust eyes of Swedenborg!

J 10:302–3. *J* 5:213 (cf. *JMN* 7:206). *J* 5:440–41 (cf. *JMN* 7:381–82). *J*
5:419–20 (cf. *JMN* 7:374). *J* 8:32–33 (cf. *JMN* 11:133–34).

Art and Criticism

This lecture might better have been called "Some Notes toward a New
Rhetoric" or "Some Notes toward a Native Style." Although Emerson sets out to
discuss a few of the "principal weapons" of the writer, he devotes himself largely
to the power of the vernacular, as distinguished from the tradition of elegance,
showy words, and neo-classical diction, his ideal being an "intermixture of the
common and the transcendental." Carlyle has made Emerson, as well as England,
conscious of a new language, in which "the vicious conventions are all dropped"
and replaced by a style so flexible, so "colloquially elastic," as to bring about a
revolution in history writing. Though Whitman is the only American writer
mentioned, among a dozen, it was apparently American usage, good and bad, that
spurred Emerson to the claim that "the language of the street is always strong"
and "some men swear with genius."

> To clothe the fiery thought
> In simple words succeeds,
> For still the craft of genius is
> To mask a king in weeds.[4]

Literature is but a poor trick, you will say, when it busies itself to make words pass for things; and yet I am far from thinking this subordinate service unimportant. The secondary services of literature may be classed under the name of Rhetoric, and are quite as important in letters as iron is in war. An enumeration of the few principal weapons of the poet or writer will at once suggest their value.

Writing is the greatest of arts, the subtilest, and of most miraculous effect; and to it the education is costliest. On the writer the choicest influences are concentrated,—nothing that does not go to his costly equipment: a war, an earthquake, revival of letters, the new dispensation by Jesus, or by Angels; Heaven, Hell, power, science, the *Néant*,[5] exist to him as colors for his brush.

In this art modern society has introduced a new element, by introducing a new audience. The decline of the privileged orders, all over the world; the advance of the Third Estate; the transformation of the laborer into reader and writer has compelled the learned and the thinkers to address them. Chiefly in this country, the common school has added two or three audiences: once, we had only the boxes; now, the galleries and the pit.

There is, in every nation, a style which never becomes obsolete, a certain mode of phraseology so consonant and congenial to the analogy and principles of its respective language as to remain settled and unaltered. This style is probably to be sought in the common intercourse of life, among those who speak only to be understood, without ambition of elegance. The polite are always catching modish innovations, and the learned depart from established forms of speech, in hope of finding or making better; those who wish for distinction forsake the vulgar, when the vulgar is right; but there is a conversation above grossness and below refinement where prosperity resides, and where Shakspeare seems to have gathered his comic dialogue. Goethe valued himself not on his learning or eccentric flights, but that he knew how to write German. And many of his poems are so idiomatic, so strongly rooted in the German soil, that they are the terror of translators, who say they cannot be rendered into any other language without loss of vigor, as we say of any darling passage of our own masters. "Le style c'est l'homme," said Buffon; and Goethe said, "Poetry here, poetry there, I have learned to speak German." And when I read of various extraordinary polyglots, self-made or college-made, who can understand fifty languages, I answer that I shall be glad and surprised to find that they know one. For if I were asked how many masters of English idiom I know, I shall be perplexed to count five.

Ought not the scholar to convey his meaning in terms as short and strong as the smith and the drover use to convey theirs? You know the history of the eminent English writer on gypsies, George Borrow; he had one clear perception, that the key to every country was command of the language of the common people. He therefore mastered the *patois* of the gypsies, called Romany, which is spoken by them in all countries where they wander, in Europe, Asia, Africa. Yet much of the raw material of the street-talk is absolutely untranslatable into print, and one must learn from Burke how to be severe without being unparliamentary. Rabelais and Montaigne are masters of this Romany, but cannot be read aloud, and so far fall short. Whitman is our American master, but has not got out of the Fire-Club and gained the *entrée* of the sitting-rooms. Bacon, if "he could out-cant a London chirurgeon," must have possessed the Romany under his brocade robes. Luther said, "I preach coarsely; that giveth content to all. Hebrew, Greek and Latin I spare, until we learned ones come together, and then we make it so curled and finical that God himself wondereth at us." He who would be powerful must have the terrible gift of familiarity,—Mirabeau, Chatham, Fox, Burke, O'Connell, Patrick Henry; and among writers, Swift, De Foe and Carlyle.

Look at this forlorn caravan of travellers who wander over Europe dumb,—never exchange a word, in the mother tongue of either, with prince or peasant; but condemned to the company of a courier and of the padrone[6] when they cannot take refuge in the society of countrymen. A well-chosen series of stereoscopic views would have served a better purpose, which they can explore at home, sauced with joyful discourse and with reference to all the books in your library.

Speak with the vulgar, think with the wise. See how Plato managed it, with an imagination so gorgeous, and a taste so patrician, that Jove, if he descended, was to speak in his style. Into the exquisite refinement of his Academy, he introduces the low-born Socrates, relieving the purple diction by his perverse talk, his gallipots, and cook, and trencher, and cart-wheels—and steadily kept this coarseness to flavor a dish else too luscious. Everybody knows the points in which the mob has the advantage of the Academy, and all able men have known how to import the petulance of the street into correct discourse. I heard, when a great bank president was expounding the virtues of his party and of the government to a silent circle of bank pensioners, a grave Methodist exclaimed "Fiddlesticks!" The whole party were surprised and cheered, except the bank president, though it would be difficult to explain the propriety of the expression, as no music or fiddle was so much as thought of.

Not only low style, but the lowest of classifying words outvalue arguments; as, upstart, dab, cockney, prig, granny, lubber, puppy, peacock—"A cocktail [pretentious] House of Commons." I remember when a venerable divine [Dr. Osgood] called the young preacher's sermon "patty cake." The *sans-culottes*[7] at Versailles cried out, "Let our little Mother Mirabeau speak!" Who has not heard in the street how forcible is bosh, gammon [humbug] and gas. The short Saxon words with which the people help themselves are better than Latin. The language of the street is always strong. I envy the boys the force of the double negative (no shoes, no money, no nothing), though clean contrary to our grammar rules, and I confess to some titillation of my ears from a rattling oath.

In the infinite variety of talents, 't is certain that some men swear with genius. I knew a poet in whose talent Nature carried this freak so far that his only graceful verses were pretty blasphemies. "The better the worse," you will say; and I own it reminds one of Vathek's[8] collection of monstrous men with humps of a picturesque peak, and horns of exquisite polish. What traveller has not listened to the vigor of the *Sacre!* of the French postilion, the *Sia ammazato!* of the Italian contadino,[9] or the deep stomach of an English drayman's execration. I remember an occasion when a proficient in this style came from North Street to Cambridge and drew a crowd of young critics in the college yard, who found his wrath so aesthetic and fertilizing that they took notes, and even overstayed the hour of the mathematical professor.

'T is odd what revolutions occur. We were educated in horror of Satan, but Goethe remarked that all men like to hear him named. Burns took him into compassion and expressed a blind wish for his reformation.

> "Ye aiblins might, I dinna ken,
> Still have a stake."[10]

And George Sand finds a whole nation who regard him as a personage who has been greatly wronged, and in which he is really the subject of a covert worship. As a study in language, the use of this word is curious, to see how words help us and must be philosophical. The Devil in philosophy is absolute negation, falsehood, nothing; and in the popular mind, the Devil is a malignant person. Yet all our speech expresses the first sense. "The Devil a monk was he," means, *he was no monk*, and "The Devil you did!" means *you did not*. Natural science gives us the inks, the shades; ink of Erebus—night of Chaos. . . .[11] Goethe, who had collected all the diabolical hints in men and nature for traits for his *Walpurgis Nacht*, continued the humor of collecting such horrors after this first occasion had passed, and professed to point his guest to his Walpurgis Sack, or Acherontian[12] Bag, in which, he said, he put all his dire hints and images, and into which, he said, he should be afraid to fall himself, lest he should be burnt up. Dante is the professor that shall teach both the noble low style, the power of working up all his experience into heaven and hell; also the sculpture of compression.

The next virtue of rhetoric is compression, the science of omitting, which makes good the old verse of Hesiod, "Fools, they did not know that half was better than the whole." The French have a neat phrase, that the secret of boring you is that of telling all,—"Le secret d'ennuyer est celui de tout dire;" which we translate short, "Touch and go." The silences, pauses, of an orator are as telling as his words. What the poet omits exalts every syllable that he writes. In good hands it will never become sterility. A good writer must convey the feeling of a flamboyant witness, and at the same time of chemic[13] selection,—as if in his densest period was no cramp, but room to turn a chariot and horses between his valid words. There is hardly danger in America of excess of condensation; there must be no cramp insufficiency, but the superfluous must be omitted. In the Hindoo mythology, "Viswaharmán" placed the sun on his lathe to grind off some of his effulgence, and in this manner reduced it to an eighth,—more was inseparable. . . .

In architecture the beauty is increased in the degree in which the material is safely diminished; as when you break up a prose wall, and leave all the strength in the poetry of columns. As soon as you read aloud, you will find what sentences drag. Blot them out, and read again, you will find the words that drag. 'T is like a pebble inserted in a mosaic. Resolute blotting rids you of all those phrases that sound like something and mean nothing, with which scriptural forms play a large part. Never say, "I beg not to be misunderstood." It is only graceful in the case when you are afraid that what is called a better meaning will be taken, and you wish to insist on a worse; a man has a right to pass, like Dean [Jonathan] Swift, for a worse man than he is, but not for a better.

And I sometimes wish that the Board of Education might carry out the project of a college for graduates of our universities, to which editors and members of Congress and writers of books might repair, and learn to sink what we could best spare of our words; to gazette those Americanisms which offend us in all journals. Some of these are odious. *Some* as an adverb—"reeled some;" *considerable* as an adverb for *much*; "quite a number;" *slim* for *bad*; the adjective *graphic*, which means *what is written*,—graphic arts and oral arts, arts of writing, and arts of speech and song,—but is used as if it meant *descriptive*: "Minerva's graphic thread." A Mr. Randall, M. C., who appeared before the committee of the House of Commons on the subject of the American mode of closing a debate, said, "that the one-hour rule worked well; made the debate short and graphic." 'T is the worst praise you can give a speech that it is as if written.

Never use the word *development*, and be wary of the whole family of Fero.[14] Dangerous words in like kind are *display, improvement, peruse, circumstances, commence* for *begin*. Vulgarisms to be gazetted, *moiety* used for *a small part*;—"nothing would answer but;" "there is none but what"—"there being scarce a person of any note in England but what some time or other paid a visit or sent a present to our Lady of Walsingham" (Bishop Parcy); "might have to go;" "I have been to Europe;" "in our midst;" *considerable*—"it is considerable of a compliment," "under considerable of a cloud;" *balance* for *remainder*—"spent the balance of his life;" "*as a general thing*;" "*after all.*" Confusions of *lie* and *lay*, *sit* and *set*, *shall* and *will*.

Persons have been named from their abuse of certain phrases, as "Pyramid" Lambert, "Finality" Russell, "Humanity" Martin, "Horizon" Turner.[15]

Every age gazettes a quantity of words which it has used up. We are now offended with "Standpoint,"[16] "Myth," "Subjective," "the Good and the True" and "the Cause."

A list might be made of showy words that tempt young writers: *asphodel, harbinger, chalice, flamboyant,*[17] *golden, diamond, amethyst, opal* and the rest of the precious stones, *carcanet, diadem.*

But these cardinal rules of rhetoric find best examples in the great masters, and are main sources of the delight they give. Shakspeare might be studied for his dexterity in the use of these weapons, if it were not for his heroic strength. There is no such master of low style as he, and therefore none can securely soar so high. I do not mean that he delights in comedy, exults in bringing the street itself, uproarious with laughter and animal joy, on to the scene, with Falstaff and Touchstone and Trinculo and the fools; but that in the conduct of the play, and the speech of the heroes, he keeps the level tone which is the tone of high and low alike, and most widely understood. A man of experience altogether, his very sonnets are as solid and close to facts as the Banker's Gazette; and the only check on the detail of each of his portraits is his own universality, which made bias or fixed ideas impossible—his impartiality is like a sunbeam.

His fun is as wise as his earnest, its foundations are below the frost. His muse is moral simply from its depth, and I value the intermixture of the common and the transcendental as in Nature. One would say Shakspeare must have been a thousand years old when he wrote his first piece; so thoroughly is his thought familiar to him, so solidly worded, as if it were already a proverb, and not only hereafter to become one. Well, that millennium is really only a little acceleration in his process of thought; his loom is better toothed, cranked and pedalled than other people's, and he can turn off a hundred yards to their one. Shakspeare is nothing but a large utterance. We cannot find that anything in his age was more worth expression than anything in ours; nor give any account of his existence, but only the fact that there was a wonderful symbolizer and expressor, who has no rival in all ages and who has thrown an accidental lustre over his time and subject.

My friend thinks the reason why the French mind is so shallow, and still to seek, running into vagaries and blind alleys, is because they do not read Shakspeare; whilst the English and Germans, who read Shakspeare and the Bible, have a great onward march. Shakspeare would have sufficed for the culture of a nation for vast periods. The Chinese have got on so long with their solitary Confucius and Mencius; the Arabs with their Mahomet; the Scandinavians with their Snorre Sturleson;[18] and if the English island had been larger and the Straits of Dover wider, to keep it at pleasure a little out of the imbroglio of Europe, they might have managed to feed on Shakspeare for some ages yet; as the camel in the desert is fed by his humps, in long absence from food.

Montaigne must have the credit of giving to literature that which we listen for in bar-rooms, the low speech,—words and phrases that no scholar coined; street-cries and war-cries; words of the boatman, the farmer and the lord; that have neatness and necessity, through their use in the vocabulary of work and appetite, like the pebbles which the incessant attrition of the sea has rounded. Every historic autobiographic trait authenticating the man adds to the value of the book. We can't afford to take the horse out of the Essays; it would take the rider too.

Herrick is a remarkable example of the low style. He is, therefore, a good example of the modernness of an old English writer. So Latimer,[19] so Chaucer, so the Bible. He found his subject where he stood, between his feet, in his house, pantry, barn, poultry-yard, in his village, neighbors' gossip and scandal. Like Montaigne in this, that his subject cost him nothing, and he knew what he spake of, and did not write up to it, but could write down (a main secret), and took his level, so that he had all his strength, the easiness of strength; he took what he knew, and "took it easy," as we say. The Germans praise in Goethe the comfortable stoutness. Herrick's merit is the simplicity and manliness of his utterance, and, rarely, the weight of his sentence. He has, and knows that he has, a noble, idiomatic English, a perfect, plain style, from which he can soar to a fine, lyric delicacy, or descend to coarsest sarcasm, without losing his firm footing. This flower of speech is accompanied with an assurance of fame. We have an artist who in this merit of which I speak will easily cope with these celebrities.

In Carlyle as in Byron one is more struck with the rhetoric than with the matter. He has manly superiority rather than intellectuality, and so makes hard hits all the time. There's more character than intellect in every sentence—herein strongly resembling Samuel Johnson. The best service Carlyle has rendered is to rhetoric, or art of writing. In his books the vicious conventions of writing are all dropped. You have no board interposed between you and the writer's mind, but he talks flexibly, now high, now low, in loud emphasis, in undertones, then laughs till the walls ring, then calmly moderates, then hints, or raises an eyebrow. He has gone nigher to the wind than any other craft.

Carlyle, with his inimitable ways of saying the thing, is next best to the inventor of the thing, and I think of him when I read the famous inscription on the pyramid, "I King Saib built this pyramid. I, when I had built it, covered it with satin. Let him who cometh after me, and says he is equal to me, cover it with mats." What he has said shall be proverb, nobody shall be able to say it otherwise. No book can any longer be tolerable in the old husky Neal-on-the-Puritans model.[20] In short, I think the revolution wrought by Carlyle is precisely parallel to that going forward in picture, by the stereoscope. Until history is interesting, it is not yet written.

Here has come into the country, three months ago, a History of Friedrich,[21] infinitely the wittiest book that ever was written; a book that, one would think, the English people would rise up in a mass to thank him for, by cordial acclamation, and signify, by crowning him with chaplet of oak-leaves, their joy that such a head existed among them, and sympathizing and much-reading America would make a new treaty or send a minister extraordinary to offer congratulations of honoring delight to England in acknowledgment of such a donation; a book holding so many memorable and heroic facts, working directly on practice; with new heroes, things unvoiced before—the German Plutarch, now that we have exhausted the Greek and Roman and British biography—with a range, too, of thought and wisdom, so large, so colloquially elastic, that we not so much read a stereotype page as we see the eyes of the writer looking into ours, whilst he is humming and chuckling, with undertones, and trumpet-tones, and shrugs, and long commanding glances, stereoscoping every figure that passes, and every hill, river, wood, hummock and pebble in the long perspective, with its wonderful mnemonics, whereby great and insignificant men are ineffaceably marked and medalled in the memory by what they were, had and did; and withal a book that is a judgment-day for its moral verdict on the men and nations and manners of modern times. And this book makes no noise. I have hardly seen a notice of it in any newspaper or journal, and you would think there was no such book. I am not aware that Mr. Buchanan has sent a special messenger to Great Cheyne Row, Chelsea; but the secret interior wits and hearts of men take note of it, not the less surely. They have said nothing lately in praise of the air, or of fire, or of the blessing of love, and yet, I suppose, they are sensible of these, and not less of this Book, which is like these.

After Low Style and Compression what the books call *Metonomy* is a principal power of rhetoric. It means, using one word or image for another. It is a low idealism. Idealism regards the world as symbolic, and all these symbols or forms as fugitive and convertible expressions. The power of the poet is in controlling these symbols; in using every fact in Nature, however great and stable, as a fluent symbol, and in measuring his strength by the facility with which he makes the mood of mind give its color to things. The world, history, the powers of Nature,—he can make them speak what sense he will.

All conversation, as all literature, appears to me the pleasure of rhetoric, or, I may say, of *metonomy*. "To make of motes mountains, and of mountains motes," Isocrates[22] said, "was the orator's office." Well, that is what poetry and thinking do. Whatever new object we see, we perceive to be only a new version of our familiar experience, and we set about translating it at once into our parallel facts. We have hereby our vocabulary.

Everything has two handles. Pindar when the victor in a race by mules offered him a trifling present, pretended to be hurt at thought of writing on demi-asses. When, however, he offered a sufficient present, he composed the poem:—

> "Hail, daughters of the tempest-footed horse,
> That skims like wind along the course."

That was the other handle. I passed at one time through a place called New City, then supposed, like each of a hundred others, to be destined to greatness. I fell in with one of the founders who showed its advantages and its river and port and the capabilities: "Sixty houses, sir, were built in a night, like tents." After Chicago had secured the confluence of the railroads to itself, I chanced to meet my founder again, but now removed to Chicago. He had transferred to that city the magnificent dreams which he had once communicated to me, and no longer remembered his first emporium. "Where is the town? Was there not," I asked, "a river and a harbor there?" "Oh yes, there was a guzzle out of a sand-bank." "And the town?" "There are still the sixty houses, but when I passed it, one owl was the only inhabitant." When Samuel Dexter, long since, argued the claims of South Boston Bridge, he had to meet loud complaints of the shutting out of the coasting-trade by the proposed improvements. "Now," said he, "I come to the grand charge that we have obstructed the commerce and naviga-tion of Roxbury Ditch." 'T is very easy to call the gracious spring "poor goody herb-wife," or to represent the farm, which stands for the organization of the gravest needs, as a poor trifle of pea-vines, turnips and hen-roosts. Everything has two handles. Shakspeare says, "A plague of opinion; a man can wear it on both sides, like a leather jerkin."

Here is my friend E.,[23] the model of opinionists. He is the April day incarnated and walking, soft sunshine and hailstones, sour east wind and flowery southwest—alternating, and each sovereign, and paint-ing all things its own color. He has it all his own way. He complains of Nature,—too many leaves, too windy and grassy, and I suppose the birds are too feathery and the horses too leggy. He thinks Egypt a humbug, and Palestine used up, and England a flash in the pan; and that the only art is landscape-painting. But when we came, in the woods, to a clump of goldenrod,—"Ah!" he says, "here they are! these things consume a great deal of time. I don't know but they are of more importance than any other of our investments." Well, this is the game that goes on every day in all companies; this is the ball that is tossed in every court of law, in every legislature and in literature, and in the history of every mind by sovereignty of thought to make facts and men obey our present humor or belief.

I designed to speak to one point more, the touching a principal question in criticism in recent times—the Classic and Romantic, or what is classic?

The art of writing is the highest of those permitted to man as drawing directly from the soul, and the means or material it uses are also of the soul. It brings man into alliance with what is great and eternal. It discloses to him the variety and splendor of his resources. And there is much in literature that draws us with a sublime charm—the superincumbent necessity by which each writer, an infirm, capricious, fragmentary soul, is made to utter his part in the chorus of humanity, is enriched by thoughts which flow from all past minds, shares the hopes of all existing minds; so that, whilst the world is made of youthful, helpless children of a day, literature resounds with the music of united vast ideas of affirmation and of moral truth.

What is the Classic? Classic art is the art of necessity; organic; modern or romantic bears the stamp of caprice or chance. One is the product of inclination, of caprice, of haphazard; the other carries its law and necessity within itself.

The politics of monarchy, when all hangs on the accidents of life and temper of a single person, may be called romantic politics. The democratic, when the power proceeds organically from the people and is responsible to them, are classic politics. The classic unfolds, the romantic adds. The classic *should*, the modern *would*. The classic is healthy, the romantic is sick. The classic draws its rule from the genius of that which it does, and not from by-ends. It does not make a novel to establish a principle of political economy.

Don't set out to please; you will displease. The Augsburg Allge-meine Zeitung [a Bavarian newspaper] deprecates an observatory founded for the benefit of navigation. Nor can we promise that our School of Design will secure a lucrative post to the pupils.

When I read Plutarch, or look at a Greek vase, I incline to accept the common opinion of scholars, that the Greeks had clearer wits than any other people. But there is anything but time in my idea of the antique. A clear or natural expression by word or deed is that which we mean when we love and praise the antique. In society I do not find it, in modern books, seldom; but when I come into the pastures, I find antiquity again. Once in the fields with the lowing cattle, the birds, trees and waters and satisfying curves of the landscape, and I cannot tell whether this is Thessaly and Enna [in Greece and Sicily], or whether Concord and Acton.

A man of genius or a work of love or beauty will not come to order, can't be compounded by the best rules, but is always a new and incalculable result, like health. Don't rattle your rules in our ears; we must behave as we can. Criticism is an art when it does not stop at the words of the poet, but looks at the order of his thoughts and the essential quality of his mind. Then the critic is poet. 'T is a question not of talents but of tone; and not particular merits, but the mood of mind into which one and another can bring us.

Natural History of Intellect and Other Papers, *W* 12:281–305; from lecture (1859) of which first quarter is missing but presumed to be included in "Art," *W* 7:37–57.

The Craft of Poetry

As a practicing poet, Emerson cogently generalized from his experience with his craft. Meter or rhythm he traced to the thought and the pulse beat of the poem. As thought and meter are "born together," so "for every thought its proper melody or rhyme exists." In true poetry, "the sense dictates the rhythm. . . . Ask the fact for the form. . . . The verse must be alive, and inseparable from its contents" (W 8:54). If the right tone permeates the whole, a poem will ring true to its inner impulse and theme. According to Jonathan Bishop, in Emerson "tone is to the mind's ear what metaphor is to the mind's eye, but it is more radical than metaphor." Bishop considers Emerson unusual as a writer because he entrusted his subject, the "Soul," to the reader's act of imaginative discovery through language: "Emerson is a prophet because he is an artist." In other words, the test of "the soul's emphasis" is at bottom a literary test: "As rhythm is the literary expression of the organic faculty, and metaphor the characteristic literary mode of action of the Soul as intellect, so the moral sentiment when it moves over into words, becomes tone."[24] Although Bishop's analysis is limited to Emerson's prose style, his chapters on metaphor and tone may readily be applied to Emerson's poetry as well.

The Poem: A Blade of Damascus Steel

1837

Do they think the composition too highly wrought? A poem should be a blade of Damascus steel, made up a mass of knife-blades and nails, and parts every one of which has had its whole surface hammered and wrought before it was welded into the sword, to be wrought over anew.

Tone in Poetry

December 9, 1868

In poetry, tone. I have been reading some of Lowell's new poems, in which he shows unexpected advance on himself, but perhaps most in technical skill and courage. It is in talent rather than in poetic tone, and rather expresses his wish, his ambition, than the uncontrollable interior impulse which is the authentic mark of a new poem, and which is unanalysable, and makes the merit of an ode of Collins, or Gray, or Wordsworth, or Herbert, or Byron,—and which is felt in the pervading tone, rather than in brilliant parts or lines; as if the sound of a bell, or a certain cadence expressed in a low whistle or booming, or humming, to which the poet first timed his step, as he looked at the sunset, or thought, was the incipient form of the piece, and was regnant through the whole.

Rhyme and Rhythm

June 1859

I learned that the rhyme is there in the theme, thought, and image, themselves. I learned that there is a beyond to every place,—and the bird moving through the air by successive dartings taught me.

June 27, 1839

Rhyme.—Rhyme; not tinkling rhyme, but grand Pindaric strokes, as firm as the tread of a horse. Rhyme that vindicates itself as an art, the stroke of the bell of a cathedral. Rhyme which knocks at prose and dullness with the stroke of a cannon ball. Rhyme which builds out into Chaos and old night a splendid architecture to bridge the impassable, and call aloud on all the children of morning that the Creation is recommencing. I wish to write such rhymes as shall not suggest a restraint, but contrariwise the wildest freedom.

And what is the weapon which the poet wields? What the materials and means of his power? Verse or metrical language. Language, the half god, language, the most spiritual of all the works of man, yet language subdued by music—an organ or engine, it must be owned, scarcely less beautiful than the world itself, a fine translation into the speech of man of breezes and waves and ripples, the form and lights of the sky, the color of clouds and leaves. As the world is round, and not square,—as bodies have shadows; and sounds, echoes; and meeting balls a rebound; as there is beauty in a row of balls, or pillars, or buildings, or trees, or statues, beyond their beauty as individuals, so is there a beauty in rhythm or metre (whereof rhyme is one instance) which has its origin in the pulse and constitution of man, and will never be quite absent from sane speech. Rhyme is one of its primary or rudest forms. The child sings or chaunts its first words, sings or chaunts before it talks, as we say. Poetry, in like manner, is found in the literature of all nations to precede prose. But the ear soon finds that there are finer measures than the coarse psalmody which tinkled in the nursery, and wondering, it listens after that sweet beauty, as the eye pines over the colors of a gem, or the transparency of water or of glass. By and by it learns the secret, that love and thought always speak in measure or music,—that with the elevation of the soul, the asperities and incoherence of speech disappear, and the language of truth is always pure music. We are very far from having reached the term of our knowledge on this subject. How can we, unless we had reached the boundaries of thought and feeling? The finer poet, the finer ear. Each new poet will as certainly invent new metres as he will have new images to clothe. In true poetry, the thought and the metre are not painfully adjusted afterward, but are born together, as the soul and the body of a child. The difference between poetry and what is called "stock poetry," I take to be this, that in *stock poetry* the metre is given and the verses are made to it, and in poetry the sense dictates the tune or march of the words.

I think a person of poetical temperament cannot indulge his veins of sentiment without perceiving that the finest rhythms and cadences of poetry are yet unfound, and that in that purer state which his thoughts prophesy, rhythms of a faery and dreamlike music shall enchant us, compared with which the happiest measures of English poetry are psalm-tunes. I think even now, that the very finest and sweetest closes and falls are not in our metres, but in the measures of prose eloquence which have greater variety and richness than verse.

J 4:278 (cf. *JMN* 5:362). *J* 10:264. *J* 9:209 (cf. *JMN* 14:296). *J* 5:226–27 (cf. *JMN* 7:219). Excerpted from "The Poet," *EL* 3:358–59, lecture (1841–42).

NOTES

1. Tyrtaeus was a seventh-century B.C. Athenian poet, whose songs are said to have inspired the Spartans to military victory.

2. *JMN* 7:374 has this additional sentence: "*Guts* is a stronger word than intestines."

3. "In my memory is fixed and now comes to my heart the dear, kind, paternal image of you when in the world, hour by hour, you taught me how man makes himself eternal." [Dante to Brunetto Latini (1212–94), Florentine author and politician] [*J*]

In 1848 Emerson brought back from England the unbound pages of Dr. John Aitken Carlyle's literal prose translation of the *Inferno*, the first American edition of which (New York, 1849) Emerson helped negotiate with Harper & Brothers. See *J* 8:33; *JMN* 11:133, n. 192; *CEC*, p. 43, p. 442 and n. 1, 447, 457.

4. From Emerson's "Merlin" (above).

5. *Néant:* The Nothingness of the universe.

6. *courier:* a travelers' attendant and agent; *padrone:* innkeeper.

7. *sans culottes:* the peasant revolutionaries in France.

8. *Vathek:* the hero of *Vathek: An Arabian Tale* by William Beckford (1759–1844), published in 1786.

9. *Sacre!* [*Sacré*]: "Damn!"; *Sia ammaz*[*z*]*ato:* literally, "Be killed!", the Italian equivalent of "Drop dead!"; *contadino:* an Italian peasant.

10. From "To the Deil" by Robert Burns.

11. *Erebus:* dark cavern on the route to Hades in Greek mythology; *Chaos:* original confusion of universe in Greek mythology.

12. From Acheron, the mythical river of Woe in Hades.

13. *chemic:* alchemical, turning base metals into gold.

14. For *development*, Mr. Emerson often used the more pleasing and picturesque *unfolding*. As for the family of *fero* and its participle *latum*, he would rather say *choice* than *preference*, *give way* than *defer*, *gather* than *infer*, *bring together* than *collate*, *render* than *translate*, with a poet's preference for simple rather than pedantic words. [*W*]

15. Johann Heinrich Lambert (1728–77), German-French mathematician, scientist, and philosopher, famous for his mathematical studies of pyramid forms; Lord John Russell (1792–1878), British statesman, nicknamed "Finality Jack" by his political opponents after a speech on electoral reform; Richard Martin (1754–1834), member of Parliament, widely known for his love of animals and for his opposition to the death penalty for forgery, first called "Humanity Martin" by George IV, his personal friend; probably Joseph M. W. Turner (1775–1850), the famous English landscape painter, although William Turner (1789–1862), artist, also preferred "wide prospects under broad atmospheric effects" (*DNB*).

16. He would say "point of view." [*W*]

17. Note that Emerson used "flamboyant" seven paragraphs earlier; here he is objecting to habitual use of the word. [*W*]

18. Snorri Sturluson (1178–1241), Icelandic historian and author of *Heimskringla* and the *Prose Edda*.

19. Hugh Latimer (1485?–1555), English Protestant martyr.

20. Reference to *History of Puritans* (1732–38), by Daniel Neal (1678–1743), a nonconformist English clergyman.

21. Carlyle's *History of Frederick the Great* (1858–65).

22. Athenian orator (436–338 B.C.).

23. William Ellery Channing, with whom Emerson often walked in the country. The Centenary Edition states that Channing had an "artistic eye," whereas Emerson preferred "wild nature."

24. Jonathan Bishop, *Emerson on the Soul*, pp. 8, 128, 138.

IV

TOWARD A MODERN
CRITICAL PERSPECTIVE

Emerging Critical Concepts

These passages illustrate and help define the authentic modernism of Emerson's response to literature. The critieria applied, all implicitly organic, are chiefly psychological, cultural, and transcendental. Aware that art expresses "the spirit of place," as D. H. Lawrence called it, and the spirit of the times, Emerson also, and not inconsistently, viewed great art as experientially *timeless or universal. Criticism at its highest level must be transcendental, treating intellectual achievements as of "one age," going behind the words to the life values they embody. "It is a greater joy to see the author's author, than himself" (W 3:233). On this level, "the literary man in this country has no critic," Emerson noted in 1836. Ten years later, he remarked that "criticism is in its infancy" in accounting for a genius such as Milton. Criticism must also become aware of the cultural roots of genius, as in Milton's Saxon origins, Renaissance (Italian) studies, and Puritan experience. The qualities and values of a writer's work stem from his character, not his talent only; Montaigne's egotism of style and attitude, for instance, reflects his picturesque character. A writer must be a man, not a fashionable wit. To be truly modern is not to be costumed in the contemporaneous mode, as in the "modern antique," but to be functionally simple with beauty that arises from within the "creative vortex" of the ordering Intellect. Similarly, it takes "experience" or insight to appreciate the superiority of high tragedy (in Greek or Shakespearean drama) over the epic poetry of Homer.*

Art Embodies the Spirit of Place

1837

The American artist who would carve a wood-god, and who was familiar with the forest in Maine, where enormous fallen pine trees "cumber the forest floor," where huge mosses depending from the trees and the mass of the timber give a savage and haggard strength to the grove, would produce a very different statue from the sculptor who only knew a European woodland—the tasteful Greek, for example.

Criticism Must Become Aware of the Cultural Roots of Genius

1846

Criticism is in its infancy. The anatomy of genius it has not unfolded. Milton in the egg, it has not found. Milton is a good apple on that tree of England. It would be impossible, by any chemistry we know, to compound that apple otherwise: it required all the tree; and out of a thousand of apples, good and bad, this specimen apple is at last procured. That is: We have a well-knit, hairy, industrious Saxon race, Londoners intent on their trade, steeped in their politics; wars of the Roses; voyages and trade to the Low Countries, to Spain, to Lepanto,[1] to Virginia, and Guiana—all bright with use and strong with success. Out of this valid stock choose the validest boy, and in the flower of this strength open to him the whole Dorian and Attic beauty and the proceeding ripeness of the same in Italy. Give him the very best of this Classic beverage. He shall travel to Florence and Rome in his early manhood: he shall see the country and the works of Dante, Angelo [Michelangelo], and Raffaelle [Raphael]. Well, on the man to whose unpalled taste this delicious fountain is opened, add the fury and concentration of the Hebraic genius, through the hereditary and already culminated Puritanism,—and you have Milton, a creation impossible before or again; and all whose graces and whose majesties involve this wonderful combination;—quite in the course of things once, but not iterated. The drill of the regiment, the violence of the pirate and smuggler, the cunning and thrift of the haberdasher's counter, the generosity of the Norman earl, are all essential to the result.

A Writer Must Have Character as well as Talent

1844

Talent alone can not make a writer. There must be a man behind the book; a personality which by birth and quality is pledged to the doctrines there set forth, and which exists to see and state things so, and not otherwise; holding things because they are things. If he can not rightly express himself to-day, the same things subsist and will open themselves to-morrow. There lies the burden on his mind,—the burden of truth to be declared,—more or less understood; and it

constitutes his business and calling in the world to see those facts
through, and to make them known. What signifies that he trips and
stammers; that his voice is harsh or hissing; that his method or his
tropes are inadequate? That message will find method and imagery,
articulation and melody. Though he were dumb it would speak. If
not,—if there be no such God's word in the man,—what care we how
adroit, how fluent, how brilliant he is?

1837

I believe the man and the writer should be one, and not diverse, as
they say Bancroft,[2] as we know Bulwer[-Lytton] is. Wordsworth
gives us the image of the true-hearted man, as Milton, Chaucer, Herbert do; not ruffled fine gentlemen who condescend to write, like
Shaftesbury, Congreve, and, greater far, Walter Scott. Let not the
author eat up the man, so that he shall be a balcony and no house.
Let him not be turned into a dapper, clerical anatomy, to be assisted
like a lady over a gutter or a stone wall. In meeting Milton, I feel that
I should encounter a real man; but Coleridge is a writer, and Pope,
Waller,[3] Addison and Swift and Gibbon, though with attributes, are
too modish. It is not man, but the fashionable wit they would be. Yet
Swift has properties. Allston[4] is respectable to me. Novalis,[5] Schiller
are only voices, no men. Dr. Johnson was a man, though he lived in
unfavorable solitude and society of one sort, so that he was an un-
leavened lump at least on which a genial unfolding had only begun.
Humanity cannot be the attribute of these people's writing; humanity, which smiles in Homer, in Chaucer, in Shakspear, in Milton, in
Wordsworth. Montaigne is a man.

1840

Originality.—Talent without character is friskiness. The charm of
Montaigne's egotism, and of his anecdotes, is, that there is a stout
cavalier, a seigneur of France, at home in his château, responsible for
all this chatting. Now suppose it should be shown and proved that the
famous "Essays" were a *jeu d'esprit* of Scaliger,[6] or other scribacious
person, written for the booksellers, and not resting on a real status,
picturesque in the eyes of all men, would not the book instantly lose
almost all its value?

Criticism Must Be Transcendental

May 18, 1840

Criticism must be transcendental, that is, must consider literature ephemeral, and easily entertain the supposition of its entire disappearance. In our ordinary states of mind, we deem not only letters in general, but most famous books parts of a pre-established harmony, fatal, unalterable, and do not go behind Dante and Shakespeare, much less behind Moses, Ezekiel, and St. John. But man is critic of all these also, and should treat the entire extant product of the human intellect as only one age, revisable, corrigible, reversible by him.

The "Creative Vortex" vs. "Modern Antiques"

1843

Critical. Do not write modern antiques like Landor's *Pericles*, or Goethe's *Iphigenia*, or Wieland's *Abderites*, or Coleridge's *Ancient Mariner*, or Scott's *Lay of the Last Minstrel*. They are paste jewels. You may well take an ancient subject where the form is incidental merely, like Shakspeare's plays, and the treatment and dialogue is simple, and most modern. But do not make much of the costume. For such things have no verity; no man will live or die by them: The way to write is to throw your body at the mark when your arrows are spent, like Cupid in Anacreon. Shakspeare's speeches in *Lear* are in the very dialect of 1843.

*   *   *

High speech of Demiurgus to his gods in the *Timaeus*. Goethe's World-Soul is a sequel of the same thought. And that does the Intellect; it goes *ordering*, distributing, and by order making beauty.

This creative vortex has not spun over London, over our modern Europe, until now in Carlyle. Humboldt is magnificent, too, as a distributing eye. His glance is stratification; geography of plants, etc.

Tragic Drama Superior to Epic Poetry

October 12, 1842

The merit of a poem or tragedy is a matter of experience. An intelligent youth can find little wonderful in the Greeks or Romans.

These tragedies, these poems, are cold and tame. Nature and all the events passing in the street are more to him, he says, than the stark, unchangeable crisis of the *Iliad* or the *Antigone*; and as for thoughts, his own thoughts are better and are more numerous. So says one, so say all. Presently, each of them tries his hand at expressing his thought; —but there is a certain stiffness, or a certain extravagance in it. All try, and all fail, each from some peculiar and different defect. The whole age of authors tries; many ages try; and in the millions and millions of experiments these confessedly tame and stark-poems of the Ancient are still the best. It seems to be certain that they will go on discontenting yet excelling the intelligent youths of the generations to come.

But always they will find their admirers, not in the creative and enthusiastic few, who will always feel their ideal inferiority, but in the elegant, cultivated and conservative class.

You praise Homer and disesteem the art that makes the tragedy. To me it seems higher—the unpopular and austere muse that casts human life into a high tragedy, *Prometheus*, *Oedipus*, *Hamlet* (midway between the Epic and the Ode)—than the art of the epic poet, which condescends more to common humanity, and approaches the ballad. Man is nine parts fool for one part wise, and therefore Homer and Chaucer more read than *Antigone*, *Hamlet*, or *Comus*.

J 4:289 (cf. *JMN* 5:373). *J* 7:213–14 (cf. *JMN* 9:440). Excerpted from "Goethe; or, The Writer," *Representative Men*, *W* 4:281–82; first published in *Representative Men* (1850), from lecture (1845–46). *J* 4:356–57 (cf. *JMN* 5:425). *J* 5:419 (cf. *JMN* 7:373–74). *J* 5:398–99 (cf. *JMN* 7:352). *J* 6:400–1 (cf. *JMN* 8:400–2). *J* 6:267–69 (cf. *JMN* 8:280).

Thoughts on Modern Literature

In an applied definition of the modern climate of opinion, Emerson identifies the new critical perspective with philosophical value questions and with the new consciousness of One Mind or the Feeling of the Infinite, an overly Romantic term. This feeling has "always been native in Germany"—in Beethoven, if not in Goethe, the latter being Emerson's chief example of the new subjective realist, yet finally rejected for accepting "the base doctrine of Fate" and for being "the poet of the Actual, not of the Ideal." The great writer transforms the actuality of a private fact or experience into the universal. Although present, in varying degree, in Byron, Wordsworth, and Shelley, this epic transcendentalism "finds its most genial climate in the American mind"; and as the prevailing "intense selfishness" and discontent are replaced by disciplined insight into Nature, love and ecstasy will characterize the "new heroic life of man." This new epistemology and aesthetics of American transcendentalism (see Part II) will serve the cultural function of literature in a radical way: "What is Austria? What is England? What is our graduated and petrified social scale of ranks and employments? Shall not a poet redeem us from these idolatries?"

* * *

In order to [obtain] any complete view of the literature of the present age, an inquiry should include what it quotes, what it writes and what it wishes to write. In our present attempt to enumerate some traits of the recent literature, we shall have somewhat to offer on each of these topics, but we cannot promise to set in very exact order what we have to say.

In the first place it has all books. It reprints the wisdom of the world. How can the age be a bad one which gives me Plato and Paul and Plutarch, Saint Augustine, Spinoza, Chapman, Beaumont and Fletcher, Donne and Sir Thomas Browne, beside its own riches? Our presses groan every year with new editions of all the select pieces of the first of mankind,—meditations, history, classifications, opinions, epics, lyrics, which the age adopts by quoting them. If we should designate favorite studies in which the age delights more than in the rest of this great mass of the permanent literature of the human race, one or two instances would be conspicuous. First; the prodigious growth and influence of the genius of Shakspeare, in the last one hundred and fifty years, is itself a fact of the first importance. It almost alone has called out the genius of the German nation into an activity which, spreading from the poetic into the scientific, religious and philosophical domains, has made theirs now at last the paramount intellectual influence of the world, reacting with great energy on England and America. And thus, and not by mechanical diffusion, does an original genius work and spread himself.

The poetry and speculation of the age are marked by a certain philosophic turn, which discriminates them from the works of earlier times. The poet is not content to see how "Fair hangs the apple from the rock," "What music a sunbeam awoke in the groves," nor of Hardiknute,[7] how

> "Stately stept he east the wa,
> And stately step he west,"

but he now revolves, What is the apple to me? and what the birds to me? and what is Hardiknute to me? and what am I? And this is called subjectiveness, as the eye is withdrawn from the object and fixed on the subject or mind.

We can easily concede that a steadfast tendency of this sort appears in modern literature. It is the new consciousness of the one mind, which predominates in criticism. It is the uprise of the soul, and not the decline. It is founded on that insatiable demand for unity, the need to recognize one nature in all the variety of objects, which always characterizes a genius of the first order. Accustomed always to behold the presence of the universe in every part, the soul will not condescend to look at any new part as a stranger, but saith,—"I know all already, and what art thou? Show me thy relations to me, to all, and I will entertain thee also."

There is a pernicious ambiguity in the use of the term *subjective*. We say, in accordance with the general view I have stated, that the single soul feels its right to be no longer confounded with numbers, but itself to sit in judgment on history and literature, and to summon all facts and parties before its tribunal. And in this sense the age is subjective.

But, in all ages, and now more, the narrow-minded have no interest in anything but in its relation to their personality. What will help them to be delivered from some burden, eased in some circumstance, flattered or pardoned or enriched; what will help to marry or to divorce them, to prolong or to sweeten life, is sure of their interest; and nothing else. Every form under the whole heaven they behold in this most partial light or darkness of intense selfishness, until we hate their being. And this habit of intellectual selfishness has acquired in our day the fine name of subjectiveness.

Nor is the distinction between these two habits to be found in the circumstance of using the first person singular, or reciting facts and feelings of personal history. A man may say I, and never refer to himself as an individual; and a man may recite passages of his life with no feeling of egotism. Nor need a man have a vicious subjectiveness because he deals in abstract propositions.

But the criterion which discriminates these two habits in the poet's mind is the tendency of his composition; namely, whether it leads us to Nature, or to the person of the writer. The great always introduce us to facts; small men introduce us always to themselves. The great man, even whilst he relates a private fact personal to him, is really leading us away from him to an universal experience. His own affection is in Nature, in *what is*, and, of course, all his communication leads outward to it, starting from whatsoever point. The great never with their own consent become a load on the minds they instruct. The more they draw us to them, the farther from them or more independent of them we are, because they have brought us to the knowledge of somewhat deeper than both them and us. The great never hinder us; for their activity is coincident with the sun and moon, with the course of the rivers and of the winds, with the stream of laborers in the street and with all the activity and well-being of the race. The great lead us to Nature, and in our age to metaphysical Nature, to the invisible awful facts, to moral abstractions, which are not less Nature than is a river, or a coal-mine—nay, they are far more Nature,—but its essence and soul.

But the weak and wicked, led also to analyze, saw nothing in thought but luxury. Thought for the selfish became selfish. They invited us to contemplate Nature, and showed us an abominable self. Would you know the genius of the writer? Do not enumerate his talents or his feats, but ask thyself, What spirit is he of? Do gladness and hope and fortitude flow from his page into thy heart? Has he led thee to Nature because his own soul was too happy in beholding her power and love? Or is his passion for the wilderness only the sensibility of the sick, the exhibition of a talent which only shines whilst you praise it; which has no root in the character, and can thus minister to the vanity but not to the happiness of the possessor; and which derives all its *éclat* from our conventional education, but would not make itself intelligible to the wise man of another age or country? The water we wash with never speaks of itself, nor does fire or wind or tree. Neither does the noble natural man: he yields himself to your occasion and use, but his act expresses a reference to universal good.

Another element of the modern poetry akin to this subjective tendency, or rather the direction of that same on the question of resources, is the Feeling of the Infinite. Of the perception now fast becoming a conscious fact,—that there is One Mind, and that all the powers and privileges which lie in any, lie in all; that I, as a man, may claim and appropriate whatever of true or fair or good or strong has anywhere been exhibited; that Moses and Confucius, Montaigne and Leibnitz, are not so much individuals as they are parts of man and parts of me, and my intelligence proves them my own,—literature is far the best expression. It is true, this is not the only nor the obvious lesson it teaches. A selfish commerce and government have caught the eye and usurped the hand of the masses. It is not to be contested that selfishness and the senses write the laws under which we live, and that the street seems to be built, and the men and women in it moving, not in reference to pure and grand ends, but rather to very short and sordid ones. Perhaps no considerable minority, no one man, leads a quite clean and lofty life. What then? We concede in sadness the fact. But we say that these low customary ways are not all that survives in human beings. There is that in us which mutters, and that which groans, and that which triumphs, and that which aspires. There are

facts on which men of the world superciliously smile, which are worth
all their trade and politics; which drive young men into gardens and
solitary places, and cause extravagant gestures, starts, distortions of
the countenance and passionate exclamations; sentiments, which
find no aliment or language for themselves on the wharves, in court,
or market, but which are soothed by silence, by darkness, by the pale
stars, and the presence of Nature. All over the modern world the
educated and susceptible have betrayed their discontent with the
limits of our municipal life, and with the poverty of our dogmas of
religion and philosophy. They betray this impatience by fleeing for
resource to a conversation with Nature, which is courted in a certain
moody and exploring spirit, as if they anticipated a more intimate
union of man with the world than has been known in recent ages.
Those who cannot tell what they desire or expect still sigh and
struggle with indefinite thoughts and vast wishes. The very child in
the nursery prattles mysticism, and doubts and philosophizes. A wild
striving to express a more inward and infinite sense characterizes the
works of every art. The music of Beethoven is said, by those who
understand it, to labor with vaster conceptions and aspirations than
music has attempted before. This feeling of the Infinite has deeply
colored the poetry of the period. This new love of the vast, always
native in Germany, was imported into France by De Staël, appeared
in England in Coleridge, Wordsworth, Byron, Shelley, Felicia Hemans, and finds a most genial climate in the American mind. Scott
and Crabbe, who formed themselves on the past, had none of this
tendency; their poetry is objective. In Byron, on the other hand, it
predominates; but in Byron it is blind, it sees not its true end—an
infinite good, alive and beautiful, a life nourished on absolute beati-
tudes, descending into Nature to behold itself reflected there. His will
is perverted, he worships the accidents of society, and his praise of
Nature is thieving and selfish.

Nothing certifies the prevalence of this taste in the people more
than the circulation of the poems—one would say most incongruously
united by some bookseller—of Coleridge, Shelley and Keats. The only
unity is in the subjectiveness and the aspiration common to the three
writers. Shelley, though a poetic mind, is never a poet. His muse is
uniformly imitative; all his poems composite. A good English scholar

he is, with ear, taste and memory; much more, he is a character full of noble and prophetic traits; but imagination, the original, authentic fire of the bard, he has not. He is clearly modern, and shares with Richter, Châteaubriand, Manzoni and Wordsworth the feeling of the Infinite, which so labors for expression in their different genius. But all his lines are arbitrary, not necessary. When we read poetry, the mind asks,—Was this verse one of twenty which the author might have written as well; or is this what that man was created to say? But whilst every line of the true poet will be genuine, he is in a boundless power and freedom to say a million things. And the reason why he can say one thing well is because his vision extends to the sight of all things, and so he describes each as one who knows many and all.

The fame of Wordsworth is a leading fact in modern literature, when it is considered how hostile his genius at first seemed to the reigning taste, and with what limited poetic talents his great and steadily growing dominion has been established. More than any poet his success has been not his own but that of the idea which he shared with his coevals, and which he has rarely succeeded in adequately expressing. The Excursion awakened in every lover of Nature the right feeling. We saw stars shine, we felt the awe of mountains, we heard the rustle of the wind in the grass, and knew again the ineffable secret of solitude. It was a great joy. It was nearer to Nature than anything we had before. But the interest of the poem ended almost with the narrative of the influences of Nature on the mind of the Boy, in the First Book. Obviously for that passage the poem was written, and with the exception of this and of a few strains of the like character in the sequel, the whole poem was dull. Here was no poem, but here was poetry, and a sure index where the subtle muse was about to pitch her tent and find the argument of her song. It was the human soul in these last ages striving for a just publication of itself. Add to this, however, the great praise of Wordsworth, that more than any other contemporary bard he is pervaded with a reverence of somewhat higher than (conscious) thought. There is in him that property common to all great poets, a wisdom of humanity, which is superior to any talents which they exert. It is the wisest part of Shakspeare and of Milton. For they are poets by the free course which they allow to the informing soul, which through their eyes beholdeth again and blesseth the things which it hath made. The soul is superior to its knowledge, wiser than any of its works.

With the name of Wordsworth rises to our recollection the name of his contemporary and friend, Walter Savage Landor—a man working in a very different and peculiar spirit, yet one whose genius and accomplishments deserve a wiser criticism than we have yet seen applied to them, and the rather that his name does not readily associate itself with any school of writers. Of Thomas Carlyle, also, we shall say nothing at this time, since the quality and energy of his influence on the youth of this country will require at our hands, ere long, a distinct and faithful acknowledgment.

But of all men he who has united in himself, and that in the most extraordinary degree, the tendencies of the era, is the German poet, naturalist and philosopher, Goethe. Whatever the age inherited or invented, he made his own. He has owed to Commerce and to the victories of the Understanding, all their spoils. Such was his capacity that the magazines of the world's ancient or modern wealth, which arts and intercourse and skepticism could command,—he wanted them all. Had there been twice so much, he could have used it as well. Geologist, mechanic, merchant, chemist, king, radical, painter, composer,—all worked for him, and a thousand men seemed to look through his eyes. He learned as readily as other men breathe. Of all the men of this time, not one has seemed so much at home in it as he. He was not afraid to live. And in him this encyclopaedia of facts, which it has been the boast of the age to compile, wrought an equal effect. He was knowing; he was brave; he was clean from all narrowness; he has a perfect propriety and taste,—a quality by no means common to the German writers. Nay, since the earth as we said had become a reading-room, the new opportunities seem to have aided him to be that resolute realist he is, and seconded his sturdy determination to see things for what they are. To look at him one would say there was never an observer before. What sagacity, what industry of observation. To read his record is a frugality of time, for you shall find no word that does not stand for a thing, and he is of that comprehension which can see the value of truth. His love of Nature has seemed to give a new meaning to that word. There was never man more domesticated in this world than he. And he is an apology for the analytic spirit of the period, because, of his analysis, always wholes were the result. All conventions, all traditions he rejected. And yet he felt his entire right and duty to stand before and try and judge every fact in Nature. He thought it necessary to dot round with his own pen the entire sphere of knowables; and for many of his stories, this seems the only reason: Here is a piece of humanity I had hitherto omitted to sketch;—take this. He does not say so in syllables, yet a sort of conscientious feeling he had to be *up* to the universe is the best account and apology for many of them. He shared also the subjectiveness of the age, and that too in both the senses I have discriminated. With the sharpest eye for form, color, botany, engraving, medals, persons and manners, he never stopped at surface, but pierced the purpose of a thing and studied to reconcile that purpose with his own being. What he could so reconcile was good; what he could not, was false. Hence a certain greatness encircles every fact he treats; for to him it has a soul, an eternal reason why it was so, and not otherwise. This is the secret of that deep realism, which went about among all objects he beheld, to find the cause why they must be what they are. It was with him a favorite task to find a theory of every institution, custom, art, work of art, which he observed. Witness his explanation of the Italian mode of reckoning the hours of the day, as growing out of the Italian climate; of the obelisk of Egypt, as growing out of a common natural fracture in the granite parallelopiped[8] in Upper Egypt; of the Doric architecture, and the Gothic; of the Venetian music of the gondolier, originating in the habit of the fishers' wives of the Lido singing on shore to their husbands on the sea; of the amphitheatre, which is the enclosure of the natural cup of heads that arranges itself round every spectacle in the street; of the coloring of Titian and Paul Veronese, which one may verify in common daylight in Venice every afternoon; of the Carnival at Rome; of the domestic rural architecture in Italy; and many the like examples.

But also that other vicious subjectiveness, that vice of the time, infected him also. We are provoked with his Olympian self-complacency, the patronizing air with which he vouchsafes to tolerate the genius and performances of other mortals, "the good Hiller," "our excellent Kant," "the friendly Wieland,"[9] etc. There is a good letter from Wieland to Merck, in which Wieland relates that Goethe read

to a select party his journal of a tour in Switzerland with the Grand
Duke, and their passage through the Vallais and over the St. Gothard.[10] "It was," says Wieland, "as good as Xenophon's Anabasis. The
piece is one of the most masterly productions, and is thought and
written with the greatness peculiar to him. The fair hearers were
enthusiastic at the nature in this piece; I liked the sly art in the
composition, whereof they saw nothing, still better. It is a true poem,
so concealed is the art too. But what most remarkably in this, as in all
his other works, distinguishes him from Homer and Shakspeare is
that the Me, the *Ille ego*, everywhere glimmers through, although
without any boasting and with an infinite fineness." This subtle
element of egotism in Goethe certainly does not seem to deform his
compositions, but to lower the moral influence of the man. He differs
from all the great in the total want of frankness. Who saw Milton,
who saw Shakspeare, saw them do their best, and utter their whole
heart manlike among their brethren. No man was permitted to call
Goethe brother. He hid himself, and worked always to astonish,
which is egotism, and therefore little.

If we try Goethe by the ordinary canons of criticism, we should say
that his thinking is of great altitude, and all level; not a succession of
summits, but a high Asiatic table-land. Dramatic power, the rarest talent in literature, he has very little. He has an eye constant to the fact
of life and that never pauses in its advance. But the great felicities, the
miracles of poetry, he has never. It is all design with him, just thought
and instructed expression, analogies, allusion, illustration, which
knowledge and correct thinking supply; but of Shakspeare and the
transcendent muse, no syllable. Yet in the court and law to which we
ordinarily speak, and without adverting to absolute standards, we
claim for him the praise of truth, of fidelity to his intellectual nature.
He is the king of all scholars. In these days and in this country, where
the scholars are few and idle, where men read easy books and sleep
after dinner, it seems as if no book could so safely be put in the hands
of young men as the letters of Goethe, which attest the incessant
activity of this man, to eighty years, in an endless variety of studies,
with uniform cheerfulness and greatness of mind. They cannot be
read without shaming us into an emulating industry. Let him have
the praise of the love of truth. We think, when we contemplate the

stupendous glory of the world, that it were life enough for one man merely to lift his hands and cry with Saint Augustine, "Wrangle who pleases, I will wonder." Well, this he did. Here was a man who, in the feeling that the thing itself was so admirable as to leave all comment behind, went up and down, from object to object, lifting the veil from every one, and did no more. What he said of Lavater,[11] may truelier be said of him, that "it was fearful to stand in the presence of one before whom all the boundaries within which Nature has circumscribed our being were laid flat." His are the bright and terrible eyes which meet the modern student in every sacred chapel of thought, in every public enclosure.

But now, that we may not seem to dodge the question which all men ask, nor pay a great man so ill a compliment as to praise him only in the conventional and comparative speech, let us honestly record our thought upon the total worth and influence of this genius. Does he represent, not only the achievement of that age in which he lived, but that which it would be and is now becoming? And what shall we think of that absence of the moral sentiment, that singular equivalence to him of good and evil in action, which discredit his compositions to the pure? The spirit of his biography, of his poems, of his tales, is identical, and we may here set down by way of comment of his genius the impressions recently awakened in us by the story of Wilhelm Meister.

All great men have written proudly, nor cared to explain. They knew that the intelligent reader would come at last, and would thank them. So did Dante, so did Macchiavel. Goethe has done this in Meister. We can fancy him saying to himself: 'There are poets enough of the Ideal; let me paint the Actual, as, after years of dreams, it will still appear and reappear to wise men. That all shall right itself in the long Morrow, I may well allow, and my novel may wait for the same regeneration. The age, that can damn it as false and falsifying, will see that it is deeply one with the genius and history of all the centuries. I have given my characters a bias to error. Men have the same. I have let mischance befall instead of good fortune. They do so daily. And out of many vices and misfortunes, I have let a great success grow, as I had known in my own and many other examples. Fierce churchmen and effeminate aspirants will chide and hate my name, but every keen beholder of life will justify my truth, and will acquit me of prejudging the cause of humanity by painting it with this morose fidelity. To a profound soul is not austere truth the sweetest flattery?'

Yes, O Goethe! but the ideal is truer than the actual. That is ephemeral, but this changes not. Moreover, because Nature is moral, that mind only can see, in which the same order entirely obtains. An interchangeable Truth, Beauty and Goodness, each wholly interfused in the other, must make the humors of that eye which would see causes reaching to their last effect and reproducing the world forever. The least inequality of mixture, the excess of one element over the other, in that degree diminishes the transparency of things, makes the world opaque to the observer, and destroys so far the value of his experience. No particular gifts can countervail this defect. In reading Meister, I am charmed with the insight; to use a phrase of Ben Jonson's, "it is rammed with life." I find there actual men and women even too faithfully painted. I am moreover instructed in the possibility of a highly accomplished society, and taught to look for great talent and culture under a gray coat. But this is all. The limits of artificial society are never quite out of sight. The vicious conventions, which hem us in like prison walls and which the poet should explode at his touch, stand for all they are worth in the newspaper. We are never lifted above ourselves, we are not transported out of the dominion of the senses, or cheered with an infinite tenderness, or armed with a grand trust.

Goethe, then, must be set down as the poet of the Actual, not of the Ideal; the poet of limitation, not of possibility; of this world, and not of religion and hope; in short; if we may say so, the poet of prose, and not of poetry. He accepts the base doctrine of Fate, and gleans what straggling joys may yet remain out of its ban. He is like a banker or a weaver with a passion for the country; he steals out of the hot streets before sunrise, or after sunset, or on a rare holiday, to get a draft of sweet air and a gaze at the magnificence of summer, but dares not break from his slavery and lead a man's life in a man's relation to Nature. In that which should be his own place, he feels like a truant, and is scourged back presently to his task and his cell. Poetry is with Goethe thus external, the gilding of the chain, the mitigation of his fate; but the Muse never assays those thunder-tones which cause to vibrate the sun and the moon, which dissipate by dreadful melody all this iron network of circumstance, and abolish the old heavens and the old earth before the free will or Godhead of man. That Goethe had not a moral perception proportionate to his other powers is not, then, merely a circumstance, as we might relate of a man that he had or had not the sense of tune or an eye for colors, but it is the cardinal fact of health or disease; since, lacking this, he failed in the high sense to be a creator, and, with divine endowments, drops by irreversible decree into the common history of genius. He was content to fall into the track of vulgar poets and spend on common aims his splendid endowments, and has declined the office proffered to now and then a man in many centuries in the power of his genius, of a Redeemer of the human mind. He has written better than other poets only as his talent was subtler, but the ambition of creation he refused. Life for him is prettier, easier, wiser, decenter, has a gem or two more on its robe, but its old eternal burden is not relieved; no drop of healthier blood flows yet in its veins. Let him pass. Humanity must wait for its physician still at the side of the road, and confess as this man goes out that they have served it better, who assured it out of the innocent hope in their hearts that a Physician will come, than this majestic Artist, with all the treasures of wit, of science, and of power at his command.

The criticism, which is not so much spoken as felt in reference to Goethe, instructs us directly in the hope of literature. We feel that a man gifted like him should not leave the world as he found it. It is true, though somewhat sad, that every fine genius teaches us how to blame himself. Being so much, we cannot forgive him for not being more. When one of these grand monads is incarnated whom Nature seems to design for eternal men and draw to her bosom, we think that the old weariness of Europe and Asia, the trivial forms of daily life will now end, and a new morning break on us all. What is Austria? What is England? What is our graduated and petrified social scale of ranks and employments? Shall not a poet redeem us from these idolatries, and pale their legendary lustre before the fires of the Divine Wisdom which burn in his heart? All that in our sovereign moments each of us has divined of the powers of thought, all the hints of omnipresence and energy which we have caught, this man should unfold, and constitute facts.

And this is the insatiable craving which alternately saddens and gladdens men at this day. The Doctrine of the Life of Man established after the truth through all his faculties;—this is the thought which the literature of this hour meditates and labors to say. This is that which tunes the tongue and fires the eye and sits in the silence of the youth. Verily it will not long want articulate and melodious expression. There is nothing in the heart but comes presently to the lips. The very depth of the sentiment, which is the author of all the cutaneous life we see, is guarantee for the riches of science and of song in the age to come. He who doubts whether this age or this country can yield any contribution to the literature of the world only betrays his own blindness to the necessities of the human soul. Has the power of poetry ceased, or the need? Have the eyes ceased to see that which they would have, and which they have not? Have they ceased to see other eyes? Are there no lonely, anxious, wondering children, who must tell their tale? Are we not evermore whipped by thoughts?

> "In sorrow steeped, and steeped in love
> Of thoughts not yet incarnated."

The heart beats in this age as of old, and the passions are busy as ever. Nature has not lost one ringlet of her beauty, one impulse of resistance and valor. From the necessity of loving none are exempt, and he that loves must utter his desires. A charm as radiant as beauty ever beamed, a love that fainteth at the sight of its object, is new to-day.

> "The world does not run smoother than of old,
> There are sad haps that must be told."[12]

Man is not so far lost but that he suffers ever the great Discontent which is the elegy of his loss and the prediction of his recovery. In the gay saloon he laments that these figures are not what Raphael and Guercino[13] painted. Withered though he stand, and trifler though he be, the august spirit of the world looks out from his eyes. In his heart he knows the ache of spiritual pain, and his thought can animate the sea and land. What, then, shall hinder the Genius of the time from speaking its thought? It cannot be silent, if it would. It will write in a higher spirit and a wider knowledge and with a grander practical aim than ever yet guided the pen of poet. It will write the annals of a changed world, and record the descent of principles into practice, of love into Government, of love into Trade. It will describe the new heroic life of man, the now unbelieved possibility of simple living and of clean and noble relations with men. Religion will bind again these that were sometime frivolous, customary, enemies, skeptics, self-seekers, into a joyful reverence for the circumambient Whole, and that which was ecstasy shall become daily bread.

Natural History of Intellect and Other Papers, *W* 12:311–36; first published as leading article in second number of the *Dial*, October 1840; based on "Literature," *EL* 2:55–68, lecture (1837). The present text incorporates Emerson's corrections of the *Dial* version.

The Novel of Character vs. the Costume Novel

Although he views the novel as a source of improved manners and dignity and praises Jane Eyre *for suggesting the great potential of this genre, Emerson deplores most novels as preoccupied with social surfaces and results, especially wealth and social position, and with overworked romantic plots. Such novels fail to deal with underlying values, with the worlds of nature and men as "analogons" of thoughts. In these few pages, no American, only British and Continental, novels are cited. (See also the passage on the novel in "Europe and European Books," below.)*

We must have idolatries, mythologies,—some swing and verge for the creative power lying coiled and cramped here, driving ardent natures to insanity and crime if it do not find vent. Without the great arts which speak to the sense of beauty, a man seems to me a poor, naked, shivering creature. These are his becoming draperies, which warm and adorn him. Whilst the prudential and economical tone of society starves the imagination, affronted Nature gets such indemnity as she may. The novel is that allowance and frolic the imagination finds. Everything else pins it down, and men flee for redress to Byron, Scott, Disraeli, Dumas, Sand, Balzac, Dickens, Thackeray and Reade. Their education is neglected; but the circulating library and the theatre, as well as the trout-fishing, the Notch Mountains, the Adirondack country, the tour to Mont Blanc, to the White Hills and the Ghauts,[14] make such amends as they can.

The imagination infuses a certain volatility and intoxication. It has a flute which sets the atoms of our frame in a dance, like planets; and once so liberated, the whole man reeling drunk to the music, they never quite subside to their old stony state. But what is the imagination? Only an arm or weapon of the interior energy, only the precursor of the reason. And books that treat the old pedantries of the world, our times, places, professions, customs, opinions, histories, with a certain freedom, and distribute things, not after the usages of America and Europe but after the laws of right reason, and with as daring a freedom as we use in dreams, put us on our feet again, enable us to form an original judgment of our duties, and suggest new thoughts for to-morrow.

Lucrezia Floriani, Le Péché de M. Antoine, Jeanne and Consuelo, of George Sand, are great steps from the novel of one termination, which we all read twenty years ago. Yet how far off from life and manners and motives the novel still is! Life lies about us dumb; the day, as we know it, has not yet found a tongue. These stories are to the plots of real life what the figures in La Belle Assemblée, which represent the fashion of the month, are to portraits. But the novel will find the way to our interiors one day, and will not always be the novel of costume merely. I do not think it inoperative now. So much novel-reading cannot leave the young men and maidens untouched; and doubtless it gives some ideal dignity to the day. The young study noble behavior; and as the player in Consuelo insists that he and his colleagues on the boards have taught princes the fine etiquette and strokes of grace and dignity which they practise with so much effect in their villas and among their dependents, so I often see traces of the Scotch or the French novel in the courtesy and brilliancy of young midshipmen, collegians and clerks. Indeed, when one observes how ill and ugly people make their loves and quarrels, 't is pity they should not read novels a little more, to import the fine generosities and the clear, firm conduct, which are as becoming in the unions and separations which love effects under shingle roofs as in palaces and among illustrious personages.

In novels the most serious questions are beginning to be discussed. What made the popularity of Jane Eyre, but that a central question was answered in some sort? The question there answered in regard to a vicious marriage will always be treated according to the habit of the party. A person of commanding individualism will answer it as Rochester does,—as Cleopatra, as Milton, as George Sand do,—magnifying the exception into a rule, dwarfing the world into an exception. A person of less courage, that is of less constitution, will answer as the heroine does,—giving way to fate, to conventionalism, to the actual state and doings of men and women.

For the most part, our novel-reading is a passion for results. We admire parks, and high-born beauties, and the homage of drawing-rooms and parliaments. They make us skeptical, by giving prominence to wealth and social position.

I remember when some peering eyes of boys discovered that the oranges hanging on the boughs of an orange-tree in a gay piazza were tied to the twigs by thread. I fear 't is so with the novelist's prosperities. Nature has a magic by which she fits the man to his fortunes, by making them the fruit of his character. But the novelist plucks this event here and that fortune there, and ties them rashly to his figures, to tickle the fancy of his readers with a cloying success or scare them with shocks of tragedy. And so, on the whole, 't is a juggle. We are cheated into laughter or wonder by feats which only oddly combine acts that we do every day. There is no new element, no power, no furtherance. 'T is only confectionery, not the raising of new corn. Great is the poverty of their inventions. *She was beautiful and he fell in love.* Money, and killing, and the Wandering Jew, and persuading the lover that his mistress is betrothed to another, these are the main-springs; new names, but no new qualities in the men and women. Hence the vain endeavor to keep any bit of this fairy gold which has rolled like a brook through our hands. A thousand thoughts awoke; great rainbows seemed to span the sky, a morning among the mountains; but we close the book and not a ray remains in the memory of evening. But this passion for romance, and this disappointment, show

how much we need real elevations and pure poetry: that which shall show us, in morning and night, in stars and mountains and in all the plight and circumstance of men, the analogons of our own thoughts, and a like impression made by a just book and by the face of Nature.

Excerpted from "Books," in *Society and Solitude* (Boston: Houghton Mifflin Co., 1911), pp. 213–17; first published in *Society and Solitude* (1870); from lecture (1859).

NOTES

1. Town on Strait of Lepanto (in Gulf of Corinth) in Greece.

2. George Bancroft (1800–1891), American historian.

3. Edmund Waller (1606–87), English poet.

4. Washington Allston (1779–1843), American painter.

5. Pseudonym of Friedrich von Hadenburg (1772–1801), German author.

6. Joseph Justus Scaliger (1540–1609), French philologist, literary critic, and chronologist.

7. Hardecanute (1019–42), king of Denmark, and the last Danish king of England.

8. *Parallelepiped:* six-sided prism whose faces are parallelograms.

9. Probably Johann Adam Hiller (1728–1804), German composer; Christoph Martin Wieland (1733–1813), German author, known as "The German Voltaire."

10. *The Vallais:* le Valais (German, Wallis), Swiss canton in the upper Rhone Valley; *the St. Gothard:* a pass in the St. Gotthard range of the Swiss Alps.

11. Johan Kaspar Lavater (1741–1801), Swiss physiognomist.

12. Source is unknown for these and previously quoted lines. [*W*]

13. *Guercino:* Giovanni Francesco Barbieri (1590?–1666), Italian painter.

14. Two ranges of mountains, Eastern Ghats and Western Ghats, bordering the coasts of southern India.

V
WRITERS AND BOOKS

Europe and European Books

This article reports on the state of the literary arts in Europe ten years after Emerson's first visit to England and the Continent in 1833. Despite the broad title, Emerson discusses only Wordsworth, Tennyson, Bulwer-Lytton, and Goethe's Wilhelm Meister. *Wordsworth's simple rural life as a poet of the commonplace—"Man and writer were not to be divided"—Emerson sees as a rebuke to the false lives and conventional ideas of his time. Tennyson's poetry, although found wanting in "rude truth," is praised for its admirable lyricism. When Emerson predicts that Leigh Hunt's "Abou ben Adhem" will have the "longest term" of any nineteenth-century poem, his enthusiasm for its theme leads him to overlook its undistinguished heroic couplets. Bulwer's* Zanoni *provides an occasion for another contrast (see Part IV) between "the novel of costume," the "standard English novel," and "the novel of character," of which* Wilhelm Meister *is the best example. A brief characterization of "the novels of Fashion" as a subgenre of "the novel of costume" ends with an ironic comment and quotation.*

It was a brighter day than we have often known in our literary calendar, when within a twelvemonth a single London advertisement announced a new volume of poems by Wordsworth, poems by Tennyson, and a play by Henry Taylor.[1] Wordsworth's nature or character has had all the time it needed in order to make its mark and supply the want of talent. We have learned how to read him. We have ceased to expect that which he cannot give. He has the merit of just moral perception, but not that of deft poetic execution. How would Milton curl his lip at such slipshod newspaper style. Many of his poems, as for example the Rylstone Doe, might be all improvised. Nothing of Milton, nothing of Marvell, of Herbert, of Dryden, could be. These are such verses as in a just state of culture should be *vers de société*, such as every gentleman could write but none would think of printing, or of claiming the poet's laurel on their merit. The Pindar, the Shakspeare, the Dante, whilst they have the just and open soul, have also the eye to see the dimmest star that glimmers in the Milky

Way, the serratures of every leaf, the test-objects of the microscope, and then the tongue to utter the same things in words that engrave them on all the ears of mankind. The poet demands all gifts, and not one or two only.

The poet, like the electric rod, must reach from a point nearer the sky than all surrounding objects, down to the earth, and into the dark wet soil, or neither is of use. The poet must not only converse with pure thought, but he must demonstrate it almost to the senses. His words must be pictures, his verses must be spheres and cubes, to be seen and smelled and handled. His fable must be a good story, and its meaning must hold as pure truth. In the debates on the Copyright Bill, in the English Parliament, Mr. Sergeant Wakley,[2] the coroner, quoted Wordsworth's poetry in derision, and asked the roaring House of Commons what that meant, and whether a man should have public reward for writing such stuff. Homer, Horace, Milton and Chaucer would defy the coroner. Whilst they have wisdom to the wise, he would see that to the external they have external meaning. Coleridge excellently said of poetry, that poetry must first be good sense; as a palace might well be magnificent, but first it must be a house.

Wordsworth is open to ridicule of this kind. And yet Wordsworth, though satisfied if he can suggest to a sympathetic mind his own mood, and though setting a private and exaggerated value on his compositions; though confounding his accidental with the universal consciousness, and taking the public to task for not admiring his poetry, is really a master of the English language, and his poems evince a power of diction that is no more rivalled by his contemporaries than is his poetic insight. But the capital merit of Wordsworth is that he has done more for the sanity of this generation than any other writer. Early in his life, at a crisis it is said in his private affairs, he made his election between assuming and defending some legal rights, with the chances of wealth and a position in the world, and the inward promptings of his heavenly genius; he took his part; he accepted the call to be a poet, and sat down, far from cities, with coarse clothing and plain fare to obey the heavenly vision. The choice he had made in his will manifested itself in every line to be real. We have poets who write the poetry of society, of the patrician and conventional Europe, as Scott and Moore,[3] and others who, like Byron or Bulwer, write the poetry of vice and disease. But Wordsworth threw himself into his place, made no reserves or stipulations; man and writer were not to be divided. He sat at the foot of Helvellyn and on the margin of Windermere, and took their lustrous mornings and their sublime midnights for his theme, and not Marlowe nor Massinger, not Horace nor Milton nor Dante. He once for all forsook the styles and standards and modes of thinking of London and Paris, and the books read there and the aims pursued, and wrote Helvellyn and Windermere and the dim spirits which these haunts harbored. There was not the least attempt to reconcile these with the spirit of fashion and selfishness, nor to show, with great deference to the superior judgment of dukes and earls, that although London was the home for men of great parts, yet Westmoreland had these consolations for such as fate had condemned to the country life,—but with a complete satisfaction he pitied and rebuked their false lives, and celebrated his own with the religion of a true priest. Hence the antagonism which was immediately felt between his poetry and the spirit of the age, that here not only criticism but conscience and will were parties; the spirit of literature and the modes of living and the conventional theories of the conduct of life were called in question on wholly new grounds—not from Platonism, not from Christianity, but from the lessons which the country muse taught a stout pedestrian climbing a mountain and following a river from its parent rill down to the sea. The Cannings and Jeffreys of the capital, the Court Journals and Literary Gazettes were not well pleased, and voted the poet a bore. But that which rose in him so high as to the lips, rose in many others as high as to the heart. What he said, they were prepared to hear and confirm. The influence was in the air, and was wafted up and down into lone and into populous places, resisting the popular taste, modifying opinions which it did not change, and soon came to be felt in poetry, in criticism, in plans of life, and at last in legislation. In this country it very early found a stronghold, and its effect may be traced on all the poetry both of England and America.

But, notwithstanding all Wordsworth's grand merits, it was a great pleasure to know that Alfred Tennyson's two volumes were coming out in the same ship; it was a great pleasure to receive them. The elegance, the wit and subtlety of this writer, his rich fancy, his power of language, his metrical skill, his independence of any living masters, his peculiar topics, his taste for the costly and gorgeous, discriminate the musky poet of gardens and conservatories, of parks and palaces. Perhaps we felt the popular objection that he wants rude truth; he is too fine. In these boudoirs of damask and alabaster, one is farther off from stern Nature and human life than in Lalla Rookh and the Loves of the Angels. Amid swinging censers and perfumed lamps, amidst velvet and glory, we long for rain and frost. Otto-of-roses is good, but wild air is better. A criticial friend of ours affirms that the vice which bereaved modern painters of their power is the ambition to begin where their fathers ended; to equal the masters in their exquisite finish, instead of their religious purpose. The painters are not willing to paint ill enough; they will not paint for their times, agitated by the spirit which agitates their country; so should their picture picture us, and draw all men after them; but they copy the technics of their predecessors, and paint for their predecessors' public. It seems as if the same vice had worked in poetry. Tennyson's compositions are not so much poems as studies in poetry, or sketches after the styles of sundry old masters. He is not the husband who builds the homestead after his own necessity, from foundation-stone to chimney-top and turret, but a tasteful bachelor who collects quaint staircases and groined ceilings. We have no right to such superfineness. We must not make our bread of pure sugar. These delicacies and splendors are then legitimate when they are the excess of substantial and necessary expenditure. The best songs in English poetry are by that heavy, hard, pedantic poet, Ben Jonson. Jonson is rude, and only on rare occasions gay. Tennyson is always fine, but Jonson's beauty is more grateful than Tennyson's. It is a natural manly grace of a robust workman. Ben's flowers are not in pots in a city florist's, arranged on a flower-stand, but he is a countryman at a harvest-home, attending his ox-cart from the fields, loaded with potatoes and apples, with grapes and plums, with nuts and berries, and stuck with boughs of hemlock and sweet-briar, with ferns and pond-lilies which the children have gathered. But let us not quarrel with our benefactors. Perhaps Tennyson is too quaint and elegant. What then? It is long since we have had as good a lyrist; it will be long before we have his superior. Godiva is a noble poem that will tell the legend a thousand years. The poem of all the poetry of the present age for which we predict the longest term is Abou ben Adhem, of Leigh Hunt. Fortune will still have her part in every victory, and it is strange that one of the best poems should be written by a man who has hardly written any other. And Godiva is a parable which belongs to the same gospel. Locksley Hall and The Two Voices are meditative poems, which were slowly written to be slowly read. The Talking Oak, though a little hurt by its wit and ingenuity, is beautiful, and the most poetic of the volume. Ulysses belongs to a high class of poetry, destined to be the highest, and to be more cultivated in the next generation. Oenone was a sketch of the same kind. One of the best specimens we have of the class is Words-worth's Laodamia, of which no special merit it can possess equals the total merit of having selected such a subject in such a spirit.

Next to the poetry, the novels, which come to us in every ship from England, have an importance increased by the immense extension of their circulation through the new cheap press, which sends them to so many willing thousands. We have heard it alleged with some evidence that the prominence given to intellectual power in Bulwer[-Lytton]'s romances has proved a main stimulus to mental culture in thousands of young men in England and America. The effect on manners cannot be less sensible, and we can easily believe that the behavior of the ballroom and of the hotel has not failed to draw some addition of dignity and grace from the fair ideals with which the imagination of a novelist has filled the heads of the most imitative class.

We are not very well versed in these books, yet we have read Mr. Bulwer enough to see that the story is rapid and interesting; he has really seen London society, and does not draw ignorant caricatures. He is not a genius, but his novels are marked with great energy and with a courage of experiment which in each instance had its degree of success. The story of Zanoni was one of those world-fables which is so agreeable to the human imagination that it is found in some form in the language of every country, and is always reappearing in litera-ture. Many of the details of this novel preserve a poetic truth. We read Zanoni with pleasure, because magic is natural. It is implied in all superior culture that a complete man would need no auxiliaries to his personal presence. The eye and the word are certainly far subtler and

stronger weapons than either money or knives. Whoever looked on the
hero would consent to his will, being certified that his aims were
universal, not selfish; and he would be obeyed as naturally as the rain
and the sunshine are. For this reason, children delight in fairy tales.
Nature is described in them as the servant of man, which they feel
ought to be true. But Zanoni pains us and the author loses our
respect, because he speedily betrays that he does not see the true
limitations of the charm; because the power with which his hero is
armed is a toy, inasmuch as the power does not flow from its
legitimate fountains in the mind, is a power for London; a divine
power converted into a burglar's false key or a highwayman's pistol to
rob and kill with.

But Mr. Bulwer's recent stories have given us who do not read
novels occasion to think of this department of literature, supposed to
be the natural fruit and expression of the age. We conceive that the
obvious division of modern romance is into two kinds: first, the novels
of costume or of circumstance, which is the old style, and vastly the
most numerous. In this class, the hero, without any particular character, is in a very particular circumstance; he is greatly in want of a
fortune or of a wife, and usually of both, and the business of the piece
is to provide him suitably. This is the problem to be solved in thousands of English romances, including the Porter novels and the more
splendid examples of the Edgeworth[4] and Scott romances.

It is curious how sleepy and foolish we are that these tales will so
take us. Again and again we have been caught in that old foolish trap.
Had one noble thought, opening the chambers of the intellect, one
sentiment from the heart of God been spoken by them, the reader had
been made a participator of their triumph; he too had been an
invited and eternal guest; but this reward granted them is property,
all-excluding property, a little cake baked for them to eat and for
none other, nay, a preference and cosseting which is rude and insult-
ing to all but the minion.

Except in the stories of Edgeworth and Scott, whose talent knew
how to give to the book a thousand adventitious graces, the novels of
costume are all one, and there is but one standard English novel, like
the one orthodox sermon, which with slight variation is repeated
every Sunday from so many pulpits.

But the other novel, of which Wilhelm Meister[5] is the best specimen, the novel of *character*, treats the reader with more respect; the
development of character being the problem, the reader is made a
partaker of the whole prosperity. Everything good in such a story
remains with the reader when the book is closed. A noble book was
Wilhelm Meister. It gave the hint of a cultivated society which we
found nowhere else. It was founded on power to do what was necessary, each person finding it an indispensable qualification of mem-
bership that he could do something useful, as in mechanics or agri-
culture or other indispensable art; then a probity, a justice was to be
its element, symbolized by the insisting that each property should be
cleared of privilege, and should pay its full tax to the state. Then a
perception of beauty was the equally indispensable element of the
association, by which each was dignified and all were dignified; then
each was to obey his genius to the length of abandonment. They
watched each candidate vigilantly, without his knowing that he was
observed, and when he had given proof that he was a faithful man,
then all doors, all houses, all relations were open to him; high behavior fraternized with high behavior, without question of heraldry,
and the only power recognized is the force of character.

The novels of Fashion, of Disraeli, Mrs. Gore, Mr. Ward,[6] belong to
the class of novels of costume, because the aim is purely external
success. Of the tales of fashionable life, by far the most agreeable and
the most efficient was Vivian Grey.[7] Young men were and still are the
readers and victims. Byron ruled for a time, but Vivian, with no tithe
of Byron's genius, rules longer. One can distinguish the Vivians in all
companies. They would quiz their father and mother and lover and
friend. They discuss sun and planets, liberty and fate, love and death,
over the soup. They never sleep, go nowhere, stay nowhere, eat
nothing, and know nobody, but are up to anything, though it were
the genesis of Nature, or the last catacylsm,—Festus-like, Faust-like,
Jove-like, and could write an Iliad any rainy morning, if fame were
not such a bore. Men, women, though the greatest and fairest, are
stupid things; but a rifle, and a mild pleasant gunpowder, a spaniel,
and a cheroot, are themes for Olympus. I fear it was in part the
influence of such pictures on living society which made the style of
manners of which we have so many pictures, as, for example, in the

following account of the English fashionist. "His highest triumph is to appear with the most wooden manners, as little polished as will suffice to avoid castigation, nay, to contrive even his civilities so that they may appear as near as may be to affronts; instead of a noble high-bred ease, to have the courage to offend against every restraint of decorum, to invert the relation in which our sex stand to women, so that they appear the attacking, and he the passive or defensive party."

We must here check our gossip in mid-volley and adjourn the rest of our critical chapter to a more convenient season.

Natural History of Intellect and Other Papers, *W* 12:365–78; first published in the *Dial*, April 1843.

Literature

Mark Van Doren's comment that English Traits *is "the wittiest work of America's wittiest writer" is complemented by Howard Mumford Jones's view that, despite its faults, "no better book by an American about Victorian England (or rather Great Britain at midcentury) has ever been written." As "a tough-minded analysis of a complex modern industrial society,"* English Traits *represents "a silent rebuke to the school of criticism that dismisses Emerson as a thin idealist."[8] The opening pages of the chapter on literature illustrate the power of Emerson's vivid characterization, as in his description of the English common sense and of Saxon speech and Renaissance poetry ("iron raised to white heat"), especially in Shakespeare, the perfect example of the union of "Saxon precision and Oriental soaring." British empiricism, as in Locke, is condemned as lacking the poetic power that derives from Platonic analogy and from "an insight of general laws" (deducing the rule "with equal precision from few subjects, or from one"). To remedy this deficiency in "the practical finality class" (the empiricists, who hate ideas, lack imagination and ideals), Emerson recommends "Oriental large-ness," or intuitive realization of universal truths. Emerson's practical idealism shows through his conclusion: that these two styles of mind, the perceptive and the practical, must interact mutually within the nation, as well as within the individual writer. In applying the transcendental test to the "English transcendental genius," by 1856 Emerson's criticism has become uncompromisingly evaluative as he relies on already formed judgments of favorite literary points of reference.*

A strong common sense, which it is not easy to unseat or disturb, marks the English mind for a thousand years: a rude strength newly applied to thought, as of sailors and soldiers who had lately learned to read.[9] They have no fancy, and never are surprised into a covert or witty word, such as pleased the Athenians and Italians, and was convertible into a fable not long after; but they delight in strong earthy expression, not mistakable, coarsely true to the human body, and, though spoken among princes, equally fit and welcome to the mob. This homeliness, veracity and plain style appear in the earliest extant works and in the latest. It imports into songs and ballads the smell of the earth, the breath of cattle, and, like a Dutch painter, seeks a household charm, though by pails and pans. They ask their constitutional utility in verse. The kail[10] and herrings are never out of sight. The poet nimbly recovers himself from every sally of the imagination. The English muse loves the farmyard, the lane and market. She says, with De Staël, "I tramp in the mire with wooden shoes, whenever they would force me into the clouds." For the Englishman has accurate perceptions; takes hold of things by the right end, and there is no slipperiness in his grasp. He loves the axe, the spade, the oar, the gun, the steam-pipe; he has built the engine he uses. He is materialist, economical, mercantile. He must be treated with sincerity and reality; with muffins, and not the promise of muffins; and prefers his hot chop, with perfect security and convenience in the eating of it, to the chances of the amplest and Frenchiest bill of fare, engraved on embossed paper. When he is intellectual, and a poet or a philosopher, he carries the same hard truth and the same keen machinery into the mental sphere. His mind must stand on a fact. He will not be baffled, or catch at clouds, but the mind must have a symbol palpable and resisting. What he relishes in Dante is the vise-like tenacity with which he holds a mental image before the eyes, as if it were a scutcheon painted on a shield. Byron "liked something craggy to break his mind upon." A taste for plain strong speech, what is called a biblical style, marks the English. It is in Alfred and the Saxon Chronicle and in the Sagas of the Northmen. Latimer was homely. Hobbes was perfect in the "noble vulgar speech." Donne, Bunyan, Milton, Taylor, Evelyn, Pepys, Hooker, Cotton and the translators wrote it. How realistic or materialistic in treatment of his subject is Swift. He describes his fictitious persons as if for the police. Defoe has no insecurity or choice. Hudibras has the same hard mentality,— keeping the truth at once to the senses and to the intellect.

It is not less seen in poetry. Chaucer's hard painting of his Canterbury pilgrims satisfies the senses. Shakspeare, Spenser and Milton, in their loftiest ascents, have this national grip and exactitude of mind. This mental materialism makes the value of English transcendental genius; in these writers and in Herbert, Henry More, Donne and Sir Thomas Browne. The Saxon materialism and narrowness, exalted into the sphere of intellect, makes the very genius of Shakspeare and Milton. When it reaches the pure element, it treads the clouds as securely as the adamant. Even in its elevations materialistic, its poetry is common sense inspired; or iron raised to white heat.

The marriage of the two qualities is in their speech. It is a tacit rule of the language to make the frame or skeleton of Saxon words, and, when elevation or ornament is sought, to interweave Roman, but sparingly; nor is a sentence made of Roman words alone, without loss of strength. The children and laborers use the Saxon unmixed. The Latin unmixed is abandoned to the colleges and Parliament. Mixture is a secret of the English island; and, in their dialect, the male principle is the Saxon, the female, the Latin; and they are combined in every discourse. A good writer, if he has indulged in a Roman roundness, makes haste to chasten and nerve his period by English monosyllables.

When the Gothic nations came into Europe they found it lighted with the sun and moon of Hebrew and of Greek genius. The tablets of their brain, long kept in the dark, were finely sensible to the double glory. To the images from this twin source (of Christianity and art), the mind became fruitful as by the incubation of the Holy Ghost. The English mind flowered in every faculty. The common sense was surprised and inspired. For two centuries England was philosophic, religious, poetic. The mental furniture seemed of larger scale: the memory capacious like the storehouse of the rains. The ardor and endurance of study, the boldness and facility of their mental construction, their fancy and imagination and easy spanning of vast distances of thought, the enterprise or accosting of new subjects, and, generally, the easy exertion of power,—astonish, like the legendary feats of Guy of Warwick. The union of Saxon precision and Oriental soaring, of which Shakspeare is the perfect example, is shared in less degree by the writers of two centuries. I find not only the great masters out of all rivalry and reach, but the whole writing of the time charged with a masculine force and freedom.

There is a hygienic simpleness, rough vigor and closeness to the matter in hand even in the second and third class of writers; and, I think, in the common style of the people, as one finds it in the citation of wills, letters and public documents; in proverbs and forms of speech. The more hearty and sturdy expression may indicate that the savageness of the Norseman was not all gone. Their dynamic brains hurled off their words as the revolving stone hurls off scraps of grit.

*   *   *

Locke, to whom the meaning of ideas was unknown, became the type of philosophy, and his "understanding" the measure, in all nations, of the English intellect. His countrymen forsook the lofty sides of Parnassus, on which they had once walked with echoing steps, and disused the studies once so beloved; the powers of thought fell into neglect. The later English want the faculty of Plato and Aristotle, of grouping men in natural classes by an insight of general laws, so deep that the rule is deduced with equal precision from few subjects, or from one, as from multitudes of lives. Shakspeare is supreme in that, as in all the great mental energies. The Germans generalize: the English cannot interpret the German mind. German science comprehends the English. The absence of the faculty in England is shown by the timidity which accumulates mountains of facts, as a bad general wants myriads of men and miles of redoubts to compensate the inspirations of courage and conduct.

The English shrink from a generalization. "They do not look abroad into universality, or they draw only a bucketful at the fountain of the First Philosophy for their occasion, and do not go to the spring-head." Bacon, who said this, is almost unique among his countrymen in that faculty; at least among the prose-writers. Milton, who was the stair or high table-land to let down the English genius from the summits of Shakspeare, used this privilege sometimes in poetry, more rarely in prose. For a long interval afterwards, it is not found. Burke was addicted to generalizing, but his was a shorter line; as his thoughts have less depth, they have less compass. Hume's abstractions are not deep or wise.

*   *   *

The essays, the fiction and the poetry of the day have the like municipal limits. Dickens, with preternatural apprehension of the language of manners and the varieties of street life; with pathos and laughter, with patriotic and still enlarging generosity, writes London tracts. He is a painter of English details, like Hogarth; local and temporary in his tints and style, and local in his aims. Bulwer, an industrious writer, with occasional ability, is distinguished for his reverence of intellect as a temporality, and appeals to the worldly ambition of the student. His romances tend to fan these low flames. Their novelists despair of the heart. Thackeray finds that God has made no allowance for the poor thing in his universe,—more's the pity, he thinks,—but 't is not for us to be wiser; we must renounce ideals and accept London.

The brilliant Macaulay, who expresses the tone of the English governing classes of the day, explicitly teaches that *good* means good to eat, good to wear, material commodity; that the glory of modern philosophy is its direction on "fruit;" to yield economical inventions; and that its merit is to avoid ideas and avoid morals. He thinks it the distinctive merit of the Baconian philosophy in its triumph over the old Platonic, its disentangling the intellect from theories of the all-Fair and all-Good, and pinning it down to the making a better sick chair and a better wine-whey for an invalid;—this not ironically, but in good faith;—that, "solid advantage," as he calls it, meaning always sensual benefit, is the only good. The eminent benefit of astronomy is the better navigation it creates to enable the fruit-ships to bring home their lemons and wine to the London grocer. It was a curious result, in which the civility and religion of England for a thousand years ends in denying morals and reducing the intellect to a sauce-pan. The critic hides his skepticism under the English cant of practical. To convince the reason, to touch the conscience, is romantic pretension. The fine arts fall to the ground. Beauty, except as luxurious commodity, does not exist. It is very certain, I may say in passing, that if Lord Bacon had been only the sensualist his critic pretends, he would never have acquired the fame which now entitles him to this patronage. It is because he had imagination, the leisures of the spirit, and basked in an element of contemplation out of all modern English atmospheric gauges, that he is impressive to the imaginations of men and has become a potentate not to be ignored. Sir David Brewster[11] sees the high place of Bacon, without finding Newton indebted to him, and thinks it a mistake. Bacon occupies it by specific gravity or levity, not by any feat he did, or by any tutoring more or less of Newton, etc., but as an effect of the same cause which showed itself more pronounced afterwards in Hooke, Boyle and Halley.[12]

Coleridge, a catholic mind, with a hunger for ideas; with eyes looking before and after to the highest bards and sages, and who wrote and spoke the only high criticism in his time, is one of those who save England from the reproach of no longer possessing the capacity to appreciate what rarest wit the island has yielded. Yet the misfortune of his life, his vast attempts but most inadequate performings, failing to accomplish any one masterpiece,—seems to mark the closing of an era. Even in him, the traditional Englishman was too strong for the philosopher, and he fell into *accommodations*; and as Burke had striven to idealize the English State,[13] so Coleridge 'narrowed his mind' in the attempt to reconcile the Gothic rule and dogma of the Anglican Church, with eternal ideas. But for Coleridge, and a lurking taciturn minority uttering itself in occasional criticism, oftener in private discourse, one would say that in Germany and in America is the best mind in England rightly respected. It is the surest sign of national decay, when the Bramins can no longer read or understand the Braminical philosophy.

In the decomposition and asphyxia that followed all this materialism, Carlyle was driven by his disgust at the pettiness and the cant into the preaching of Fate. In comparison with all this rottenness, any check, any cleansing, though by fire, seemed desirable and beautiful. He saw little difference in the gladiators, or "the causes" for which they combated; the one comfort was, that they were all going speedily into the abyss together. And his imagination, finding no nutriment in any creation, avenged itself by celebrating the majestic beauty of the laws of decay. The necessities of mental structure force all minds into a few categories; and where impatience of the tricks of men makes Nemesis amiable, and builds altars to the negative Deity, the inevitable recoil is to heroism or the gallantry of the private heart, which decks its immolation with glory, in the unequal combat of will against fate.

*   *   *

Thus poetry is degraded and made ornamental. Pope and his school wrote poetry fit to put round frosted cake. What did Walter Scott write without stint? a rhymed traveller's guide to Scotland. And the libraries of verses they print have this Birmingham character. How many volumes of well-bred metre we must jingle through, before we can be filled, taught, renewed! We want the miraculous; the beauty which we can manufacture at no mill,—can give no account of; the beauty of which Chaucer and Chapman had the secret. The poetry of course is low and prosaic; only now and then, as in Wordsworth, conscientious; or in Byron, passional; or in Tennyson, factitious. But if I should count the poets who have contributed to the Bible of existing England sentences of guidance and consolation which are still glowing and effective,—how few! Shall I find my heavenly bread in the reigning poets? Where is great design in modern English poetry? The English have lost sight of the fact that poetry exists to speak the spiritual law, and that no wealth of description or of fancy is yet essentially new and out of the limits of prose, until this condition is reached. Therefore the grave old poets, like the Greek artists, heeded their designs, and less considered the finish. It was their office to lead to the divine sources, out of which all this, and much more, readily springs; and, if this religion is in the poetry, it raises us to some purpose and we can well afford some staidness or hardness, or want of popular tune in the verses.

The exceptional fact of the period is the genius of Wordsworth. He had no master but nature and solitude. "He wrote a poem," says

Landor, "without the aid of war." His verse is the voice of sanity in a worldly and ambitious age. One regrets that his temperament was not more liquid and musical. He has written longer than he was inspired. But for the rest, he has no competitor.

Tennyson is endowed precisely in points where Wordsworth wanted. There is no finer ear, nor more command of the keys of language. Color, like the dawn, flows over the horizon from his pencil, in waves so rich that we do not miss the central form. Through all his refinements, too, he has reached the public,—a certificate of good sense and general power, since he who aspires to be the English poet must be as large as London, not in the same kind as London, but in his own kind. But he wants a subject, and climbs no mount of vision to bring its secrets to the people. He contents himself with describing the Englishman as he is, and proposes no better. There are all degrees in poetry and we must be thankful for every beautiful talent. But it is only a first success, when the ear is gained. The best office of the best poets has been to show how low and uninspired was their general style, and that only once or twice they have struck the high chord.

That expansiveness which is the essence of the poetic element, they have not. It was no Oxonian, but Hafiz, who said, "Let us be crowned with roses, let us drink wine, and break up the tiresome old roof of heaven into new forms." A stanza of the song of nature the Oxonian has no ear for, and he does not value the salient and curative influence of intellectual action, studious of truth without a by-end.

By the law of contraries, I look for an irresistible taste for Orientalism in Britain. For a self-conceited modish life, made up of trifles, clinging to a corporeal civilization, hating ideas, there is no remedy like the Oriental largeness. That astonishes and disconcerts English decorum. For once, there is thunder it never heard, light it never saw, and power which trifles with time and space. I am not surprised then to find an Englishman like Warren Hastings, who had been struck with the grand style of thinking in the Indian writings, deprecating the prejudices of his countrymen while offering them a translation of the Bhagvat. "Might I, an unlettered man, venture to prescribe bounds to the latitude of criticism, I should exclude, in estimating the merit of such a production, all rules drawn from the ancient or modern literature of Europe, all references to such sentiments or manners as are become the standards of propriety for opinion and action in our own modes, and, equally, all appeals to our revealed tenets of religion and moral duty." He goes to bespeak indulgence to "ornaments of fancy unsuited to our taste, and passages elevated to a tract of sublimity into which our habits of judgment will find it difficult to pursue them."

Meantime, I know that a retrieving power lies in the English race which seems to make any recoil possible; in other words, there is at all times a minority of profound minds existing in the nation, capable of appreciating every soaring of intellect and every hint of tendency. While the constructive talent seems dwarfed and superficial, the criticism is often in the noblest tone and suggests the presence of the invisible gods. I can well believe what I have often heard, that there are two nations in England; but it is not the Poor and the Rich, nor is it the Normans and Saxons, nor the Celt and the Goth. These are each always becoming the other; for Robert Owen does not exaggerate the power of circumstance. But the two complexions, or two styles of mind,—the perceptive class, and the practical finality class, —are ever in counterpoise, interacting mutually: one in hopeless minorities; the other in huge masses; one studious, contemplative, experimenting; the other, the ungrateful pupil, scornful of the source whilst availing itself of the knowledge for gain; these two nations, of genius and of animal force, though the first consist of only a dozen souls and the second of twenty millions, forever by their discord and their accord yield the power of the English State.

English Traits, *W* 5:232–36, 243–44, 246–50, 255–260; first published in *English Traits* (1856).

Preface to *Parnassus*

Not generally available, this preface to Emerson's anthology of poetry in English (including some translations) represents his final effort at evaluative criticism of poetry. At the urging of James R. Osgood, the publisher, and with the help of his daughter, Mrs. Edith Emerson Forbes, Emerson prepared Parnassus *to complement the anthologies by Palgrave, Anderson, and Chalmers. Holmes praised the "golden words" of the introduction, and Longfellow found it very interesting and pleasurable, but neither remarked on the selections or the criteria of choice. Emerson says he chose poems for their historical importance, weight of sense, magic of style or musical expression, or wealth of truth. In his conclusion, he emphasizes that whereas a poem need not have rhyme or meter, it must have a "special music or tone," which is "the union of nature with thought," as in all great poetry, good ballads, German hymns, the "Marseillaise," and old church chants.*

An outgrowth of an old habit of copying "certain gems of pure lustre," this anthology contains old favorites from a lifetime of reading—memorable lines, lyrics, and narrative and reflective verse. The absence of any consistently high or objective standard of choice is evident in the very conventional thematic or subject-matter grouping of the contents, implying a popular, parlor-table use (and, for that, the book sold well). Section titles include Nature, Narratives, Ballads, Portraits, Songs, Dirges and Pathetic Poems, Comic and Satirical Verses, Oracles and Counsels, and even Poetry of Terror (mainly passages from Shakespeare's plays). Among the poets more generously represented are Shakespeare with eighty-eight (including nine sonnets); Byron, thirty-three; Scott, twenty-eight; Burns, twenty-four; Herrick, twenty-three; Jonson, twenty-two; Herbert, sixteen; Milton, fourteen; Thomas Moore, nine; Bryant, eight; Channing, eight; Holmes, seven; Longfellow, seven; Whittier, seven; Marvell, seven; Lowell, seven. Among the less well represented are Arnold, one; Shelley, two; Pope, two; Blake, three; the Brownings, three each; Thoreau, four; Spenser, six; Keats, six; and Coleridge, six. Conspicuously missing are Poe, Whitman, Melville, Freneau, Anne Bradstreet, Emerson himself, and a score of lesser American poets. Whereas Emerson omitted "The Rime of the Ancient Mariner," possibly because of its length, he included his brother Edward's "The Last Farewell," Forceythe Willson's "In State," and the trite verses of Felicia Hemans. Although the selection is generally consistent with the primacy of a "metre-making argument," at times his Puritan distrust of rhetorical ornament led him to favor depth of feeling and thought even when expressed in mediocre or unmusical language. Beyond these limitations lie the shortcomings attributable to Emerson's failing memory.

The Preface consists mainly of pithy judgments on Chaucer, Jonson, Shakespeare, Wordsworth, Byron, and Tennyson, with lesser comments on Herbert, Herrick, Pope, Scott, two minor Americans, Forceythe Willson, and H. H. (Helen Hunt Jackson), and a poem by Sarah Palfrey. The paragraphs on Wordsworth are almost identical with those in "Europe and European Books."

This volume took its origin from an old habit of copying any poem or lines that interested me into a blank book. In many years, my selections filled the volume, and required another; and still the convenience of commanding all my favorites in one album, instead of searching my own and other libraries for a desired song or verse, and the belief that what charmed me probably might charm others, suggested the printing of my enlarged selection. I know the convenience and merits of the existing anthologies, and the necessity of printing in every collection many masterpieces which all English-speaking men have agreed in admiring. Each has its merits; but I have found that the best of these collections do not contain certain gems of pure lustre, whilst they admit many of questionable claim. The voluminous octavos of Anderson and Chalmers[14] have the same fault of too much mass and too little genius; and even the more select "Golden Treasury" of Mr. Palgrave omits too much that I cannot spare. I am aware that no two readers would make the same selection. Of course, I shall gladly hail with the public a better collection than mine.

Poetry teaches the enormous force of a few words, and, in proportion to the inspiration, checks loquacity. It requires that splendor of expression which carries with it the proof of great thoughts. Great thoughts insure musical expressions. Every word should be the right word. The poets are they who see that spiritual is greater than any material force, that thoughts rule the world. The great poets are judged by the frame of mind they induce; and to them, of all men, the severest criticism is due.

Some poems I have inserted for their historical importance; some, for their weight of sense; some, for single couplets or lines, perhaps even for a word; some, for magic of style; and I have admitted verses, which, in their structure, betray a defect of poetic ear, but have a wealth of truth which ought to have created melody. I know the peril of didactics to kill poetry, and that Wordsworth runs fearful risks to save his mental experiences. Some poems are external, like Moore's, and have only a superficial melody: others, like Chaucer's, have such internal music as to forgive a roughness to the modern ear, which, in the mouth of the bard, his contemporaries probably did not detect. To Chaucer may be well applied the word of Heraclitus, that "Harmony latent is of greater value than that which is patent."

There are two classes of poets,—the poets by education and practice, these we respect; and poets by nature, these we love. Pope is the best type of the one class: he had all the advantage that taste and wit could give him, but never rose to grandeur or to pathos. Milton had all its advantages, but was also poet born. Chaucer, Shakspeare, Jonson (despite all the pedantic lumber he dragged with him), Herbert, Herrick, Collins, Burns,—of the other. Then there are poets who rose slowly, and wrote badly, and had yet a true calling, and, after a hundred failures, arrived at pure power; as Wordsworth, encumbered for years with childish whims, but at last, by his religious insight, lifted to genius.

Scott was a man of genius, but only an accomplished rhymer (poet on the same terms as the Norse bards and minstrels), admirable chronicler, and master of the ballad, but never crossing the threshold of the epic, where Homer, Dante, Shakspeare, and Milton dwell.

The task of selection is easiest in poetry. What a signal convenience is fame! Do we read all authors to grope our way to the best? No; but the world selects for us the best, and we select from these our best.

Chaucer fulfils the part of the poet, possesses the advantage of being the most cultivated man of his time, and so speaks always sovereignly and cheerfully. Often the poetic nature, being too susceptible, is over-acted on by others. The religious sentiment teaching the immensity of every moment, the indifference of magnitude, the present is all, the soul is God;—this lesson is great and greatest. Yet this, also, has limits for humanity. One must not seek to dwell in ethereal contemplation: so should the man decline into a monk, and stop short of his possible enlargement. The intellect is cheerful.

Chaucer's antiquity ought not to take him out of the hands of intelligent readers. No lover of poetry can spare him, or should grudge the short study required to command the archaisms of his English, and the skill to read the melody of his verse. His matter is excellent, his story told with vivacity, and with equal skill in the pathos and in triumph. I think he has lines of more force than any English writer, except Shakspeare. If delivered by an experienced reader, the verses will be found musical as well as wise, and fertile in invention. He is always strong, facile, and pertinent, and with what vivacity of style through all the range of his pictures, comic or tragic! He knows the language of joy and of despair.

Of Shakspeare what can we say, but that he is and remains an exceptional mind in the world; that a universal poetry began and ended with him; and that mankind have required the three hundred and ten years since his birth to familiarize themselves with his supreme genius? I should like to have the Academy of Letters propose a prize for an essay on Shakspeare's poem, "*Let the bird of loudest lay,*" and the "*Threnos*" with which it closes; the aim of the essay being to explain, by a historical research into the poetic myths and tendencies of the age in which it was written, the frame and allusions of the poem. I have not seen Chester's "*Love's Martyr,*" and "the Additional Poems" (1601), in which it appeared.[15] Perhaps that book will suggest all the explanation this poem requires. To unassisted readers, it would appear to be a lament on the death of a poet, and of his poetic mistress. But the poem is so quaint, and charming in diction, tone, and allusions, and in its perfect metre and harmony, that I would gladly have the fullest illustration yet attainable. I consider this piece a good example of the rule, that there is a poetry for bards proper, as well as a poetry for the world of readers. This poem, if published for the first time, and without a known author's name, would find no general reception. Only the poets would save it.

To the modern reader, Ben Jonson's plays have lost their old attraction; but his occasional poems are full of heroic thought, and his songs are among the best in the language. His life interests us from the wonderful circle of companions with whom he lived,—with Camden, Shakspeare, Beaumont, Fletcher, Bacon, Chapman, Herbert, Herrick, Cowley, Suckling, Drayton, Donne, Carew, Selden, —and by whom he was honored. Cowley tells us, "I must not forget Ben's reading: it was delicious: never was poetry married to more exquisite music:" and the Duchess of Newcastle relates, that her husband, himself a good reader, said he "never heard any man read well but Ben Jonson."

Spence reports, that Pope said to him, "Crashaw is a worse sort of Cowley: Herbert is lower than Crashaw,"—an opinion which no reader of their books at this time will justify. Crashaw, if he be the translator of the 'Sospetto d'Herode,' has written masterly verses never learned from Cowley, some of which I have transcribed; and Herbert is the psalmist dear to all who love religious poetry with exquisite refinement of thought. So much piety was never married to so much wit. Herbert identifies himself with Jewish genius, as Michael Angelo did when carving or painting prophets and patriarchs, not merely old men in robes and beards, but with the sanctity and the character of the Pentateuch and the prophecy conspicuous in them. His wit and his piety are genuine, and are sure to make a lifelong friend of a good reader.

Herrick is the lyric poet, ostentatiously choosing petty subjects, petty names for each piece, and disposing of his theme in a few lines, or in a couplet; is never dull, and is the master of miniature painting. On graver themes, in his "Sacred Numbers," he is equally successful.

Milton's "Paradise Lost" goes so surely with the Bible on to every book-shelf, that I have not cited a line; but I could not resist the insertion of the "Comus," and the "Lycidas," which are made of pure poetry, and have contented myself with extracts from the grander scenes of "Samson Agonistes."

The public sentiment of the reading world was long divided on the merits of Wordsworth. His early poems were written on a false theory of poetry; and the critics denounced them as childish. He persisted long to write after his own whim; and, though he arrived at unexpected power, his readers were never safe from a childish return upon himself and an unskilful putting-forward of it. How different from the absolute concealment of Shakspeare in all his miraculous dramas, and even in his love-poems, in which, of course, the lover must be perpetually present, but always by thought, and never by his buttons or pitifulness! Montaigne is delightful in his egotism. Byron is always egotistic, but interesting thereby, through the taste and genius of his confession or his defiance.

Wordsworth has the merit of just moral perception, but not that of deft poetic execution. How would Milton curl his lip at such slipshod newspaper style! Many of his poems, as, for example, "The Rylstone Doe," might be all improvised: nothing of Milton, nothing of Marvell, of Herbert, of Dryden, could be. These are verses such as many country gentlemen could write; but few would think of claiming the poet's laurel on their merit. Pindar, Dante, Shakspeare, whilst they have the just and open soul, have also the eye to see the dimmest star, the serratures of every leaf, the test objects of the microscope, and then the tongue to utter the same things in words that engrave them on the ears of all mankind.

The poet demands all gifts, and not one or two only. Like the electric rod, he must reach from a point nearer to the sky than all surrounding objects, down to the earth, and into the wet soil, or neither is of use. The poet must not only converse with pure thought, but he must demonstrate it almost to the senses. His words must be pictures: his verses must be spheres and cubes, to be seen and handled. His fable must be a good story, and its meaning must hold as pure truth. In the debates on the Copyright Bill, in the English parliament, Mr. Sergeant Wakley, the coroner, quoted Wordsworth's poetry in derision, and asked the roaring House of Commons, "what that meant, and whether a man should have a public reward for writing such stuff?"—Homer, Horace, Milton and Chaucer would defy the coroner. Whilst they have wisdom to the wise, he would see that to the external they have external meaning. Coleridge rightly said that "poetry must first be good sense, as a palace might well be magnificent, but first it must be a house." Wordsworth is open to ridicule of this kind; and yet, though satisfied if he can suggest to a sympathetic mind his own mood, and though setting a private and exaggerated value on his compositions, and taking the public to task for not admiring his poetry, he is really a master of the English language; and his best poems evince a power of diction that is no more rivalled by his contemporaries than is his poetic insight. But his capital merit is, that he has done more for the sanity of his generation than any other writer.

"Laodamia" is almost entitled to that eminence in his literary performance which Landor gave it when he said, that "Wordsworth had now written a poem which might be fitly read in Elysium, and the gods and heroes might gather round to listen." I count that and the "Ode on Immortality" as the best.

Wordsworth has a religious value for his thoughts; but his inspirations are casual and insufficient, and he persists in writing after they are gone. No great poet needs so much a severely critical selection of the noble numbers from the puerile into which he often falls. Leigh Hunt said of him, that "he was a fine lettuce with too many outer leaves."

Byron's rare talent is conspicuously partial. He has not sweetness, nor solid knowledge, nor lofty aim. He had a rare skill for rhythm, unmatched facility of expression, a firm, ductile thread of gold. His rhymes do not suggest any restraint, but the utmost freedom, as the rules of the dance do not fetter the good dancer, but exhibit his natural grace. In his isolation he is starved for a purpose; and finding no material except of romance,—first, of corsairs, and Oriental robbers and harems, and, lastly, of satire,—he revenges himself on society for its supposed distrust of him, by cursing it, and throwing himself on the side of its destroyers. His life was wasted; and its only result was this brilliant gift of song with which he soothed his chosen exile. I do not know that it can retain for another generation the charm it had for his contemporaries; but the security with which he pours these perfectly modulated verses to any extent, without any sacrifice of sense for the sake of metre, surprises the reader.

Tennyson has incomparable felicity in all poetic forms, surpassing in melody also, and is a brave, thoughtful Englishman, unmatched in rhythmic power and variety. The thoroughness with which the fable has been thought out, as in the account of the supreme influence of Arthur on his knights, is only one of his triumphs. The passion of love in his "Maud" found a new celebration, which woke delight wherever the English language is known; the "Dirge of Wellington" was a more magnificent monument than any or all of the histories that record that commander's life. Then the variety of his poems discloses the wealth and the health of his mind. Nay, some of his words are poems.

The selections from American writers are necessarily confined to the present century; but some of them have secured a wide fame. Some of them are recent, and have yet to earn their laurels. I have inserted only one of the remarkable poems of Forceythe Willson, a young Wisconsin poet of extraordinary promise, who died very soon after this was written. The poems of a lady who contents herself with the initials H. H. in her book published in Boston (1874) have rare merit of thought and expression, and will reward the reader for the careful attention which they require. The poem of "Sir Pavon and Saint Pavon," by another hand, has a dangerous freedom of style, but carries in it rare power and pathos.[16]

The imagination wakened brings its own language, and that is always musical. It may or may not have rhyme or a fixed metre; but it will always have its special music or tone. Whatever language the bard uses, the secret of tone is at the heart of the poem. Every great master is such by this power,—Chaucer and Shakspeare and Raleigh and Milton and Collins and Burns and Byron and Tennyson and Wolfe. The true inspiration always brings it. Perhaps it cannot be analyzed; but we all yield to it. It is the life of the good ballads; it is in the German hymns which Wesley translated; it is in the "Marseillaise" of Rouget de Lisle; it gave their value to the chants of the old Romish and of the English Church; and it is the only account we can give of their wonderful power on the people. Poems may please by their talent and ingenuity; but, when they charm us, it is because they have this quality, for this is the union of nature with thought.

R. W. E.

Parnassus (Boston, 1874), pp. iii–xi.

Chaucer

Although in some measure a public reading, this early lecture identifies "the gifts of Chaucer" as good sense, clear insight, kindness, and reformist sympathy. Chaucer's "English sincerity and homeliness and humor" are praised and generously illustrated. An example of Emerson's concern for democratic values is the importance attached to "gentilesse," formerly a product of noble birth and education, now a matter of "gentle behavior" to the English and American mind. In discussing Chaucer's indebtedness to Colonna and Boccaccio, Emerson sets forth a theory of borrowing based on the view that "there never was an original writer." The poet is like a marble fountain into and out of which the waters flow in a process of "universal receiving" and "universal giving." Thus, because truth is ever present in the world, the simple lover of truth will not trouble himself with the question of authorship. Copernicus, Jesus, Jefferson, Homer, and Aristotle are examples of great men who assimilated the wisdom of their age. So Chaucer, never hiding his sources, is "a luminous mind collecting and imparting to us the religion, the wit, and humanity of a whole age." In the 1874 Preface to Parnassus, *Emerson again paid tribute to Chaucer's vital humanity and vivacity of style.*

But the poems of Chaucer have great merits of their own. They are the compositions of a man of the world who has much knowledge both of books and of men. They exhibit strong sense, humor, pathos, and a dear love of nature. He is a man of strong and kindly genius possessing all his faculties in that balance and symmetry neither too little nor too much which constitute an individual a sort of Universal Man and fit him to take up into himself without egotism all the wit and character of his age and to stand for his age before posterity. He possesses many of the highest gifts of genius and those too whose value is most intelligible to all men. The milk of human kindness flows always in his veins. The hilarity of good sense joined with the best health and temper never forsakes him. He possesses that clear insight into life which ever and anon perceives under the play of the thousand interests and follies and caprices of man the adamantine framework of Nature on which all the decoration and activity of life is hung.

He possesses the most authentic property of genius, that of sympathy with his subjects so that he describes every object with a delight in the thing itself. It has been observed that it does not argue genius that a man can write well on himself, or on topics connected with his personal relations. It is the capital deduction from Lord Byron that his poems have but one subject: himself. It is the burden of society, that very few men have sufficient strength of mind to speak of any truth or sentiment and hardly even of facts and persons clean of any reference to themselves and their personal history. But the wise man and much more the true Poet quits himself and throws his spirit into whatever he contemplates and enjoys the making it speak that it would say. This power belonged to Chaucer.

With these endowments he writes though often playfully yet always as a sincere man who has an earnest meaning to express and nowise (at least in those poems on which his fame is founded) as an idle and irresponsible rhymer. He acknowledges in House of Fame that he prefers "sentence," that is, sense, to skill of numbers. He would make

> the rime agreeable
> Tho some verse fail in a syllable
> And though I do no diligence
> To show crafte but sentence.
>
> [ll. 1097–1100]

But he felt and maintained the dignity of the laurel and restored it in England to its honor.

* * *

No one can read Chaucer in his grave compositions without being struck with his consciousness of his poetic duties. He never writes with timidity. He speaks like one who knows the law, and has a right to be heard. He is a philanthropist, a moralist, a reformer. He lashes the vices of the clergy. He wrote a poem of stern counsel to King Richard. He exposes the foibles and tricks of all pretenders in science [and] the professions, and his prophetic wisdom is found on the side of good sense and humanity.

I do not feel that I have closed the enumeration of the gifts of Chaucer until it is added as a cause of his permanent fame in spite of the obsoleteness of his style (now 500 years old) that his virtues and genius are singularly agreeable to the English mind; that in him they find their prominent tastes and prejudices. He has the English sincerity and homeliness and humor, and his Canterbury tales are invaluable as a picture of the domestic manners of the fourteenth century. Shakspear and Milton are not more intrinsically national poets than is Chaucer. He has therefore contributed not a little to deepen and fix in the character of his countrymen those habits and sentiments which inspired his early song.

The humor with which the English race is so deeply tinged, which constitutes the genius of so many of their writers, as, of the author of Hudibras, Smollett, Fielding, Swift, and Sterne, and which the English maintain to be inseparable from genius, effervesces in every page of Chaucer. The prologue to the Canterbury Tales is full of it. A pleasing specimen of it is the alarm in the farmyard in the Fable of the Cock and the Fox.

> The sely widow and her daughters two
> Herden these hennes crien and make wo
> And out at the dores they sterten anon
> And saw the fox toward the wood is gon
> And bare upon his back the cock away
> They crieden out Harow and Wala way!
> A ha the fox! and after him they ran
> And eke with staves many another man
> Ran Col our dog and Talbot and Girland
> And Malkin with the distaff in her hand
> Ran cow and calf and eke the very hogs
> So fered were for barking of the dogs
> And shouting of the men and women eke
> They ronnen so them thought their hearts would break
> The duckes crieden as men would them quell
> The geese for fear flewen over the trees
> Out of the hive came the swarm of bees
> Of bras they broten beemes and of box
> A horn and bone in which they blew and pooped
> And therewithal they shrieked and they whooped
> It seemed as if the very Heaven would fall.[17]

In Chaucer are conspicuous some of those ideas which reappear continually in the Saxon race. One of these is that of Gentilesse, or the doctrine of gentle behaviour founded upon Honor, which adheres in all times and fortunes to the English mind. Mr. Coleridge has remarked that "Chaucer represents a very high and romantic style of society among the gentry."[18] But beyond his delineation of actual manners he is possessed with the idea of the gentleman in no less strength and clearness than it existed in the minds of Spenser, Sidney, Milton, Clarendon and Addison and Burke.

*   *   *

Chaucer is a teacher of this doctrine expressly and by implication throughout his works. In the Wife of Bath's tale he has given us excellent advice which embodies the most liberal and republican creed:

> But for ye speken of such gentillesse
> As is descended out of old richesse
> That therefore shullen ye be gentilmen
> Such arrogance n'is not worth an hen.
> [ll. D 1109–12]

*   *   *

The influence of Chaucer I have remarked already is very conspicuous on all our early literature. Not only Pope, Dryden, and Milton have been indebted to him but a large unacknowledged debt is easily traced. From Chaucer succeeding writers have borrowed the English versions of the celebrated classic mythology. Phebus, Diana and Mars, Priam, Hector, Troilus, Dido, Theseus, Ariadne reign as much in his poems as in those of the ancients, though in quite new costume of manners and speech. Chaucer however did not invent this modern dress for the old gods and heroes. In the year 1260 Guido de Colonna, a native of Messina in Sicily, published a grand prose romance in Latin in fifteen books, called Historia de Bello Trojano. This was founded on the apocryphal Greek history of Dares Phrygius and enriched by all paraphrases from Ovid and Statius. This is Chaucer's chief magazine. This is the book which was turned into English poetry by Lydgate at the command of Henry V and translated into

English prose by Caxton the printer in 1471. Chaucer's other sources are Petrarch, Boccacio, Lollius, and the Provençal poets. The Romaunt of the Rose is translated from William of Lorris and John of Meun. Troilus and Creseide from Lollius of Urbino. The House of Fame is from the French or Italian. The Cock and the Fox is from the Lais of Marie a French poetess.[19] And the extent of Chaucer's obligations to his foreign contemporaries and predecessors is so great as to induce the inquiry whether he can claim the praise of an original writer.

The truth is all works of literature are Janus faced and look to the future and to the past. Shakspear, Pope, and Dryden borrow from Chaucer and shine by his borrowed light. Chaucer reflects Boccacio and Colonna and the Troubadours; Boccacio and Colonna elder Greek and Roman authors, and these in their turn others if only history would enable us to trace them. There never was an original writer. Each is a link in an endless chain. To receive and to impart are the talents of the poet and he ought to possess both in equal degrees. He is merely the marble mouth of a fountain into which the waters ascend and out of which they flow. This is but the nature of man, universal, receiving to the end of universal giving. The great theory of the Solar System published by Copernicus in the sixteenth century is but the revival of a very ancient system of astronomy known to Archimedes, and in his writings attributed to Aristarchus of Samos. The sublime prayer which Jesus taught his disciples, Grotius has shown to be a compilation of existing Jewish petitions,[20] and learned oriental scholars find the leading thought of many of his precepts in Hebrew proverbs current in his time. Where is the doctrine of the newest sect of religion or philosophy that we cannot match with its counterpart from some primeval verse or proverb? Jefferson is not less the author of the Declaration of Independence because every clause of it had been suggested by some Memorial or Remonstrance of the period.

* * *

Morality is concerned only with the spirit in which it is done; if the writer appropriates the praise and conceals the debt he is a plagiarist. If he generously feel that the thought most strictly his own is not his own and recognizes with awe the perpetual suggestion of God he then makes even the oldest thoughts new and fresh when he speaks them. Chaucer is never anxious to hide his obligations; he frankly acknowledges in every page or whenever he wants a rhyme that his author or the old book says so; and thus is to us in the remote past a luminous mind collecting and imparting to us the religion, the wit, and humanity of a whole age.

EL 1:272–73, 274–76, 278, 283–85, 286, lecture (1835).

Bacon

Bacon's Essays, *an early favorite, became for Emerson a model of beauty of style and nobility of sentiment. In 1824, mentioning Bacon as one of the "wisdom" writers, Emerson expressed a desire to write "A Sequel to Bacon." The following pages on the* Essays *repeat earlier appreciations, this time with exemplary sentences quoted, but emphasize the lack of "intrinsic Unity," especially in comparison with a play like* Hamlet. *Although here Emerson noticed "a mean cunning" in the essays, as a defect of Bacon's moral character, in* English Traits *he placed Bacon among the analogists or Platonists. In 1869 he called Bacon "a great generous thinker" whose every sentence "gave the mind a lift, filled the horizon, was a fine generalization."[21]*

The book of Lord Bacon that gets out of libraries into parlors and chambers and travelling carriages and into camps, is his Essays. Few books ever written contain so much wisdom and will bear to be read so many times. Each reader is struck with the truth of the observations on that subject with which he happens to be most familiar. Yet almost all the topics are such as interest all men. They are clothed meantime in a style of so much splendor that imaginative persons find sufficient delight in the beauty of expression.

They delight us by the dignity of the sentiments whenever he surrenders himself to his genius, as when he writes in the first Essay,

"Certainly it is heaven upon earth to have a man's mind move in charity, rest in Providence and turn upon the poles of truth." How profound the observation in this passage! "This same truth is a naked and open daylight that doth not show the masks and mummeries and triumphs of the world half so stately and daintily as candle lights. Truth may perhaps come to the price of a pearl that showeth best by day, but it will not rise to the price of a diamond or carbuncle that showeth best in varied lights. A mixture of a lie doth ever add pleasure. Doth any man doubt that if there were taken out of men's minds vain opinions, flattering hopes, false valuations, imaginations as one would and the like, but it would leave the minds of a number of men poor shrunken things, full of melancholy and indisposition and unpleasing to themselves?" And let us believe that the following sentence contains his own apology to himself for submitting to the mortifications of ambition. "Power to do good is the true and lawful end of aspiring; for good thoughts though God accept them yet towards men are no better than good dreams except they be put in act, and that cannot be, without power and place, as the vantage and commanding ground."

How noble is the view which he takes of personal deformity as being more a spur to virtue than a cause of malevolence: "Because there is in man an election touching the frame of his mind and a necessity in the frame of his body, the stars of natural inclination are sometimes obscured by the sun of discipline and virtue; therefore it is good to consider of deformity not as a sign which is most deceivable but as a cause which seldom faileth of the effect."

The uses of Friendship are nobly set forth: "Certain it is that whosoever hath his mind fraught with many thoughts, his wits and understanding do clarify and break up in the communicating and discoursing with another; he tosseth his thoughts more easily; he marshalleth them more orderly; he seeth how they look when they are turned into words; finally he waxeth wiser than himself and that more by an hour's discourse than by a day's meditation."

The defects of this book stand in glaring contrast to its merits. Out breaks at intervals a mean cunning like the hiss of a snake amid the discourse of angels. But these passages need no index and no brand. The finger of a child can point them out.

What wisdom is shown in the essay on Travel and in that of Studies! What criticism on manners in that on Ceremonies and Respects! What nicety and curiosity of taste in those on Gardens and Masks and Buildings!

If I may adventure a criticism upon Lord Bacon's writings, it would be to remark a fault not easily separable from so colossal undertakings. His works have not that highest perfection of literary works, an intrinsic Unity, a method derived from the Mind. If a comparison were to be instituted between the Instauration and the Epic of Milton or the Hamlet of Shakspear I think the preference must remain with these last as the production of higher faculties. They are the mind's own Creation and are perfect according to certain inward canons which the mind must always acknowledge. But Bacon's method is not within in the work itself, but without. This might be expected in his Natural History but not in his elaborated compositions. Yet in his Essays it is the same. All his work lies along the ground, a vast unfinished city. He did not arrange but unceasingly collect facts. His own Intellect often acts little on what he collects. Very much stands as he found it—mere lists of facts material or spiritual. All of his work is therefore somewhat fragmentary. The fire has hardly passed over it and given it fusion and a new order from his own mind. It is sand without lime. It is a vast collection of proverbs, all wise but the order is much of it quite mechanical, things on one subject being thrown together; the order of a shop and not that of a tree or an animal where perfect assimilation has taken place and all the parts have a perfect unity. The Novum Organon has taken this form of separate propositions and the Essays would bear to be printed in the form of Solomon's proverbs, that is, in total disconnection.

So loose a method had this advantage, that it allowed of perpetual amendment and addition. And every one of his works was a gradual growth. Three times he published the Essays with large additions. Twelve times he wrote over the Novum Organon, that is once every year from 1607. Many fragments remain to us among his works, by which we may see the manner in which all his works were written. Works of this sort which consist of detached observations and to which the mind has not imparted a system of its own, are never ended. Each of Shakspear's dramas is perfect, hath an immortal integrity. To make Bacon's works complete, he must live to the end of the world.

From "Lord Bacon," *EL* 1:333–35, lecture (1835).

Montaigne

In these pages, Emerson gives a brilliant description of the qualities of mind and language that distinguish Montaigne's Essays: *candor and integrity under a superficial levity, and a preference and feeling for the genuine, the familiar, the personal, the everyday experienced reality. The realism of such an experiential outlook on life is caught in a style like "the shower of bullets" attributed to Montaigne's conversational writing. "No book before or since was ever so much to me as that," Emerson wrote in his journal. This selection is literary criticism on the level of the artistic essay itself. Emerson's own cheek flushes and his style rises to passion, as he said of Montaigne's writing about Socrates.*

* * *

A single odd volume of Cotton's translation of the Essays remained to me from my father's library, when a boy. It lay long neglected, until, after many years, when I was newly escaped from college, I read the book, and procured the remaining volumes. I remember the delight and wonder in which I lived with it. It seemed to me as if I had myself written the book, in some former life, so sincerely it spoke to my thought and experience.

* * *

Montaigne is the frankest and honestest of all writers. His French freedom runs into grossness; but he has anticipated all censure by the bounty of his own confessions. In his times, books were written to one

sex only, and almost all were written in Latin; so that in a humorist a
certain nakedness of statement was permitted, which our manners, of
a literature addressed equally to both sexes, do not allow. But though
a biblical plainness coupled with a most uncanonical levity may
shut his pages to many sensitive readers, yet the offense is superficial.
He parades it: he makes the most of it: nobody can think or say worse
of him than he does. He pretends to most of the vices; and, if there be
any virtue in him, he says, it got in by stealth. There is no man, in his
opinion, who has not deserved hanging five or six times; and he
pretends no exception in his own behalf. "Five or six as ridiculous
stories," too, he says, "can be told of me, as of any man living." But,
with all this really superfluous frankness, the opinion of an invincible
probity grows into every reader's mind. "When I the most strictly
and religiously confess myself, I find that the best virtue I have has in
it some tincture of vice; and I, who am as sincere and perfect a lover of
virtue of that stamp as any other whatever, am afraid that Plato, in
his purest virtue, if he had listened and laid his ear close to himself,
would have heard some jarring sound of human mixture; but faint and
remote and only to be perceived by himself."

Here is an impatience and fastidiousness at color or pretence of any
kind. He has been in courts so long as to have conceived a furious
disgust at appearances; he will indulge himself with a little cursing
and swearing; he will talk with sailors and gipsies, use flash and street
ballads; he has stayed in-doors till he is deadly sick; he will to the
open air, though it rain bullets. He has seen too much of gentlemen of
the long robe, until he wishes for cannibals; and is so nervous, by
factitious life, that he thinks the more barbarous man is, the better he
is. He likes his saddle. You may read theology, and grammar, and
metaphysics elsewhere. Whatever you get here shall smack of the
earth and of real life, sweet, or smart, or stinging. He makes no
hesitation to entertain you with the records of his disease, and his
journey to Italy is quite full of that matter. He took and kept this
position of equilibrium. Over his name he drew an emblematic pair
of scales, and wrote *Que sçais je?*[22] under it. As I look at his effigy
opposite the title-page, I seem to hear him say, 'You may play old
Poz, if you will;[23] you may rail and exaggerate,—I stand here for
truth, and will not, for all the states and churches and revenues and

personal reputations of Europe, overstate the dry fact, as I see it; I will rather mumble and prose about what I certainly know,—my house and barns; my father, my wife and my tenants; my old lean bald pate; my knives and forks; what meats I eat and what drinks I prefer, and a hundred straws just as ridiculous,—than I will write, with a fine crow-quill, a fine romance. I like gray days, and autumn and winter weather. I am gray and autumnal myself, and think an undress and old shoes that do not pinch my feet, and old friends who do not constrain me, and plain topics where I do not need to strain myself and pump my brains, the most suitable. Our condition as men is risky and ticklish enough. One cannot be sure of himself and his fortune an hour, but he may be whisked off into some pitiable or ridiculous plight. Why should I vapor and play the philosopher, instead of ballasting, the best I can, this dancing balloon? So, at least, I live within compass, keep myself ready for action, and can shoot the gulf at last with decency. If there be anything farcical in such a life, the blame is not mine: let it lie at fate's and nature's door.'

The Essays, therefore, are an entertaining soliloquy on every random topic that comes into his head; treating every thing without ceremony, yet with masculine sense. There have been men with deeper insight; but, one would say, never a man with such abundance of thoughts: he is never dull, never insincere, and has the genius to make the reader care for all that he cares for.

The sincerity and marrow of the man reaches to his sentences. I know not anywhere the book that seems less written. It is the language of conversation transferred to a book. Cut these words, and they would bleed; they are vascular and alive. One has the same pleasure in it that he feels in listening to the necessary speech of men about their work, when any unusual circumstance gives momentary importance to the dialogue. For blacksmiths and teamsters do not trip in their speech; it is a shower of bullets. It is Cambridge men who correct themselves and begin again at every half sentence, and, moreover, will pun, and refine too much, and swerve from the matter to the expression.[24] Montaigne talks with shrewdness, knows the world and books and himself, and uses the positive degree; never shrieks, or protests, or prays: no weakness, no convulsion, no superlative: does not wish to jump out of his skin, or play any antics, or annihilate space or time, but is stout and solid; tastes every moment of the day; likes pain because it makes him feel himself and realize things; as we pinch ourselves to know that we are awake. He keeps the plain; he rarely mounts or sinks; likes to feel solid ground and the stones underneath. His writing has no enthusiasms, no aspiration; contented, self-respecting and keeping the middle of the road. There is but one exception,—in his love for Socrates. In speaking of him, for once his cheek flushes and his style rises to passion.

From "Montaigne; or, The Skeptic," in *Representative Men*, *W* 4:162, 164–69; first published in *Representative Men* (1850); from lecture (1846).

Shakespeare

From an early journal entry in 1822 to the Preface to Parnassus *of 1874, Emerson expressed an almost unqualified enthusiasm for Shakespeare. In 1838, after reading* Lear *and* Hamlet *again, he exclaimed with wonder and admiration at the inimitable characterization of Hamlet and Lear and at the "mightier magic than any learning" that is the deep source of Shakespeare's creativity. Similarly, in 1864, for the three hundredth anniversary celebration of Shakespeare's birth by the Saturday Club, Emerson composed an eloquent tribute to "the first poet of the world," mythical as Homer, and "the most robust and potent thinker that ever was," speaking "the pure sense of humanity" without egotism. "He dwarfs all writers without a solitary exception." In addition to his universality, in the 1864 journal (J 10:27–31) Shakespeare is praised for "pure poetic power," his transcendental "mythologizing [of] every fact of the common life," his intellectual courage and power, his mastery of language, and an "Aristotelian" as well as a courtly "poetic Culture" behind the sonnets. But then there is the problem of how to read the plays, "for the interest of the story is sadly in the way of poetry. It is safer, therefore, to read the play backwards." Because neither of the two lectures on Shakespeare in December 1835 (EL 1:287–304, 305–19) was incorporated into this piece, they deserve passing mention. The first treated Shakespeare as a poet of imaginative power; as a philosopher of reflective power, capable not only of self-scrutiny but also of linking the world of truth with the world of nature and humanity; and as a practical man sympathetic with common sense and ordinary life. The second lecture, by contrast, dealt with the rhythm, language, characters, and wise sentences of the plays, sufficient evidence that Shakespeare was a true composer, not a mere rhapsodist or improviser. Being public readings in part, these introductory lectures lack the cogency and depth of this major essay. Because the greatest genius has "a heart in unison with his time and country," Shakespeare embodied both the zeitgeist and his culture; he was responsive to the popular tradition of the Elizabethan drama and owed much to others ("all originality is relative"). The neglect of Shakespeare's life story in the records implies that his genius had communal roots. No biographical facts will explain the plays. "Shakspeare is the only biographer of Shakspeare; and even he can tell nothing, except to the Shakspeare in us." He is man thinking, recording his great insights on life, death, love, and the mysteries which defy science. But despite his creative power and wisdom, he was, finally, deficient in transcendental vision to the extent that "he was master of the revels of mankind" and failed to turn natural objects into emblems of his thoughts ("He rested in their beauty"). Apparently Shakespeare's life in and of the world of the theater, where he "led an obscure and profane life, using his genius for the public amusement," troubled Emerson's moral sense as well. This conclusion is the only negative note in an otherwise very laudatory lecture, and is but a minor qualification of Emerson's characteristic view of Shakespeare as a transcendental poet of Nature, a poet whose great vision implied a universality and equality among men.*

Great men are more distinguished by range and extent than by originality. If we require the originality which consists in weaving, like a spider, their web from their own bowels; in finding clay and making bricks and building the house; no great men are original. Nor does valuable originality consist in unlikeness to other men. The hero is in the press of knights and the thick of events; and seeing what men want and sharing their desire, he adds the needful length of sight and of arm, to come at the desired point. The greatest genius is the most indebted man. A poet is no rattle-brain, saying what comes uppermost, and, because he says every thing, saying at last something good; but a heart in unison with his time and country. There is nothing whimsical and fantastic in his production, but sweet and sad earnest, freighted with the weightiest convictions and pointed with the most determined aim which any man or class knows of in his times.

The Genius of our life is jealous of individuals, and will not have any individual great, except through the general. There is no choice to genius. A great man does not wake up on some fine morning and say, 'I am full of life, I will go to sea and find an Antartic continent: to-day I will square the circle: I will ransack botany and find a new food for man: I have a new architecture in my mind: I foresee a new mechanic power:' no, but he finds himself in the river of thoughts and events, forced onward by the ideas and necessities of his contemporaries. He stands where all the eyes of men look one way, and their hands all point in the direction in which he should go. The Church has reared him amidst rites and pomps, and he carries out the advice which her music gave him, and builds a cathedral needed by her chants and processions. He finds a war raging: it educates him, by trumpet, in barracks, and he betters the instruction. He finds two counties groping to bring coal, or flour, or fish, from the place of production to the place of consumption, and he hits on a railroad. Every master has found his materials collected, and his power lay in his sympathy with his people and in his love of the materials he wrought in. What an economy of power! and what a compensation for the shortness of life! All is done to his hand. The world has brought him thus far on his way. The human race has gone out before him, sunk the hills, filled the hollows and bridged the rivers. Men, nations, poets, artisans, women, all have worked for him, and he enters into their labors. Choose any other thing, out of line of tendency, out of the national feeling and history, and he would have all to do for himself: his powers would be expended in the first preparations. Great genial power, one would almost say, consists in not being original at all; in being altogether receptive; in letting the world do all, and suffering the spirit of the hour to pass unobstructed through the mind.

Shakspeare's youth fell in a time when the English people were importunate for dramatic entertainments. The court took offence easily at political allusions and attempted to suppress them. The Puritans, a growing and energetic party, and the religious among the Anglican church, would suppress them. But the people wanted them.

Inn-yards, houses without roofs, and extemporaneous enclosures at country fairs were the ready theatres of strolling players. The people had tasted this new joy; and, as we could not hope to suppress newspapers now,—no, not by the strongest party,—neither then could king, prelate, or puritan, alone or united, suppress an organ which was ballad, epic, newspaper, caucus, lecture, Punch and library, at the same time. Probably king, prelate and puritan, all found their own account in it. It had become, by all causes, a national inter- est,—by no means conspicuous, so that some great scholar would have thought of treating it in an English history,—but not a whit less considerable because it was cheap and of no account, like a baker's- shop. The best proof of its vitality is the crowd of writers which suddenly broke into this field; Kyd, Marlow, Greene, Jonson, Chap- man, Dekker, Webster, Heywood, Middleton, Peele, Ford, Mas- singer, Beaumont and Fletcher.

The secure possession, by the stage, of the public mind, is of the first importance to the poet who works for it. He loses no time in idle experiments. Here is audience and expectation prepared. In the case of Shakspeare there is much more. At the time when he left Stratford and went up to London, a great body of stage-plays of all dates and writers existed in manuscript and were in turn produced on the boards. Here is the Tale of Troy, which the audience will bear hearing some part of, every week; the Death of Julius Caesar, and other stories out of Plutarch, which they never tire of; a shelf full of English history, from the chronicles of Brut[25] and Arthur, down to the royal Henries, which men hear eagerly; and a string of doleful trag- edies, merry Italian tales and Spanish voyages, which all the Lon- don 'prentices know. All the mass has been treated, with more or less skill, by every playwright, and the prompter has the soiled and tattered manuscripts. It is now no longer possible to say who wrote them first. They have been the property of the Theatre so long, and so many rising geniuses have enlarged or altered them, inserting a speech or a whole scene, or adding a song, that no man can any longer claim copyright in this work of numbers. Happily, no man wishes to. They are not yet desired in that way. We have few readers, many spectators and hearers. They had best lie where they are.

Shakspeare, in common with his comrades, esteemed the mass of old plays waste stock, in which any experiment could be freely tried. Had the *prestige* which hedges about a modern tragedy existed, nothing could have been done. The rude warm blood of the living England circulated in the play, as in street-ballads, and gave body which he wanted to his airy and majestic fancy. The poet needs a ground in popular tradition on which he may work, and which, again, may restrain his art within the due temperance. It holds him to the people, supplies a foundation for his edifice, and in furnishing so much work done to his hand, leaves him at leisure and in full strength for the audacities of his imagination. In short, the poet owes to his legend what sculpture owed to the temple. Sculpture in Egypt and in Greece grew up in subordination to architecture. It was the ornament of the temple wall; at first a rude relief carved on pediments, then the relief became bolder and a head or arm was projected from the wall; the groups being still arranged with reference to the building, which serves also as a frame to hold the figures; and when at last the greatest freedom of style and treatment was reached, the prevailing genius of architecture still enforced a certain calmness and continence in the statue. As soon as the statue was begun for itself, and with no reference to the temple or palace, the art began to decline: freak, extravagance and exhibition took the place of the old temperance. This balance-wheel, which the sculptor found in architecture, the perilous irritability of poetic talent found in the accumulated dramatic materials to which the people were already wonted, and which had a certain excellence which no single genius, however extraordinary, could hope to create.

In point of fact it appears that Shakspeare did owe debts in all directions, and was able to use whatever he found; and the amount of indebtedness may be inferred from Malone's[26] laborious computations in regard to the First, Second and Third parts of Henry VI., in which, "out of 6043 lines, 1771 were written by some author preceding Shakspeare, 2373 by him, on the foundation laid by his predecessors, and 1899 were entirely his own." And the proceeding investigation hardly leaves a single drama of his absolute invention. Malone's sentence is an important piece of external history. In Henry VIII. I think I see plainly the cropping out of the original rock on which his own finer stratum was laid. The first play was written by a superior, thoughtful man, with a vicious ear. I can mark his lines, and know well their cadence. See Wolsey's soliloquy, and the following scene with Cromwell, where instead of the metre of Shakspeare, whose secret is that the thought constructs the tune, so that reading for the sense will best bring out the rhythm,— here the lines are constructed on a given tune, and the verse has even a trace of pulpit eloquence. But the play contains through all its length unmistakable traits of Shakspeare's hand, and some passages, as the account of the coronation, are like autographs. What is odd, the compliment to Queen Elizabeth is in the bad rhythm.

Shakspeare knew that tradition supplies a better fable than any invention can. If he lost any credit of design, he augmented his resources; and, at that day, our petulant demand for originality was not so much pressed. There was no literature for the million. The universal reading, the cheap press, were unknown. A great poet who appears in illiterate times, absorbs into his sphere all the light which is any where radiating. Every intellectual jewel, every flower of sentiment it is his fine office to bring to his people; and he comes to value his memory equally with his invention. He is therefore little solicitous whence his thoughts have been derived; whether through translation, whether through tradition, whether by travel in distant countries, whether by inspiration; from whatever source, they are equally welcome to his uncritical audience. Nay, he borrows very near home. Other men say wise things as well as he; only they say a good many foolish things, and do not know when they have spoken wisely. He knows the sparkle of the true stone, and puts it in high place, wherever he finds it. Such is the happy position of Homer perhaps; of Chaucer, of Saadi. They felt that all wit was their wit. And they are librarians and historiographers, as well as poets. Each romancer was heir and dispenser of all the hundred tales of the world,—

> "Presenting Thebes' and Pelops' line
> And the tale of Troy divine."
>
> [*Il Penseroso*, ll. 99–100]

The influence of Chaucer is conspicuous in all our early literature; and more recently not only Pope and Dryden have been beholden to him, but, in the whole society of English writers, a large unacknowledged debt is easily traced. One is charmed with the opulence which feeds so many pensioners. But Chaucer is a huge borrower. Chaucer, it seems, drew continually, through Lydgate and Caxton, from Guido di Colonna, whose Latin romance of the Trojan war was in turn a compilation from Dares Phrygius, Ovid and Statius. Then Petrarch, Boccaccio and the Provençal poets are his benefactors; the Romaunt of the Rose is only judicious translation from William of Lorris and John of Meung: Troilus and Creseide, from Lollius of Urbino: The Cock and the Fox, from the *Lais* of Marie: The House of Fame, from the French or Italian: and poor Gower he uses as if he were only a brick-kiln or stone-quarry out of which to build his house.[27] He steals by this apology,—that what he takes has no worth where he finds it and the greatest where he leaves it. It has come to be practically a sort of rule in literature, that a man having once shown himself capable of original writing, is entitled thenceforth to steal from the writings of others at discretion. Thought is the property of him who can entertain it and of him who can adequately place it. A certain awkwardness marks the use of borrowed thoughts; but as soon as we have learned what to do with them they become our own.

Thus all originality is relative. Every thinker is retrospective. The learned member of the legislature, at Westminster or at Washington, speaks and votes for thousands. Show us the constituency, and the now invisible channels by which the senator is made aware of their wishes; the crowd of practical and knowing men, who, by correspondence or conversation, are feeding him with evidence, anecdotes and estimates, and it will bereave his fine attitude and resistance of something of their impressiveness. As Sir Robert Peel and Mr. Webster vote, so Locke and Rousseau think, for thousands; and so there were fountains all around Homer, Menu, Saadi, or Milton, from which they drew; friends, lovers, books, traditions, proverbs, —all perished—which, if seen, would go to reduce the wonder. Did the bard speak with authority? Did he feel himself overmatched by any companion? The appeal is to the consciousness of the writer. Is there at last in his breast a Delphi whereof to ask concerning any thought or thing, whether it be verily so, yea or nay? and to have answer, and to rely on that? All the debts which such a man could contract to other wit would never disturb his consciousness of originality; for the ministrations of books and of other minds are a whiff of smoke to that most private reality with which he has conversed.

It is easy to see that what is best written or done by genius in the world, was no man's work, but came by wide social labor, when a thousand wrought like one, sharing the same impulse. Our English Bible is a wonderful specimen of the strength and music of the English language. But it was not made by one man, or at one time; but centuries and churches brought it to perfection. There never was a time when there was not some translation existing. The Liturgy, admired for its energy and pathos, is an anthology of the piety of ages and nations, a translation of the prayers and forms of the Catholic church,—these collected, too, in long periods, from the prayers and meditations of every saint and sacred writer all over the world. Grotius[28] makes the like remark in respect to the Lord's Prayer, that the single clauses of which it is composed were already in use in the time of Christ, in the Rabbinical forms. He picked out the grains of gold. The nervous language of the Common Law, the impressive forms of our courts and the precision and substantial truth of the legal distinctions, are the contribution of all the sharp-sighted, strong-minded men who have lived in the countries where these laws govern. The translation of Plutarch gets its excellence by being translation on translation. There never was a time when there was none. All the truly idiomatic and national phrases are kept, and all others successively picked out and thrown away. Something like the same process had gone on, long before, with the originals of these books. The world takes liberties with world-books. Vedas, Aesop's Fables, Pilpay, Arabian Nights, Cid, Iliad, Robin Hood, Scottish Minstrelsy, are not the work of single men. In the composition of such works the time thinks, the market thinks, the mason, the carpenter, the merchant, the farmer, the fop, all think for us. Every book supplies its time with one good word; every municipal law, every trade, every folly of the day; and the generic catholic genius who is not afraid or ashamed to owe his originality to the originality of all, stands with the next age as the recorder and embodiment of his own.

We have to thank the researches of antiquaries, and the Shakspeare Society, for ascertaining the steps of the English drama, from the Mysteries celebrated in churches and by churchmen, and the final detachment from the church, and the completion of secular plays, from Ferrex and Porrex, and Gammer Gurton's Needle,[29] down to the possession of the stage by the very pieces which Shakspeare altered, remodelled and finally made his own. Elated with success and piqued by the growing interest of the problem, they have left no bookstall unsearched, no chest in a garret unopened, no file of old yellow accounts to decompose in damp and worms, so keen was the hope to discover whether the boy Shakspeare poached or not, whether he held horses at the theatre door, whether he kept school, and why he left in his will only his second-best bed to Ann Hathaway, his wife.

There is somewhat touching in the madness with which the passing age mischooses the object on which all candles shine and all eyes are turned; the care with which it registers every trifle touching Queen Elizabeth and King James, and the Essexes, Leicesters, Burleighs and Buckinghams; and lets pass without a single valuable note the founder of another dynasty, which alone will cause the Tudor dynasty to be remembered,—the man who carries the Saxon race in him by the inspiration which feeds him, and on whose thoughts the foremost people of the world are now for some ages to be nourished, and minds to receive this and not another bias. A popular player;—nobody suspected he was the poet of the human race; and the secret was kept as faithfully from poets and intellectual men as from courtiers and frivolous people. Bacon, who took the inventory of the human understanding for his times, never mentioned his name. Ben Jonson, though we have strained his few words of regard and panegyric, had no suspicion of the elastic fame whose first vibrations he was attempting. He no doubt thought the praise he has conceded to him generous, and esteemed himself, out of all question, the better poet of the two.

If it need wit to know wit, according to the proverb, Shakspeare's time should be capable of recognizing it. Sir Henry Wotton was born four years after Shakspeare, and died twenty-three years after him; and I find, among his correspondents and acquaintances, the following persons: Theodore Beza, Isaac Casaubon, Sir Philip Sidney, the Earl of Essex, Lord Bacon, Sir Walter Raleigh, John Milton, Sir Henry Vane, Isaac Walton, Dr. Donne, Abraham Cowley, Bellar-

mine, Charles Cotton, John Pym, John Hales, Kepler, Vieta, Alber-
icus Gentilis, Paul Sarpi, Arminius,[30] with all of whom exists some
token of his having communicated, without enumerating many
others whom doubtless he saw,—Shakspeare, Spenser, Jonson, Beaumont, Massinger, the two Herberts, Marlow, Chapman and the rest.
Since the constellation of great men who appeared in Greece in the
time of Pericles, there was never any such society;—yet their genius
failed them to find out the best head in the universe. Our poet's mask
was impenetrable. You cannot see the mountain near. It took a
century to make it suspected; and not until two centuries had passed,
after his death, did any criticism which we think adequate begin to
appear. It was not possible to write the history of Shakspeare till now;
for he is the father of German literature: it was with the introduction
of Shakspeare into German, by Lessing, and the translation of his
works by Wieland and Schlegel, that the rapid burst of German
literature was most intimately connected. It was not until the nineteenth century, whose speculative genius is a sort of living Hamlet,
that the tragedy of Hamlet could find such wondering readers. Now,
literature, philosophy and thought are Shakspearized. His mind is
the horizon beyond which, at present, we do not see. Our ears are
educated to music by his rhythm. Coleridge and Goethe are the only
critics who have expressed our convictions with any adequate fidelity: but there is in all cultivated minds a silent appreciation of his
superlative power and beauty, which, like Christianity, qualifies the
period.

  The Shakspeare Society have inquired in all directions, advertised
the missing facts, offered money for any information that will lead to
proof,—and with what result? Beside some important illustration of
the history of the English stage, to which I have adverted, they have
gleaned a few facts touching the property, and dealings in regard to
property, of the poet. It appears that from year to year he owned a
larger share in the Blackfriars' Theatre:[31] its wardrobe and other
appurtenances were his: that he bought an estate in his native village
with his earnings as writer and shareholder; that he lived in the best
house in Stratford; was intrusted by his neighbors with their com-
missions in London, as of borrowing money, and the like; that he was
a veritable farmer. About the time when he was writing Macbeth, he

sues Philip Rogers, in the borough-court of Stratford, for thirty-five shillings, ten pence, for corn delivered to him at different times; and in all respects appears as a good husband, with no reputation for eccentricity or excess. He was a good-natured sort of man, an actor and shareholder in the theatre, not in any striking manner distinguished from other actors and managers. I admit the importance of this information. It was well worth the pains that have been taken to procure it.

But whatever scraps of information concerning his condition these researches may have rescued, they can shed no light upon that infinite invention which is the concealed magnet of his attraction for us. We are very clumsy writers of history. We tell the chronicle of parentage, birth, birth-place, schooling, school-mates, earning of money, marriage, publication of books, celebrity, death; and when we have come to an end of this gossip, no ray of relation appears between it and the goddess-born; and it seems as if, had we dipped at random into the "Modern Plutarch,"[32] and read any other life there, it would have fitted the poems as well. It is the essence of poetry to spring, like the rainbow daughter of Wonder, from the invisible, to abolish the past and refuse all history. Malone, Warburton, Dyce and Collier[33] have wasted their oil. The famed theatres, Covent Garden, Drury Lane, the Park and Tremont have vainly assisted. Betterton, Garrick, Kemble, Kean and Macready[34] dedicate their lives to this genius; him they crown, elucidate, obey and express. The genius knows them not. The recitation begins; one golden word leaps out immortal from all this painted pedantry and sweetly torments us with invitations to its own inaccessible homes. I remember I went once to see the Hamlet of a famed performer, the pride of the English stage; and all I then heard and all I now remember of the tragedian was that in which the tragedian had no part; simply Hamlet's question to the ghost:—

> "What may this mean,
> That thou, dead corse, again in complete steel
> Revisit'st thus the glimpses of the moon?"
>
> [*Hamlet* 1.4.51–53]

That imagination which dilates the closet he writes in to the world's dimension, crowds it with agents in rank and order, as quickly reduces the big reality to be the glimpses of the moon. These tricks of his magic spoil for us the illusions of the green-room.[35] Can any biography shed light on the localities into which the Midsummer Night's Dream admits me? Did Shakspeare confide to any notary or parish recorder, sacristan, or surrogate in Stratford, the genesis of that delicate creation? The forest of Arden, the nimble air of Scone Castle, the moonlight of Portia's villa, "the antres vast and desarts idle" of Othello's captivity,—where is the third cousin, or grand-nephew, the chancellor's file of accounts, or private letter, that has kept one word of those transcendent secrets? In fine, in this drama, as in all great works of art,—in the Cyclopaean architecture of Egypt and India, in the Phidian sculpture, the Gothic minsters,[36] the Italian painting, the Ballads of Spain and Scotland,—the Genius draws up the ladder after him, when the creative age goes up to heaven, and gives way to a new age, which sees the works and asks in vain for a history.

Shakspeare is the only biographer of Shakspeare; and even he can tell nothing, except to the Shakspeare in us, that is, to our most apprehensive and sympathetic hour. He cannot step from off his tripod[37] and give us anecdotes of his inspirations. Read the antique documents extricated, analyzed and compared by the assiduous Dyce and Collier,[38] and now read one of these skyey sentences,—aerolites [meteorites],—which seem to have fallen out of heaven, and which not your experience but the man within the breast has accepted as words of fate, and tell me if they match; if the former account in any manner for the latter; or which gives the most historical insight into the man.

Hence, though our external history is so meagre, yet, with Shakspeare for biographer, instead of Aubrey and Rowe,[39] we have really the information which is material; that which describes character and fortune, that which, if we were about to meet the man and deal with him, would most import us to know. We have his recorded convictions on those questions which knock for answer at every heart,—on life and death, on love, on wealth and poverty, on the prizes of life and the ways whereby we come at them; on the characters of men, and the influences, occult and open, which affect their fortunes; and on those mysterious and demoniacal powers which defy our science and which yet interweave their malice and their gift in our brightest hours. Who ever read the volume of the Sonnets without finding that the poet had there revealed, under masks that are no masks to the intelligent, the lore of friendship and of love; the confusion of sentiments in the most susceptible, and, at the same time, the most intellectual of men? What trait of his private mind has he hidden in his dramas? One can discern, in his ample pictures of the gentleman and the king, what forms and humanities pleased him; his delight in troops of friends, in large hospitality, in cheerful giving. Let Timon, let Warwick, let Antonio[40] the merchant answer for his great heart. So far from Shakspeare's being the least known, he is the one person, in all modern history, known to us. What point of morals, of manners, of economy, of philosophy, of religion, of taste, of the conduct of life, has he not settled? What mystery has he not signified his knowledge of? What office, or function, or district of man's work, has he not remembered? What king has he not taught state, as Talma[41] taught Napoleon? What maiden has not found him finer than her delicacy? What lover has he not outloved? What sage has he not outseen? What gentleman has he not instructed in the rudeness of his behavior?

Some able and appreciating critics think no criticism on Shakspeare valuable that does not rest purely on the dramatic merit; that he is falsely judged as poet and philosopher. I think as highly as these critics of his dramatic merit, but still think it secondary. He was a full man, who liked to talk; a brain exhaling thoughts and images, which, seeking vent, found the drama next at hand. Had he been less, we should have had to consider how well he filled his place, how good a dramatist he was,—and he is the best in the world. But it turns out that what he has to say is of that weight as to withdraw some attention from the vehicle; and he is like some saint whose history is to be rendered into all languages, into verse and prose, into songs and pictures, and cut up into proverbs; so that the occasion which gave the saint's meaning the form of a conversation, or of a prayer, or of a code of laws, is immaterial compared with the universality of its application. So it fares with the wise Shakspeare and his book of life. He wrote the airs for all our modern music: he wrote the text of modern life; the text of manners: he drew the man of England and Europe; the father of the man in America; he drew the man, and described the day, and what is done in it: he read the hearts of men and women, their probity, and their second thought and wiles; the wiles of innocence, and the transitions by which virtues and vices slide into their contraries: he could divide the mother's part from the father's part in the face of the child, or draw the fine demarcations of freedom and of fate: he knew the laws of repression which make the police of nature: and all the sweets and all the terrors of human lot lay in his mind as truly but as softly as the landscape lies on the eye. And the importance of this wisdom of life sinks the form, as of Drama or Epic, out of notice. 'T is like making a question concerning the paper on which a king's message is written.

Shakspeare is as much out of the category of eminent authors, as he is out of the crowd. He is inconceivably wise; the others, conceivably. A good reader can, in a sort, nestle into Plato's brain and think from thence; but not into Shakspeare's. We are still out of doors. For executive faculty, for creation, Shakspeare is unique. No man can imagine it better. He was the farthest reach of subtlety compatible with an individual self,—the subtilest of authors, and only just within the possibility of authorship. With this wisdom of life is the equal endowment of imaginative and of lyric power. He clothed the creatures of his legend with form and sentiments as if they were people who had lived under his roof; and few real men have left such distinct characters as these fictions. And they spoke in language as sweet as it was fit. Yet his talents never seduced him into an ostentation, nor did he harp on one string. An omnipresent humanity co-ordinates all his faculties. Give a man of talents a story to tell, and his partiality will presently appear. He has certain observations, opinions, topics, which have some accidental prominence, and which he disposes all to exhibit. He crams this part and starves that other part, consulting not the fitness of the thing, but his fitness and strength. But Shakspeare has no peculiarity, no importunate topic; but all is duly given; no veins, no curiosities; no cow-painter, no bird-fancier, no mannerist is he: he has no discoverable egotism: the great he tells greatly; the small subordinately. He is wise without emphasis or assertion; he is strong, as nature is strong, who lifts the land into mountain slopes without effort and by the same rule as she floats a bubble in the air, and likes as well to do the one as the other. This makes that equality of power in farce, tragedy, narrative, and love-songs; a merit so incessant that each reader is incredulous of the perception of other readers.

This power of expression, or of transferring the inmost truth of things into music and verse, makes him the type of the poet and has added a new problem to metaphysics. This is that which throws him into natural history, as a main production of the globe, and as announcing new eras and ameliorations. Things were mirrored in his poetry without loss or blur: he could paint the fine with precision, the great with compass, the tragic and the comic indifferently and without any distortion or favor. He carried his powerful execution into minute details, to a hair point; finishes an eyelash or a dimple as firmly as he draws a mountain; and yet these, like nature's, will bear the scrutiny of the solar microscope.

In short, he is the chief example to prove that more or less of production, more or fewer pictures, is a thing indifferent. He had the power to make one picture. Daguerre[42] learned how to let one flower etch its image on his plate of iodine, and then proceeds at leisure to etch a million. There are always objects; but there was never representation. Here is perfect representation, at last; and now let the world of figures sit for their portraits. No recipe can be given for the making of a Shakspeare; but the possibility of the translation of things into song is demonstrated.

His lyric power lies in the genius of the piece. The sonnets, though their excellence is lost in the splendor of the dramas, are as inimitable as they; and it is not a merit of lines, but a total merit of the piece; like the tone of voice of some incomparable person, so is this a speech of poetic beings, and any clause as unproducible now as a whole poem.

Though the speeches in the plays, and single lines, have a beauty which tempts the ear to pause on them for their euphuism, yet the sentence is so loaded with meaning and so linked with its foregoers and followers, that the logician is satisfied. His means are as admirable as his ends; every subordinate invention, by which he helps himself to connect some irreconcilable opposites, is a poem too. He is not reduced to dismount and walk because his horses are running off with him in some distant direction: he always rides.

The finest poetry was first experience; but the thought has suffered a transformation since it was an experience. Cultivated men often attain a good degree of skill in writing verses; but it is easy to read, through their poems, their personal history: any one acquainted with the parties can name every figure; this is Andrew and that is Rachel. The sense thus remains prosaic. It is a caterpillar with wings, and not yet a butterfly. In the poet's mind the fact has gone quite over into the new element of thought, and has lost all that is exuvial. This generosity abides with Shakspeare. We say, from the truth and closeness of his pictures, that he knows the lesson by heart. Yet there is not a trace of egotism.

One more royal trait properly belongs to the poet. I mean his cheerfulness, without which no man can be a poet,—for beauty is his aim. He loves virtue, not for its obligation but for its grace: he delights in the world, in man, in woman, for the lovely light that sparkles from them. Beauty, the spirit of joy and hilarity, he sheds over the universe. Epicurus relates that poetry hath such charms that a lover might forsake his mistress to partake of them. And the true bards have been noted for their firm and cheerful temper. Homer lies in sunshine; Chaucer is glad and erect; and Saadi says, "It was rumored abroad that I was penitent; but what had I to do with repentance?" Not less sovereign and cheerful,—much more sovereign and cheerful, is the tone of Shakspeare. His name suggests joy and emancipation to the heart of men. If he should appear in any company of human souls, who would not march in his troop? He touches nothing that does not borrow health and longevity from his festal style.

And now, how stands the account of man with this bard and benefactor, when, in solitude, shutting our ears to the reverberations of his fame, we seek to strike the balance? Solitude has austere lessons; it can teach us to spare both heroes and poets; and it weighs Shakspeare also, and finds him to share the halfness and imperfection of humanity.

Shakspeare, Homer, Dante, Chaucer, saw the splendor of meaning that plays over the visible world; knew that a tree had another use than for apples, and corn another than for meal, and the ball of the earth, than for tillage and roads: that these things bore a second and finer harvest to the mind, being emblems of its thoughts, and conveying in all their natural history a certain mute commentary on human life. Shakspeare employed them as colors to compose his picture. He rested in their beauty; and never took the step which seemed inevitable to such genius, namely to explore the virtue which resides in these symbols and imparts this power:—what is that which they themselves say? He converted the elements which waited on his command, into entertainments. He was master of the revels to mankind. Is it not as if one should have, through majestic powers of science, the comets given into his hand, or the planets and their moons, and should draw them from their orbits to glare with the municipal fireworks on a holiday night, and advertise in all towns, "Very superior pyrotechny this evening"? Are the agents of nature, and the power to understand them, worth no more than a street serenade, or the breath of a cigar? One remembers again the trumpet-text in the Koran,—"The heavens and the earth and all that is between them, think ye we have created them in jest?" As long as the question is of talent and mental power, the world of men has not his equal to show. But when the question is, to life and its materials and its auxiliaries, how does he profit me? What does it signify? It is but a Twelfth Night, or Midsummer-Night's Dream, or Winter Evening's Tale: what signifies another picture more or less? The Egyptian verdict of the Shakspeare Societies comes to mind; that he was a jovial actor and manager. I can not marry this fact to his verse. Other admirable men have led lives in some sort of keeping with their thought; but this man, in wide contrast. Had he been less, had he reached only the common measure of great authors, of Bacon, Milton, Tasso, Cervantes, we might leave the fact in the twilight of human fate: but that this man of men, he who gave to the science of mind a new and larger subject than had ever existed, and planted the standard of humanity some furlongs forward into Chaos,—that he should not be wise for himself;—it must even go into the world's history that the best poet led an obscure and profane life, using his genius for the public amusement.

Well, other men, priest and prophet, Israelite, German and Swede, beheld the same objects: they also saw through them that which was contained. And to what purpose? The beauty straightway vanished; they read commandments, all-excluding mountainous duty; an obligation, a sadness, as of piled mountains, fell on them, and life became ghastly, joyless, a pilgrim's progress, a probation, beleaguered round with doleful histories of Adam's fall and curse behind us; with doomsdays and purgatorial and penal fires before us; and the heart of the seer and the heart of the listener sank in them.

It must be conceded that these are half-views of half-men. The world still wants its poet-priest, a reconciler, who shall not trifle, with Shakspeare the player, nor shall grope in graves, with Swedenborg the mourner; but who shall see, speak, and act, with equal inspiration. For knowledge will brighten the sunshine; right is more beautiful than private affection; and love is compatible with universal wisdom.

"Shakspeare; or, The Poet," in *Representative Men*, *W* 4:187–220; first published in *Representative Men* (1850); origin in "Shakespeare," lecture at Exeter Hall, London (1848) and lecture in Boston (1846).

Milton

The excerpts from this appreciation deal with Milton the writer only, omitting the pages on Milton's physical traits, speech, schooling, character, austere habits, heroic and Christian qualities, and his championing of political, religious, and domestic freedom. Milton's prose tracts are found rhetorically excellent but not integrated; brilliant in expression but uncompromising in point of view. Superlative as Areopagitica *may be, that and the theology of* Paradise Lost *have faded into the polemical and sectarian past, whereas the poems have been the object of new sensitive recitations and criticism. More important is Milton's commanding intellect reading "the laws of the moral sentiment to the new-born race," raising "the idea of Man" to a transcendental level, superior to that of Bacon, Locke, Pope, Johnson, Franklin, Homer, and Shakespeare. A writer, said Milton, "ought himself to be a true poem." Because "the man is paramount to the poet," Emerson regards Milton's writings as identifiably autobiographical. But the argument as well as the style of Milton's prose is poetic; that is, it seeks to create an ideal world, as in his essay pleading for freedom of divorce. Both Milton and his work represent an attempt "to carry out the life of man to new heights of spiritual grace and dignity."*

I framed his tongue to music,
I armed his hand with skill,
I moulded his face to beauty,
And his heart the throne of will.[43]

*   *   *

The fame of a great man is not rigid and stony like his bust. It changes with time. It needs time to give it due perspective. It was very easy to remark an altered tone in the criticism when Milton reappeared as an author, fifteen years ago, from any that had been bestowed on the same subject before. It implied merit indisputable and illustrious; yet so near to the modern mind as to be still alive and life-giving. The aspect of Milton, to this generation, will be part of the history of the nineteenth century. There is no name in English literature between his age and ours that rises into any approach to his own. And as a man's fame, of course, characterizes those who give it, as much as him who receives it, the new criticism indicated a change in the public taste, and a change which the poet himself might claim to have wrought.

The reputation of Milton had already undergone one or two revolutions long anterior to its recent aspects. In his lifetime, he was little or not at all known as a poet, but obtained great respect from his contemporaries as an accomplished scholar and a formidable pamphleteer. His poem fell unregarded among his countrymen. His prose writings, especially the Defense of the English People,[44] seem to have been read with avidity. These tracts are remarkable compositions. They are earnest, spiritual, rich will allusion, sparkling with innumerable ornaments; but as writings designed to gain a practical point, they fail. They are not effective, like similar productions of Swift and Burke; or, like what became also controversial tracts, several masterly speeches in the history of the American Congress. Milton seldom deigns a glance at the obstacles that are to be overcome before that which he proposes can be done. There is no attempt to conciliate,—no mediate, no preparatory course suggested,—but, peremptory and impassioned, he demands, on the instant, an ideal justice. Therein they are discriminated from modern writings, in which a regard to the actual is all but universal.

Their rhetorical excellence must also suffer some deduction. They have no perfectness. These writings are wonderful for the truth, the learning, the subtility and pomp of the language; but the whole is sacrificed to the particular. Eager to do fit justice to each thought, he does not subordinate it so as to project the main argument. He writes whilst he is heated; the piece shows all the rambles and resources of indignation, but he has never *integrated* the parts of the argument in his mind. The reader is fatigued with admiration, but is not yet master of the subject.

Two of his pieces may be excepted from this description, one for its faults, the other for its excellence. The Defence of the People of England, on which his contemporary fame was founded, is, when divested of its pure Latinity, the worst of his works. Only its general aim, and a few elevated passages, can save it. We could be well content if the flames to which it was condemned at Paris, at Toulouse, and at London, had utterly consumed it. The lover of his genius will always regret that he should not have taken counsel of his own lofty heart at this, as at other times, and have written from the deep convictions of love and right, which are the foundations of civil liberty. There is little poetry or prophecy in this mean and ribald scolding. To insult Salmasius, not to acquit England, is the main design. What under heaven had Madame de Saumaise, or the manner of living of Saumaise, or Salmasius, or his blunders of grammar, or his niceties of diction, to do with the solemn question whether Charles Stuart had been rightly slain? Though it evinces learning and critical skill, yet, as an historical argument, it cannot be valued with similar disquisitions of Robertson and Hallam,[45] and even less celebrated scholars. But when he comes to speak of the reason of the thing, then he always recovers himself. The voice of the mob is silent, and Milton speaks. And the peroration, in which he implores his countrymen to refute this adversary by their great deeds, is in a just spirit. The other piece is his Areopagitica, the discourse, addressed to the Parliament, in favor of removing the censorship of the press; the most splendid of his prose works. It is, as Luther said of one of Melancthon's[46] writings, "alive, hath hands and feet,—and not like Erasmus's sentences, which were made, not grown." The weight of the thought is equalled by the vivacity of the expression, and it cheers

as well as teaches. This tract is far the best known and the most read
of all, and is still a magazine of reasons for the freedom of the press. It
is valuable in history as an argument addressed to a government to
produce a practical end, and plainly presupposes a very peculiar state
of society.

But deeply as that peculiar state of society, in which and for which
Milton wrote, has engraved itself in the remembrance of the world, it
shares the destiny which overtakes everything local and personal in
Nature; and the accidental facts on which a battle of principles was
fought have already passed, or are fast passing, into oblivion. We
have lost all interest in Milton as the redoubted disputant of a sect;
but by his own innate worth this man has steadily risen in the world's
reverence, and occupies a more imposing place in the mind of men at
this hour than ever before.

It is the aspect which he presents to this generation, that alone
concerns us. Milton the polemic has lost his popularity long ago; and
if we skip the pages of Paradise Lost where "God the Father argues
like a school divine,"[47] so did the next age to his own. But, we are
persuaded, he kindles a love and emulation in us which he did not in
foregoing generations. We think we have seen and heard criticism
upon the poems, which the bard himself would have more valued
than the recorded praise of Dryden, Addison and Johnson, because
it came nearer to the mark; was finer and closer appreciation; the
praise of intimate knowledge and delight; and, of course, more welcome to the poet than the general and vague acknowledgment of his
genius by those able but unsympathizing critics. We think we have
heard the recitation of his verses by genius which found in them that
which itself would say; recitation which told, in the diamond sharp-
ness of every articulation, that now first was such perception and
enjoyment possible; the perception and enjoyment of all his varied
rhythm, and his perfect fusion of the classic and the English styles.
This is a poet's right; for every masterpiece of art goes on for some
ages reconciling the world unto itself, and despotically fashioning the
public ear. The opposition to it, always greatest at first, continually
decreases and at last ends; and a new race grows up in the taste and
spirit of the work, with the utmost advantage for seeing intimately its
power and beauty.

But it would be great injustice to Milton to consider him as enjoy-
ing merely a critical reputation. It is the prerogative of this great man
to stand at this hour foremost of all men in literary history, and so
(shall we not say?) of all men, in the power *to inspire*. Virtue goes out of
him into others. Leaving out of view the pretensions of our contemporaries (always an incalculable influence), we think no man can be
named whose mind still acts on the cultivated intellect of England
and America with an energy comparable to that of Milton. As a poet,
Shakspeare undoubtedly transcends, and far surpasses him in his
popularity with foreign nations; but Shakspeare is a voice merely;
who and what he was that sang, that sings, we know not. Milton
stands erect, commanding, still visible as a man among men, and
reads the laws of the moral sentiment to the new-born race. There is
something pleasing in the affection with which we can regard a man
who died a hundred and sixty years ago in the other hemisphere, who,
in respect to personal relations, is to us as the wind, yet by an
influence purely spiritual makes us jealous for his fame as for that of a
near friend. He is identified in the mind with all select and holy
images, with the supreme interests of the human race. If hereby we
attain any more precision, we proceed to say that we think no man in
these later ages, and few men ever, possessed so great a conception of
the manly character. Better than any other he has discharged the
office of every great man, namely, to raise the idea of Man in the
minds of his contemporaries and of posterity—to draw after Nature a
life of man, exhibiting such a composition of grace, of strength and of
virtue, as poet had not described nor hero lived. Human nature in
these ages is indebted to him for its best portrait. Many philosophers
in England, France and Germany have formally dedicated their
study to this problem; and we think it impossible to recall one in those
countries who communicates the same vibration of hope, of self-
reverence, of piety, of delight in beauty, which the name of Milton
awakens. Lord Bacon, who has written much and with prodigious
ability on this science, shrinks and falters before the absolute and
uncourtly Puritan. Bacon's Essays are the portrait of an ambitious
and profound calculator,—a great man of the vulgar sort. Of the
upper world of man's being they speak few and faint words. The man
of Locke is virtuous without enthusiasm, and intelligent without

poetry. Addison, Pope, Hume and Johnson, students, with very unlike temper and success, of the same subject, cannot, taken together, make any pretension to the amount or the quality of Milton's inspirations. The man of Lord Chesterfield is unworthy to touch his garment's hem. Franklin's man is a frugal, inoffensive, thrifty citizen, but savors of nothing heroic. The genius of France has not, even in her best days, yet culminated in any one head—not in Rousseau, not in Pascal, not in Fénelon—into such perception of all the attributes of humanity as to entitle it to any rivalry in these lists. In Germany, the greatest writers are still too recent to institute a comparison; and yet we are tempted to say that art and not life seems to be the end of their effort. But the idea of a purer existence than any he saw around him, to be realized in the life and conversation of men, inspired every act and every writing of John Milton. He defined the object of education to be, "to fit a man to perform justly, skilfully and magnanimously all the offices, both private and public, of peace and war." He declared that "he who would aspire to write well hereafter in laudable things, ought himself to be a true poem; that is, a composition and pattern of the best and honorablest things, not presuming to sing high praises of heroic men or famous cities, unless he have in himself the experience and the practice of all that which is praiseworthy."[48] Nor is there in literature a more noble outline of a wise external education than that which he drew up, at the age of thirty-six, in his Letter to Samuel Hartlib. The muscles, the nerves and the flesh with which this skeleton is to be filled up and covered exist in his works and must be sought there.

*   *   *

The perception we have attributed to Milton, of a purer ideal of humanity, modifies his poetic genius. The man is paramount to the poet. His fancy is never transcendent, extravagant; but as Bacon's imagination was said to be "the noblest that ever contented itself to minister to the understanding," so Milton's ministers to the character. Milton's sublimest song, bursting into heaven with its peals of melodious thunder, is the voice of Milton still. Indeed, throughout his poems, one may see, under a thin veil, the opinions, the feelings, even the incidents of the poet's life, still reappearing. The sonnets are all

occasional poems. L'Allegro and Il Penseroso are but a finer autobiography of his youthful fancies at Harefield; the Comus a tran-
script, in charming numbers, of that philosophy of chastity, which, in
the Apology for Smectymnuus, and in the Reason of Church Government, he declares to be his defence and religion. The Samson
Agonistes is too broad an expression of his private griefs to be mistak-
en, and is a version of the Doctrine and Discipline of Divorce. The
most affecting passages in Paradise Lost are personal allusions; and
when we are fairly in Eden, Adam and Milton are often difficult to be
separated. Again, in Paradise Regained, we have the most distinct
marks of the progress of the poet's mind, in the revision and enlargement of his religious opinions. This may be thought to abridge his
praise as a poet. It is true of Homer and Shakspeare that they do not
appear in their poems; that those prodigious geniuses did cast themselves so totally into their song that their individuality vanishes, and
the poet towers to the sky, whilst the man quite disappears. The fact is
memorable. Shall we say that in our admiration and joy in these
wonderful poems we have even a feeling of regret that the men knew
not what they did; that they were too passive in their great service;
were channels through which streams of thought flowed from a
higher source, which they did not appropriate, did not blend with
their own being? Like prophets, they seem but imperfectly aware of
the import of their own utterances. We hesitate to say such things,
and say them only to the unpleasing dualism, when the man and the
poet show like a double consciousness. Perhaps we speak to no fact,
but to mere fables, of an idle mendicant Homer, and of a Shakspeare
content with a mean and jocular way of life. Be it how it may, the
genius and office of Milton were different, namely, to ascend by the
aids of his learning and his religion—by an equal perception, that is,
of the past and the future—to a higher insight and more lively delineation of the heroic life of man. This was his poem; whereof all his
indignant pamphlets and all his soaring verses are only single cantos
or detached stanzas. It was plainly needful that his poetry should be a
version of his own life, in order to give weight and solemnity to his
thoughts; by which they might penetrate and possess the imagination
and the will of mankind. The creations of Shakspeare are cast into the
world of thought to no further end than to delight. Their intrinsic

beauty is their excuse for being. Milton, fired "with dearest charity to infuse the knowledge of good things into others,"[49] tasked his giant imagination and exhausted the stores of his intellect for an end beyond, namely, to teach. His own conviction it is which gives such authority to his strain. Its reality is its force. If out of the heart it came, to the heart it must go. What schools and epochs of common rhymers would it need to make a counterbalance to the severe oracles of his muse:—

> "In them is plainest taught and easiest learnt,
> What makes a nation happy, and keeps it so."[50]

The lover of Milton reads one sense in his prose and in his metrical compositions; and sometimes the muse soars highest in the former, because the thought is more sincere. Of his prose in general, not the style alone but the argument also is poetic; according to Lord Bacon's definition of poetry, following that of Aristotle, "Poetry, not finding the actual world exactly conformed to its idea of good and fair, seeks to accommodate the shows of things to the desires of the mind, and to create an ideal world better than the world of experience."[51] Such certainly is the explanation of Milton's tracts. Such is the apology to be entered for the plea for freedom of divorce; an essay, which, from the first, until now, has brought a degree of obloquy on his name. It was a sally of the extravagant spirit of the time, overjoyed, as in the French Revolution, with the sudden victories it had gained, and eager to carry on the standard of truth to new heights. It is to be regarded as a poem on one of the griefs of man's condition, namely, unfit marriage. And as many poems have been written upon unfit society, commending solitude, yet have not been proceeded against, though their end was hostile to the state; so should this receive that charity which an angelic soul, suffering more keenly than others from the unavoidable evils of human life, is entitled to.

We have offered no apology for expanding to such length our commentary on the character of John Milton; who, in old age, in solitude, in neglect, and blind, wrote the Paradise Lost; a man whom labor or danger never deterred from whatever efforts a love of the supreme interests of man prompted. For are we not the better; are not all men fortified by the remembrance of the bravery, the purity, the temperance, the toil, the independence and the angelic devotion of this man, who, in a revolutionary age, taking counsel only of himself, endeavored, in his writings and in his life, to carry out the life of man to new heights of spiritual grace and dignity, without any abatement of its strength?

Natural History of Intellect and Other Papers, *W* 12:247–79; first published in *The North American Review*, July 1838; presumably from reworking of lecture (1835).

Burns

Delivered at the celebration of the Burns Centenary in Boston, this speech praises Burns as person, reformer, and poet. Holmes, Lowell, and other listeners were deeply impressed by Emerson's passionate eloquence, as if he were speaking extemporaneously. The evaluative criteria applied here are twofold: Burns's values—independence, labor, common sense, reform, nature—and the melody and dialect of Burns's songs. As general-essay criticism, this is Emerson almost at his best.

> "His was the music to whose tone
>   The common pulse of man keeps time
> In cot or castle's mirth or moan,
>   In cold or sunny clime.
>
> Praise to the bard! his words are driven,
>   Like flower-seeds by the far winds sown,
> Where'er, beneath the sky of heaven,
>   The birds of fame have flown."

Halleck.[52]

Mr. President, and Gentlemen: I do not know by what untoward accident it has chanced, and I forbear to inquire, that, in this accomplished circle, it should fall to me, the worst Scotsman of all, to receive your commands, and at the latest hour too, to respond to the sentiment just offered, and which indeed makes the occasion. But I am told there is no appeal, and I must trust to the inspirations of the theme to make a fitness which does not otherwise exist. Yet, Sir, I heartily feel the singular claims of the occasion. At the first announcement, from I know not whence, that the 25th of January was the hundredth anniversary of the birth of Robert Burns, a sudden consent warmed the great English race, in all its kingdoms, colonies and states, all over the world, to keep the festival. We are here to hold our parliament with love and poesy, as men were wont to do in the Middle Ages. Those famous parliaments might or might not have had more stateliness and better singers than we,—though that is yet to be known,—but they could not have better reason. I can only explain this singular unanimity in a race which rarely acts together, but rather after their watchword, Each for himself,—by the fact that Robert Burns, the poet of the middle class, represents in the mind of men to-day that great uprising of the middle class against the armed and privileged minorities, that uprising which worked politically in the American and French Revolutions, and which, not in governments so much as in education and social order, has changed the face of the world.

In order for this destiny, his birth, breeding and fortunes were low. His organic sentiment was absolute independence, and resting as it should on a life of labor. No man existed who could look down on him. They that looked into his eyes saw that they might look down the sky as easily. His muse and teaching was common sense, joyful, aggressive, irresistible. Not Latimer, nor Luther struck more telling blows against false theology than did this brave singer. The Confession of Augsburg, the Declaration of Independence, the French Rights of Man, and the Marseillaise, are not more weighty documents in the history of freedom than the songs of Burns. His satire has lost none of its edge. His musical arrows yet sing through the air. He is so substantially a reformer that I find his grand plain sense in close chain with the greatest masters,—Rabelais, Shakspeare in comedy, Cervantes, Butler, and Burns. If I should add another name, I find it only in a living countryman of Burns [i.e., Thomas Carlyle].

He is an exceptional genius. The people who care nothing for literature and poetry care for Burns. It was indifferent—they thought who saw him—whether he wrote verse or not: he could have done anything else as well. Yet how true a poet is he! And the poet, too, of poor men, of gray hodden and the guernsey coat and the blouse. He has given voice to all the experiences of common life; he has endeared the farmhouse and cottage, patches and poverty, beans and barley; ale, the poor man's wine; hardship; the fear of debt; the dear society of weans and wife, of brothers and sisters, proud of each other, knowing so few and finding amends for want and obscurity in books and thoughts. What a love of Nature, and, shall I say it? of middle-class Nature. Not like Goethe, in the stars, or like Byron, in the ocean, or Moore, in the luxurious East; but in the homely landscape which the poor see around them,—bleak leagues of pasture and stubble, ice and sleet and rain and snow-choked brooks; birds, hares, field-mice, thistles and heather, which he daily knew. How many "Bonny Doons" and "John Anderson my jo's" and "Auld lang synes" all around the earth have his verses been applied to! And his love-songs still woo and melt the youths and maids; the farm-work, the country holiday, the fishing-cobble are still his debtors to-day.

And as he was thus the poet of the poor, anxious, cheerful, working humanity, so had he the language of low life. He grew up in a rural district, speaking a *patois* unintelligible to all but natives, and he has made the Lowland Scotch a Doric dialect of fame. It is the only example in history of a language made classic by the genius of a single man. But more than this. He had that secret of genius to draw from the bottom of society the strength of its speech, and astonish the ears of the polite with these artless words, better than art, and filtered of all offence through his beauty. It seemed odious to Luther that the devil should have all the best tunes; he would bring them into the churches; and Burns knew how to take from fairs and gypsies, black-smiths and drovers, the speech of the market and street, and clothe it with melody. But I am detaining you too long. The memory of Burns,—I am afraid heaven and earth have taken too good care of it to leave us anything to say. The west winds are murmuring it. Open the windows behind you, and hearken for the incoming tide, what the waves say of it. The doves perching always on the eaves of the Stone Chapel opposite, may know something about it. Every name in broad Scotland keeps his fame bright. The memory of Burns,—every man's, every boy's and girl's head carries snatches of his songs, and they say them by heart, and, what is strangest of all, never learned them from a book, but from mouth to mouth. The wind whispers them, the birds whistle them, the corn, barley, and bulrushes hoarsely rustle them, nay, the music-boxes at Geneva are framed and toothed to play them; the hand-organs of the Savoyards in all cities repeat them, and the chimes of bells ring them in the spires. They are the property and the solace of mankind.

From "Robert Burns," *Miscellanies*, *W* 11:436–43; from speech (25 January 1853).

Byron

Beginning in 1818 and through the early 1820s Emerson read most of Byron's poetry, probably aware of the controversy over Byron in the literary reviews. In 1821 Emerson found "Manfred" a "sublime dramatic poem" and in 1822 he thought Byron's "intensity of feeling" and "impassioned earnestness" praiseworthy and his heroes no longer vicious but of "redeeming gentle affections." But in 1823–24 he deplored "the profligate Byron" and repudiated Don Juan as a breaker of moral law and Byron's poetry as a poisonous influence. In his 1836 lecture, from which these excerpts are drawn, a favorable judgment is supported by examples of Byron's lyrical flow and true sentiment. But while praising the purity and power of Byron's language, Emerson deplored the pride, the selfishness, and the malevolent and morbid feelings expressed. Thereafter, Emerson limited his occasional comments on Byron to a paragraph, as in "Thoughts on Modern Literature," where the "Feeling of the Infinite" is said to predominate in Byron, though in him it is blind. In the journal of 1846 (J 7:163; JMN 9:376) appears Emerson's most severe transcendental judgment: "Byron is no poet: what did he know of the world and its law and Lawgiver?" In the 1874 Preface to Parnassus, Byron's verses, though felicitous and musical, are judged wanting in "solid knowledge" and "lofty aims"—essentially the same criticism as in 1836. Yet the choice of thirty-three of Byron's poems for Parnassus is itself a high tribute.

Lord Byron's genius attracted so much attention a few years since, that the ear is almost weary of the topic, and the more so that men begin to feel that his claims to a permanent popularity are more than dubious.

He owed his strong popularity to something. Certainly his knowledge is very little; his truth of sentiment very little; his taste was just; his power of language and that peculiar gift of making it flexible to all the compass and variety of his emotion without ever marring the purity of his diction, is as remarkable in him as in any English writer since Dryden. No structure of verse seemed laborious to him. How perfect is the flow in the difficult stanza of Childe Harold. He could not speak more simply in prose:

> I twine
> My hopes of being remembered in my line
> With my land's language if too fond and far
> These aspirations in their scope incline
> If my fame should be as my fortunes are
> Of hasty growth and blight and dull oblivion bar
>
> My name from out the temple where the dead
> Are honored by the nations let it be
> And light the laurels on a loftier head
> And be the Spartan's epitaph on me
> Sparta hath many a worthier son than he.
>
> [*Childe Harold*, 4:9–10]

This power of language is a very compound faculty and involving as it does a certain facility of association is one of the rarest and best gifts of the poet. But in Byron, as if merely from moral faults, from the pride and selfishness which made him an incurious observer, it was hindered of its use, it lacked food. Instead of marrying his Muse to Nature after the ordination of God, he sought to make words and emotions suffice alone, until our interest dies of a famine of meaning. We must try his pretensions by the old and stern interrogatories of higher literature.

What faculties does he excite? What feelings does he awaken? What impressions does he leave? The malevolent feelings certainly have their interest and their place in poetry but only for a short time or in company with and under the counteraction of others. Volumes upon volumes of morbid emotion disgust.

    Cursing will soon be sufficient in the most skilful variety of diction. Yet several of his [poems are] little else. I know no more signal example of failure from this cause than in the celebrated imprecation in the Fourth Canto of Childe Harold which begun and continued with great magniloquence ends in utter nonsense, not from the fault of the writer who is certainly a great genius but from the poverty of thought. When a man knows nothing let him say nothing. Occasionally, he utters a true and natural sentiment; as in that burst of bitter remembrance in which the spirit of beauty and youth seem to return upon us:

> No more no more oh never more on me
> The freshness of the heart can fall like dew
> Which out of all the lovely things we see
> Extracts emotions beautiful and new
> Hived in our bosoms like the bag o' the bee
> Think'st thou the honey with those objects grew
> Alas 'twas not in them but in thy power
> To double even the sweetness of a flower
>
> No more no more oh never more my heart
> Canst thou be my sole world my universe
> Once all in all but now a thing apart
> Thou canst not be my blessing or my curse
> The illusion's gone forever.

[Don Juan, 1:214–15]

    The fourth Canto of Childe Harold surpasses his earlier productions and he had made some improvement in his knowledge by his travels so that he had at last another subject than himself, and that Canto is the best guidebook to the traveller who visits Venice, Florence, and Rome.[53]

    I think the Island one of the most pleasing of his poems; but how painful is it to feel on looking back at the writings of one who should have been a clear and beneficent genius to guide and cheer human nature the emotions which a gang of pirates and convicts suggest.

Excerpted from "Modern Aspects of Letters," EL 1:372–74, lecture (1836).

Shelley

From his earliest Journals *comment, incorporated in "Thoughts on Modern Literature" (1840), through the later comments here, Emerson's view of Shelley as poet remained largely unchanged. Shelley, he recognized, was "clearly modern," a man of his age, a "man of aspiration" and of "heroic character." He shares with Wordsworth and others "the feeling of the Infinite." But, despite his poetic mind and his imagination, he is "never a poet . . . all his lines are arbitrary, not necessary." By comparison, "Keats* had *poetic genius." In* Parnassus, *Emerson reprinted "The Cloud" and "To a Skylark," the only exceptions to the negative judgment above. Although puzzled and surprised at the wide acceptance of Shelley's poetry, Emerson attempts no analysis of his verse, making only one lecture comment, the paragraph in "Thoughts" (see Part IV).*

1841

The Age. Shelley is wholly unaffecting to me. I was born a little too soon: but his power is so manifest over a large class of the best persons, that he is not to be overlooked.

1842

Elizabeth Hoar says that Shelley is like shining sand; it always looks attractive and valuable, but, try never so many times, you cannot get anything good. And yet the mica-glitter will still remain after all.

1868

*   *   *

Meantime, the Critical Essays[54] not coming, it occurred that other copies might swim, if mine had lodged; I sent to an importer & was so fortunate as to procure a copy, which I have carefully read. The Analysis of Macaulay is excellent: The "Coleridge" painful, though I fear irrefutable. Yet he was so efficient a benefactor to that generation of which he had the teaching, that I think his merits understated. The

"Tennyson" is a magnificent statue,—the first adequate work of its kind,—his real traits & superiorities rightly shown.—But Shelley,—was he the poet? He was a man in whom the spirit of the Age was poured,—man of aspiration, heroic character; but poet? Excepting a few well known lines about a cloud & a skylark, I could never read one of his hundreds of pages, and, though surprised by your estimate, despair of a re-attempt. Keats *had* poetic genius, though I could well spare the whole Endymion. The doubt has crossed my mind once or twice, that your friendships hoodwink your dangerous eyes.

*   *   *

With great regard, yours,
R. W. Emerson

J. H. Stirling, Esq.

J 6:114–15 (cf. *JMN* 8:61). *J* 6:213 (cf. *JMN* 8:178). *L* 6:19.

Tennyson

Emerson owned Tennyson's Poems, Chiefly Lyrical *as early as 1831, obtained the 1833* Poems *while in England, and in 1838 tried unsuccessfully to have Tennyson's poems republished in the United States. In his journals, his comments range from delight to distrust. In 1842 the* Dial *published Emerson's review of Tennyson's* Poems. *Although appreciably longer than any other of Emerson's commentaries on Tennyson, it is omitted here, being no better than the standard fare of the day. Emerson is satisfied to praise and illustrate Tennyson's "gorgeous music" and "picturesque representation," his "serene wisdom," "simplicity," "grace," and "nobleness and individuality of thoughts." In the following year, in "Europe and European Books," after the usual tribute to Tennyson's elegance, wit, felicity, and rhythmic power and variety, Emerson complained of the lack of "rude truth." Tennyson is "too fine . . . we have no right to such superfineness." In "The Poet" the passage on "a recent writer of lyrics" (W 3:9) probably refers to Tennyson as an example of one whose technical skill is primary, argument (idea or meaning) secondary. In 1859, however, after read-ing* Idylls of the King, *he tossed aside all reservations: "At last in Tennyson, a national soul comes to the Olympic games" and triumphs by completing the "Arthur Epic" begun by Chaucer.*

1838

I have read the second volume of poems [*Poems*, 1832] by Tenny-son, with like delight to that I found in the first and with like criticism. Drenched he is in Shakspear, born, baptized and bred in Shakspear, yet has his own humor, and original rhythm, music and images. How ring his humorsome lines in the ear,—

> "In the afternoon they came unto a land
> In which it seemèd always afternoon."[55]

The Old Year's Death[56] pleases me most. But why I speak of him now is because he had a line or two that looked like the moral strain amaranthine I spake of.

1855

Then what to say of Tennyson? When I read "Maud" then I say, Here is one of those English heads again such as in the Elizabethan days were rammed full of delightful fancies. What colouring like Titian, colour like the dawn.

1859

Tennyson. England is solvent, no matter what rubbish and hypoc-risy of Palmerstons and Malmesburys and Disraelis she may have, for here comes Tennyson's poem [first four of the *Idylls of the King*], indi-cating a supreme social culture, a perfect insight, and the posses-sion of all the weapons and all the functions of a man, with the skill to wield them which Homer, Aristophanes, or Dante had. The long promise to pay that runs over Ages from Chaucer, Spenser, Milton, Ben Jonson,—the long promise to write the national poem of Arthur, Tennyson at last keeps, in these low self-despising times; Taliessin and Ossian are at last edited, revised, expurgated, distilled. The national poem needed a national man. And the blood is still so rich, and healthful, that at last in Tennyson, a national soul comes to the

Olympic games,—equal to the task. He is the Pisistratus, who collects and publishes the Homer, ripened at last by the infusion of so many harvests, and henceforth unchangeable and immortal.

A collection there should be of those fables which are agreeable to the human mind. One is the orator or singer who can control all minds. The Perfect Poet again is described in Taliessin's *Songs*, in the *Mabinogion*. Tennyson has drawn Merlin.

England forever! What a secular genius is that which begins its purpose of writing the Arthur Epic with Chaucer, and slowly ripens it until now, in 1859, it is done! And what a heart-whole race is that which in the same year can turn out two such sovereign productions as the *History of Frederick*, and *The Four Idylls*.

Channing's remark is that there is a prose tone running through the book, and certainly he has flat lines, e.g., the four lines, "Forgetful of his promise to the King," etc., which contrasts badly with a similar iteration in Shakspeare's *Henry VI*, the dying soliloquy of Warwick, which is alive.[57]

But he has known how to universalize his fable and fill it with his experience and wisdom. The eternal moral shines. But what landscape, and what words!—"the stammering thunder."

January 1, 1870

Tennyson's Saint Grail.[58] Tennyson has abundant invention, but contents himself with the just enough; is never obscure or harsh in a new or rare word. Then he has marked virility, as if a surgeon or practical physiologist had no secrets to teach him, but he deals with these as Abraham or Moses would, and without prudery or pruriency. His inventions are adequate to the dignity of the fable. The gift of adequate expression is his; [Bacchic phrensy in *Maud*. A nightingale drunken with his overflowing melody, an animal heat in the verse, and its opulent continuations.] The priest is astonished to find a holiness in this knight-errant which he himself never knew, and rubs his eyes. The fine invention of Tennyson is in crowding into an hour the slow creations and destructions of centuries. It suggests besides, in the coming and vanishing of cities and temples, what really befalls in long durations on earth. How science of Ethnology limps after these enchantments! Miracles of cities and temples made by Merlin, like thoughts.

What I wrote on the last leaf concerning Tennyson is due perhaps to the first reading,—to the new wine of his imagination,—and I may not enjoy it, or rate it so highly again.

October 1871
The only limit to the praise of Tennyson as a lyric poet is, that he is alive. If he were an ancient, there would be none.

J 4:411–12 (cf. *JMN* 5:463). *J* 6:218 (cf. *JMN* 13:404–5). *J* 9:207–9 (cf. *JMN* 14:287–89). *J* 10:240–41.

Wordsworth

It has been said that "Coleridge touched Emerson's intellect. . . . Wordsworth touched his soul," and that from Coleridge Emerson learned the art of literary criticism, from Wordsworth the art of lyric poetry.[59] Initially, however, Emerson undervalued Wordsworth, as did others; not until 1828–29, when he reread him, did Emerson cautiously reconsider his view. Even so, though he had praised the "Immortality" ode for its latent Platonism in 1826, in 1828 he faulted Wordsworth for being too direct in his treatment of poetic subjects, and in 1832 referred to him as "a genius that hath epilepsy, a deranged angel." In 1831 he praised "Ode to Duty," among several poems by Wordsworth; in 1832 he felt that poem and "Tintern Abbey" to be seriously flawed in language. The 1833 visit with Wordsworth is reprinted here as a commentary on the poet, the man, and his "very narrow and English mind." Most memorable were Wordsworth's opinions of America, Goethe, Carlyle, and Coleridge, and his comments on and recitation of his own poems. From 1833 to 1836, Emerson's views continued mixed, with occasional outbursts crowning Wordsworth as "a divine man," a true genius, a "divine savage," and "the great philosophical poet of the present day" (EL 1:140), once rating Wordsworth as "a more original poet" than Milton (JMN 4:312–13). In 1837 he listed his choice of Wordsworth's best poems from the years 1798 to 1820, omitting "The Prelude," not available in full until 1850. "Modern Literature" (1840) singles out "The Excursion," especially the passage on the boy in Book I, as a source of "great joy" . . . in its

*"right feeling" for nature; otherwise, "the poem as a whole was dull." Words-
worth's "wisdom of humanity" ranks him with Shakespeare and Milton. In
"Europe and European Books" (1843), despite a lack of "deft poetic execution,"
Wordsworth is praised for his moral perception, the power of his diction, his
insight into the beauty of the commonplace, and for being the critic and conscience
of his time. The 1855 account of his second visit with Wordsworth in 1848,
while regretting the lack of grace and scope in the poems, expresses admiration for
his plain living, his consistent adherence to his revolution in poetic language, and
his "Ode on Immortality" as "the high-water mark which the intellect has
reached in this age" (see W 5:294–98 and JMN 14:99). That sentiment is
echoed in the lecture excerpt printed here, where this ode is called "the best
modern essay on the subject" of immortality, as well as in the 1874 Preface to*
Parnassus. *Despite the fifty-year history of the influence of this ode on Emerson,
one finds no extended criticism of it by him, nor any record of his "reading" of
"The Prelude," which he described as "a poetical pamphlet; though proceeding
from a new & genuine experience" (see JMN 14:202), nor any essay or lecture
on Wordsworth comparable to those pieces on Goethe, Milton, and Shakespeare.*

1828

A fault that strikes the readers of Mr. Wordsworth is the direct
pragmatical analysis of objects, in their nature *poetic*, but which all
other poets touch incidentally. He mauls the moon and the waters
and the bulrushes, as his main business. Milton and Shakspeare
touch them gently, as illustrations or ornament. Beds of flowers send
up a most grateful scent to the passenger who hastens by them, but let
him pitch his tent among them and he will find himself grown
insensible to their fragrance. And it must have occurred frequently to
our reader that brilliant moonlight will not bear acquaintance.
Nothing is more glorious than the full moon to those who ride or walk
under its beams. But whoso goes out of doors expressly to see it returns
disappointed. Mr. Wordsworth is a poet with the same error that
wasted the genius of the alchemists and astrologers of the Middle
Age. These attempted to extort by direct means the principle of life,
the secret substance of matter from material things; and those to
extract intelligence from remoter nature, instead of observing that
science is ever approximating to truth by dint of application to
present wants, and not by search after general and recondite Truth.

Mr. Wordsworth is trying to distil the essence of poetry from poetic things, instead of being satisfied to adorn common scenes with such lights from these sources of poetry as nature will always furnish to her true lovers. We feel the same sort of regret that is occasioned when Aristotle forsakes the Laws of the Intellect and the Principles of Ethics for researches into the nature of mind.

> "The man who shows his heart
> Is hooted for his nudities, and scorned."
>
> Young[60]

There's a great difference between good poetry and everlasting poetry.

December 1, 1832

I never read Wordsworth without chagrin; a man of such great powers and ambition, so near to the *Dii majores*, to fail so meanly in every attempt! A genius that hath epilepsy, a deranged archangel. The Ode to Duty, conceived and expressed in a certain high, severe style, does yet miss of greatness and of all effect by such falsities or falses as,

> "And the most ancient heavens thro' thee are fresh
> and strong,"

which is throwing dust in your eyes, because they have no more to do with duty than a dung-cart has. So that fine promising passage about "the mountain winds being free to blow upon thee," etc., flats out into "*me and my bendictions.*" If he had cut in his Dictionary for words, he could hardly have got worse.

On the 28th August [1833] I went to Rydal Mount, to pay my respects to Mr. Wordsworth. His daughters called in their father, a plain, elderly, white-haired man, not prepossessing, and disfigured by green goggles. He sat down, and talked with great simplicity. He had just returned from a journey. His health was good, but he had broken a tooth by a fall, when walking with two lawyers, and had said that he was glad it did not happen forty years ago; whereupon they had praised his philosophy.

He had much to say of America, the more that it gave occasion for his favorite topic,— that society is being enlightened by a superficial tuition [teaching or custom], out of all proportion to its being restrained by moral culture. Schools do no good. Tuition is not education. He thinks more of the education of circumstances than of tuition. 'T is not question whether there are offences of which the law takes cognizance, but whether there are offences of which the law does not take cognizance. Sin is what he fears,—and how society is to escape without gravest mischiefs from this source. He has even said, what seemed a paradox, that they needed a civil war in America, to teach the necessity of knitting the social ties stronger. "There may be," he said, "in America some vulgarity in manner, but that's not important. That comes of the pioneer state of things. But I fear they are too much given to the making of money; and secondly, to politics; that they make political distinction the end and not the means. And I fear they lack a class of men of leisure,—in short, of gentlemen,—to give a tone of honor to the community. I am told that things are boasted of in the second class of society there, which, in England,— God knows, are done in England every day, but would never be spoken of. In America I wish to know not how many churches or schools, but what newspapers? My friend Colonel Hamilton, at the foot of the hill, who was a year in America, assures me that the newspapers are atrocious, and accuse members of Congress of stealing spoons!" He was against taking off the tax on newspapers in England,—which the reformers represent as a tax upon knowledge,—for this reason, that they would be inundated with base prints. He said he talked on political aspects, for he wished to impress on me and all good Americans to cultivate the moral, the conservative, etc., etc., and never to call into action the physical strength of the people, as had just now been done in England in the Reform Bill,—a thing prophesied by Delolme.[61] He alluded once or twice to his conversation with Dr. Channing,[62] who had recently visited him (laying his hand on a particular chair in which the Doctor had sat).

The conversation turned on books. Lucretius he esteems a far higher poet than Virgil; not in his system, which is nothing, but in his power of illustration. Faith is necessary to explain anything and to reconcile the foreknowledge of God with human evil. Of Cousin[63] (whose lectures we had all been reading in Boston), he knew only the name.

I inquired if he had read Carlyle's critical articles and translations. He said he thought him sometimes insane. He proceeded to abuse Goethe's Wilhelm Meister heartily. It was full of all manner of fornication. It was like the crossing of flies in the air. He had never gone farther than the first part; so disgusted was he that he threw the book across the room. I deprecated this wrath, and said what I could for the better parts of the book, and he courteously promised to look at it again. Carlyle he said wrote most obscurely. He was clever and deep, but he defied the sympathies of every body. Even Mr. Coleridge wrote more clearly, though he had always wished Coleridge would write more to be understood. He led me out into his garden, and showed me the gravel walk in which thousands of his lines were composed. His eyes are much inflamed. This is no loss except for reading, because he never writes prose, and of poetry he carries even hundreds of lines in his head before writing them. He had just returned from a visit to Staffa, and within three days had made three sonnets on Fingal's Cave,[64] and was composing a fourth when he was called in to see me. He said, "If you are interested in my verses perhaps you will like to hear these lines." I gladly assented, and he recollected himself for a few moments and then stood forth and repeated, one after the other, the three entire sonnets with great animation. I fancied the second and third more beautiful than his poems are wont to be. The third is addressed to the flowers, which, he said, especially the ox-eye daisy, are very abundant on the top of the rock. The second alludes to the name of the cave, which is "Cave of Music;" the first to the circumstance of its being visited by the promiscuous company of the steamboat.

This recitation was so unlooked for and surprising,—he, the old Wordsworth, standing apart, and reciting to me in a garden-walk, like a school-boy declaiming,—that I at first was near to laugh; but recollecting myself, that I had come thus far to see a poet and he was chanting poems to me, I saw that he was right and I was wrong, and gladly gave myself up to hear. I told him how much the few printed extracts had quickened the desire to possess his unpublished poems. He replied he never was in haste to publish; partly because he corrected a good deal, and every alteration is ungraciously received after printing; but what he had written would be printed, whether he lived or died. I said Tintern Abbey appeared to be the favorite poem with the public, but more contemplative readers preferred the first books of the Excursion, and the Sonnets. He said, "Yes, they are better." He preferred such of his poems as touched the affections, to any others; for whatever is didactic—what theories of society, and so on—might perish quickly; but whatever combined a truth with an affection was κτῆμα ἐς ἀεί [a gain forever], good to-day and good forever. He cited the sonnet, On the feelings of a highminded Spaniard, which he preferred to any other (I so understood him), and the Two Voices;[65] and quoted, with evident pleasure, the verses addressed To the Sky-lark. In this connection he said of the Newtonian theory that it might yet be superseded and forgotten; and Dalton's atomic theory.

When I prepared to depart he said he wished to show me what a common person in England could do, and he led me into the enclosure of his clerk, a young man to whom he had given this slip of ground, which was laid out, or its natural capabilities shown, with much taste. He then said he would show me a better way towards the inn; and he walked a good part of a mile, talking and ever and anon stopping short to impress the word or the verse, and finally parted from me with great kindness and returned across the fields.

Wordsworth honored himself by his simple adherence to truth, and was very willing not to shine; but he surprised by the hard limits of his thought. To judge from a single conversation, he made the impression of a narrow and very English mind; of one who paid for his rare elevation by general tameness and conformity. Off his own beat, his opinions were of no value. It is not very rare to find persons of loving sympathy and ease, who expiate their departure from the common in one direction, by their conformity in every other.

October 21, 1835

It is the comfort I have in taking up those new poems of Words-worth,[66] that I am sure here to find thoughts in harmony with the great frame of Nature, the placid aspect of the Universe. I may find dulness and flatness, but I shall not find meanness and error.

October 22, 1835

What platitudes I find in Wordsworth!

"I, poet, bestow my verse
On this and this and this."

Scarce has he dropped the smallest piece of an egg, when he fills the barnyard with his cackle.

May 25, 1837

"My dear sir, clear your mind of cant," said Dr. Johnson. Wordsworth, whom I read last night, is garrulous and weak often, but quite free from cant. I think I could easily make a small selection from his volumes which should contain all their poetry. It would take Fidelity, Tintern Abbey, Cumberland Beggar, Ode to Duty, September, The Force of Prayer, Lycoris, Lines on the Death of Fox, Dion, Happy Warrior, Laodamia, the Ode.

* * *

I mean that I am a better believer, and all serious souls are better believers in the immortality, than we can give grounds for. The real evidence is too subtle, or is higher than we can write down in propositions, and therefore Wordsworth's Ode is the best modern essay on the subject.

* * *

J 2:232–33 (cf. *JMN* 3:39–40). *J* 3:534–35 (cf. *JMN* 4:63). Excerpted from "First Visit to England," in *English Traits*, *W* 5:19–24; first published in *English Traits* (1856). *J* 3:560 (cf. *JMN* 5:99). *J* 3:561 (cf. *JMN* 5:100). *J* 4:246 (cf. *JMN* 5:335). Excerpted from "Immortality," in *Letters and Social Aims*, *W* 8:346; first published in *Letters and Social Aims* (1883); from lecture (1861).

Carlyle

The rhetorical style of Carlyle's essays and histories left Emerson both wonder-struck and disturbed, as illustrated by his comments in "Diction and Style" (Part III above). Emerson read Carlyle's essays as early as 1827, when they were published anonymously. Carlyle was unknown in the United States until 1829, when his translation of Goethe's Wilhelm Meister *appeared. As described in* English Traits, *Emerson's first visit with Carlyle and his wife was a delightful one. In 1834 he found inspiring the "divine pages" of* Sartor Resartus *by the "fantastical Scotchman," whom in 1835 he called "the best thinker of his age." The following selection is the first part of a letter thanking Carlyle for a gift copy of* The French Revolution, *which Emerson hails with an intensity, verve, and tone not unlike Carlyle's own. Broad strokes sketch the qualities of the work—its energy, style, interest ("Gothically efflorescent"), its embodiment of "a mind," and "the copresence of Humanity." By comparison, Emerson's review of the same work in the* Christian Examiner, *January 1838, seems pallid.[67] In 1840 Emerson confided to his journal that although "every history . . . will be indebted to him," the writing of Carlyle is so powerfully descriptive it leaves nothing to suggestion. This dual criticism rings out again and again in the journals. After 1837 Emerson stopped trying to reform Carlyle's style; instead, he concluded that Carlyle was a manly and heroic individualist, but not an intellect or philosopher (see* W 5:15–18, 249–50; 10:487–98). *In 1843* Past and Present *was praised not only for its style but also as a work of "honest" and "brave" criticism, based as it was on the assumption that "the dynasty of labor is replacing the old nobilities . . . a remarkable book . . . full of treason" (*W 12:379–91). *In his remarks on the* History of Frederick the Great *in 1859, Emerson again lauded the "colloquially elastic" rhetoric and the revolution in history writing, an appreciation confirmed in 1865 (*W 12:297–99; *see also "Art and Criticism" in Part III;* J 10:122–23).*

Concord
13 September, 1837

My dear friend,

Such a gift as the French Revolution demanded a speedier acknowledgement. But you mountaineers that can scale Andes before breakfast for an airing, have no measures for the performance of lowlanders & valetudinarians. I am ashamed to think & will not tell what little things have kept me silent.

The "French Revolution" did not reach me until three weeks ago, having had at least two long pauses by the way, as I find, since landing. Between many visits received & some literary haranguing done, I have read two volumes & half the third: and I think you a very good giant; disporting yourself with an original & vast ambition of fun; pleasure & peace not being strong enough for you, you choose to suck pain also, & teach fever & famine to dance & sing. I think you have written a wonderful book which will last a very long time. I see that you have created a history, which the world will own to be such. You have recognized the existence of other persons than officers & of other relations than civism. You have broken away from all books, & written a mind. It is a brave experiment & the success is great. We have men in your story & not names merely; always men, though I may doubt sometimes whether I have the historic men. We have great facts—and selected facts—truly set down. We have always the co-presence of Humanity along with the imperfect damaged individuals. The soul's right of Wonder is still left to us; and we have righteous praise & doom awarded, assuredly without cant: yes comfort your self on that particular, O ungodliest divine man! Thou cantest never. Finally, we have not—a dull word. Never was there a style so rapid as yours—which no reader can outrun; and so it is for the most intelligent. I suppose nothing will astonish more than the audacious wit of cheerfulness which no tragedy & no magnitude of events can overpower or daunt. Henry VIII loved a Man,[68] and I see with joy my bard always equal to the crisis he re-presents. And so I thank you for your labor, and feel that your cotemporaries ought to say, All hail, Brother! live forever; not only in the great Soul which thou largely inhalest, but also as a named person in this thy definite deed.

I will tell you more of the book when I have once got it at focal distance—if that can ever be, and muster my objections when I am sure of their ground. I insist, of course, that it might be more simple, less Gothically efflorescent. You will say no rules for the illumination of windows can apply to the aurora borealis. However, I find refreshment when every now & then a special fact slips into the narrative couched in sharp business like terms. This character-drawing in the book is certainly admirable; the lines are ploughed furrows; but there was cake & ale before, though thou be virtuous.[69] Clarendon surely drew sharp outlines for me in Falkland, Hampden, & the rest, without defiance or skyvaulting.[70] I wish I could talk with you face to face for one day & know what your uttermost frankness would say concerning the book.

* * *

CEC, pp. 166–68.

Coleridge

Although brief comments on Coleridge are scattered throughout Emerson's works, none contains a more considered or more substantial appreciation than these pages from an early lecture. To Emerson, Coleridge is less a poet than a thinker and critic, especially in this tribute summarizing his achievement as a Platonist philosopher and as a social, moral, intellectual, and literary critic of the first rank. Neither his aristocratic views nor "his excessive bigotry toward the Constitution of the Church of England" diminished his great accomplishments in poetry, criticism, and philosophy, so Emerson maintains. (A similar but briefer comment appears in J 4:152; JMN 5:252). Emerson's first visit with Coleridge (1833) is described in English Traits (W 5:10–14). The Preface to Parnassus makes no reference to Coleridge's poetry—surely an oversight—and only "Kubla Khan" and a few minor verses are anthologized.

The grave has only recently received the body of Samuel Taylor Coleridge, a man whose memory may comfort the philanthropist as he showed genius and depth of thought to be still possible which but for this solitary scholar we might think not genial and native to our age.

It is very certain that Coleridge was not popular in his lifetime. That fact certainly warrants the charge we make upon the times, of superficialness or deficiency of interest in profound inquiries, though it does not at all affect him. He was a person of great reading and a passion for learning that made him a profound scholar in books of a philosophical character, though his learning certainly was not of that robust and universal character as that of the famous scholars of England such as Bentley[71] and Gibbon. It was a lake that had some flats, and some fathomless places, and not one whose waters were everywhere overhead. His interest in all sciences was equal. He was of that class of philosophers called Platonists, that is, of the most Universal school; of that class that take the most enlarged and reverent views of man's nature. His eye was fixed upon Man's Reason as the faculty in which the very Godhead manifested itself or the Word was anew made flesh. His reverence for the Divine Reason was truly philosophical and made him regard every man as the most sacred object in the Universe, the Temple of Deity. An aristocrat in his politics, this most republican of all principles secured his unaffected interest in lowly and despised men the moment a religious sentiment or a philosophical principle appeared. Witness his reverential remembrance of George Fox; Behme; De Thoyras;[72] of his poor miner; his private soldier of the Parliament, from whom he drew the sublime passage in the Friend; and of so many of his poetic persons.[73]

His true merit undoubtedly is not that of a philosopher or of a poet but a critic. I think the biography of Coleridge is written in that sentence of Plato, "He shall be as a god to me who shall rightly define and divide."[74] He possessed extreme subtlety of discrimination; and of language he was a living dictionary, surpassing all men in the fineness of distinctions he could indicate, touching his mark with a needle's point.

And that is the most valuable work he has done for his contemporaries and for all who hereafter shall read the English tongue, that he has taken a survey of the moral, intellectual, and social world as it interests us at this day, and has selected a great number of conspicuous points therein and has set himself to fix their true position and bearings.

He has made admirable definitions, and drawn indelible lines of distinction between things heretofore confounded. He thought and thought truly that all confusion of thought tended to confusion in action; and said that he had never observed an abuse of terms obtain currency without being followed by some practical error. He has enriched the English language and the English mind with an explanation of the object of Philosophy; of the all-important distinction between Reason and Understanding; the distinction of an Idea and a Conception; between Genius and Talent; between Fancy and Imagination; of the nature and end of Poetry; of the Idea of a State.[75]

But what definitions and distinctions are these to the reader of his fervent page? How unlike the defining of school logic and formal metaphysicians! Out of every one of his distinctions comes life and heat. They light the road of common duty: they arm the working hand with skill. They fill the mind with emotions of awe and delight at the perception of its own depth. Take the single example of the distinction so scientifically drawn by him between Reason and Understanding. We do not read the popular writers of our own day, those I mean of the best class in this country, without seeing what confusion of thought the study of this one subject would have saved them, and that with his theory of Reason he could not fail to impart to them his own sublime confidence in Man.

In like manner, his singular book called Biographia Literaria, or his own literary life and opinions, is undoubtedly the best body of criticism in the English language. Nay for the importance and variety of the questions treated; for the clearness with which the truth is pointed and the beauty that adorns the whole road,

> Pitching her tents before us as we walk
> An hourly neighbor,[76]

I do not know a book on criticism in any language to which a modern scholar can be so much indebted. His works are of very unequal interest; the Aids to Reflexion, though a useful book I suppose, is the least valuable. In his own judgment, half the Biography and the third volume of the Friend from the beginning of the Essay on Method to the end with a few of his poems were all that he would preserve of his works. In this judgment, if you add the invaluable little book called Church and State which was written afterwards, I suppose all good judges would concur.

The unpopularity of Coleridge during his lifetime is undoubtedly to be attributed very much to the abstruseness of the speculations in which he delighted and which tasked the intellect too sorely to be the favorite reading of the loungers in reading rooms. Undoubtedly his genius is disfigured by some faults which his critics were glad to lay hold on as reasons for dislike and contempt. He indulges much in expressions of censure and contempt at the low state of philosophical and ethical studies in England; and at the impatience of the public of any writings exacting severe thought; and especially at the arrogance and unscrupulousness of the periodical critical journals. As he had himself some private griefs to complain of, his lovers will always regret that he should have allowed the supercilious remarks upon his writings in the Reviews or the very limited circulation of his own books to affect his serenity. We feel that a man of his discernment should know that by the eternal law of Providence the Present and the Future are always rivals; he who writes for the wise alone writes for few at any one time and writing for eternity he does not write for the mixed throng that make up a nation today. Another fault with which he is taxed in this country is his excessive bigotry to the Constitution of the Church of England. This is so apparent and so separate from the general tendency and texture of his philosophy that it will never disturb the student who is accustomed to watch his moods of thought and will skip the unnecessary pages. But [the] disinterestedness with which he put behind him all the baits of lucre and pleasure, the heartiness of his patriotism, the manliness of his sympathy with all great and generous thoughts and actions, the piercing sight which made the world transparent to him, and the kindling eloquence with which both in speech and in writing this old man eloquent[ly] masters our minds and hearts promises him an enduring dominion.

But death hath now set his seal upon him, and already his true character and greatness begin to be felt. Already he quits the throng of his contemporaries and takes his lofty station in that circle of sages whom he loved: Heraclitus, Hermes, Plato, Giordano Bruno, St. Augustine.

Excerpted from "Modern Aspects of Letters," *EL* 1:377–80, lecture (1836).

Dickens

In 1839 the fictional appeal and social criticism of Oliver Twist *were lost on Emerson, for whom an "acute eye for costume" and other surfaces was hardly less negative a quality than the lack of insight into character. Three years later, he found* American Notes *readable, but false as a picture of American manners. Later still he came to see Dickens's criticism of American bad manners as needed and beneficial (* W *6:174) and his "humanity" as the intention of his work (* W *10:339).*

1839

I have read *Oliver Twist* in obedience to the opinions of so many intelligent people as have praised it. The author has an acute eye for costume; he sees the expression of dress, of form, of gait, of personal deformities; of furniture, of the outside and inside of houses; but his eye rests always on surfaces; he has no insight into character. For want of key to the moral powers the author is fain to strain all his stage trick of grimace, of bodily terror, of murder, and the most approved performances of Remorse. It all avails nothing, there is nothing memorable in the book except the *flash*, which is got at a police office, and the dancing of the madman which strikes a momentary terror. Like Cooper and Hawthorne he has no dramatic talent. The moment he attempts dialogue the improbability of life hardens to wood and stone. And the book begins and ends without a poetic ray, and so perishes in the reading.

November 25, 1842

Yesterday I read Dickens's *American Notes*. It answers its end very well, which plainly was to make a readable book, nothing more. Truth is not his object for a single instant, but merely to make good points in a lively sequence, and he proceeds very well. As an account of America it is not to be considered for a moment: it is too short, and too narrow, too superficial, and too ignorant, too slight, and too fabulous, and the man totally unequal to the work. A very lively rattle on that nuisance, a sea voyage, is the first chapter; and a pretty fair example of the historical truth of the whole book. We can hear throughout every page the dialogue between the author and his publisher,—"Mr. Dickens, the book must be entertaining—that is the essential point. Truth? Damn truth! I tell you, it must be entertaining." As a picture of American manners nothing can be falser. No such conversations ever occur in this country in real life, as he relates. He has picked up and noted with eagerness each odd local phrase that he met with, and, when he had a story to relate, has joined them together, so that the result is the broadest caricature; and the scene might as truly have been laid in Wales or in England as in the States. Monstrous exaggeration is an easy secret of romance. But Americans who, like some of us Massachusetts people, are not fond of spitting, will go from Maine to New Orleans, and meet no more annoyance than we should in Britain or France. So with "yes," so with "fixings," so with soap and towels; and all the other trivialities which this trifler detected in travelling over half the world. The book makes but a poor apology for its author, who certainly appears in no dignified or enviable position.

J 5:261 (cf. *JMN* 7:244–45). *J* 6:312 (cf. *JMN* 8:222–23).

Scott

Emerson always honored Scott the man and affectionately remembered his poems and novels, calling them "the delight of generous boys." In the two commentaries reprinted here, one early and one late, Emerson characteristically uses public speech for literary criticism by generalization, always with an eye for the generous observation and the democratic value. Of a dozen Scott works that he had read by 1825, he expressed enthusiasm for Lay of the Last Minstrel, Rokeby, The Abbott, Quentin Durward—*"a very respectable novel" —and especially* The Bride of Lammermoor. *By the late 1820s the novel seemed to him a second-rate genre and Scott "the grandpa of the grown-up children." The passage from the lecture of 1836 is largely negative in its view of Scott's imagination, dialogue, characters, and aim. The commemorative remarks of 1871, chiefly favorable, praise Scott's ballads for their effective use of social verse and the novels for their representation of the common people as well as aristocratic values. As a novel of fate,* The Bride of Lammermoor *is found comparable to a tragedy by Aeschylus.*

The debt of all the civilized world to Sir Walter Scott, [the] entertainment he has given to solitude, the relief to headache and heartache which he has furnished, make it ungrateful to speak of him but with cheerful respect. Though a very careless and incorrect writer he is always simple and unaffected. Strong sense never leaves him; his good nature is infinite; he has humor; he has fancy; and unsleeping observation. In the high and strict sense of Imagination he can scarcely be said to exercise that faculty. The Lear and Hamlet and Richard are sublime from themselves; Ravenswood and Meg Merrilies, Norna, only from situation and costume.[77] Jeanie Deans, Di Vernon, Burley, certainly have a degree of interest from character also, but it is not very deep and we do not remember anything they say. That in which he is unrivalled, is, the skill of combining dramatic situations of painful interest.

The dialogue, though far superior in natural grace and dignity to the tone of vulgar romances, is often quite artificial and pedantic. He rarely makes us shed a tear; but sometimes he does. The fate of Fergus, the devotion of Evan Maccombich, the trial of Effie Deans, I think must be admitted to be passages of genuine pathos.

If Scott is advanced from the crowd of his contemporaries and compared with the standard English authors, I apprehend, it will be found that he has done little for permanent literature. He has been content to amuse us. He has not aimed to teach. Let it not be said that this is not to be expected from the novelist. Truth will come from every writer, let the form be what it may, who writes in earnest. "Fictions have often been the vehicle of sublimest verities." What Scott has to contribute is not brought from deep places of the mind and of course cannot reach thither. Always we ought to hear sounding in our ears that first canon of criticism: "What comes from the heart that alone goes to the heart: what proceeds from a divine impulse that the Godlike alone can awaken."[78] The vice of his literary effort is that the whole structure was artificial. Scott is no lover or carer for absolute truth. The conventions of society are sufficient for him and he never pondered with the higher order of minds, Milton, Jonson, Wordsworth, De Stael, Rousseau, the enterprise of presenting a purer and truer system of social life. He was content instead to have an idol. His taste and humor happened to be taken with the ringing of old ballads and the shape and glitter and rust of old armor, and the turrets of old castles frowning among Scottish hills and he said, I will make these tricks of my fancy so great and so gay that for a time they shall take the attention of men like truths and things. By the force of talent he accomplished his purpose but the design was not natural and true and daily loses its interest as swarms of new writers appear.

Remarks at the Celebration by the Massachusetts Historical Society of the Centennial Anniversary of His Birth, August 15, 1871

SCOTT, the delight of generous boys.

As far as Sir Walter Scott aspired to be known for a fine gentleman, so far our sympathies leave him. . . . Our concern is only with the residue, where the man Scott was warmed with a divine ray that clad with beauty every sheet of water, every bald hill in the country he looked upon, and so reanimated the well-nigh obsolete feudal history and illustrated every hidden corner of a barren and disagreeable territory.

Lecture, "Being and Seeing," 1838.[79]

The memory of Sir Walter Scott is dear to this Society, of which he was for ten years an honorary member. If only as an eminent antiquary who has shed light on the history of Europe and of the English race, he had high claims to our regard. But to the rare tribute of a centennial anniversary of his birthday, which we gladly join with Scotland, and indeed with Europe, to keep, he is not less entitled—perhaps he alone among literary men of this century is entitled—by the exceptional debt which all English-speaking men have gladly owed to his character and genius. I think no modern writer has inspired his readers with such affection to his own personality. I can well remember as far back as when The Lord of the Isles was first republished in Boston, in 1815,—my own and my school-fellows' joy in the book. Marmion and The Lay[80] had gone before, but we were then learning to spell. In the face of the later novels, we still claim that his poetry is the delight of boys. But this means that when we reopen these old books we all consent to be boys again. We tread over our youthful grounds with joy. Critics have found them to be only rhymed prose. But I believe that many of those who read them in youth, when, later, they come to dismiss finally their school-days' library, will make some fond exception for Scott as for Byron.

It is easy to see the origin of his poems. His own ear had been charmed by old ballads crooned by Scottish dames at firesides, and written down from their lips by antiquaries; and finding them now outgrown and dishonored by the new culture, he attempted to dignify and adapt them to the times in which he lived. Just so much thought, so much picturesque detail in dialogue or description as the old ballad required, so much suppression of details and leaping to the event, he would keep and use, but without any ambition to write a high poem after a classic model. He made no pretension to the lofty style of Spenser, or Milton, or Wordsworth. Compared with their purified songs, purified of all ephemeral color or material, his were *vers de société*. But he had the skill proper to *vers de société*,—skill to fit his verse to his topic, and not to write solemn pentameters alike on a hero or a spaniel. His good sense probably elected the ballad to make his audience larger. He apprehended in advance the immense enlargement of the reading public, which almost dates from the era of his books,—which his books and Byron's inaugurated; and which, though until then unheard of, has become familiar to the present time.

If the success of his poems, however large, was partial, that of his novels was complete. The tone of strength in Waverley at once announced the master, and was more than justified by the superior genius of the following romances, up to the Bride of Lammermoor,[81] which almost goes back to Aeschylus for a counterpart as a painting of Fate,—leaving on every reader the impression of the highest and purest tragedy.

His power on the public mind rests on the singular union of two influences. By nature, by his reading and taste an aristocrat, in a time and country which easily gave him that bias, he had the virtues and graces of that class, and by his eminent humanity and his love of labor escaped its harm. He saw in the English Church the symbol and seal of all social order; in the historical aristocracy the benefits to the state which Burke claimed for it; and in his own reading and research such store of legend and renown as won his imagination to their cause. Not less his eminent humanity delighted in the sense and virtue and wit of the common people. In his own household and neighbors he found characters and pets of humble class, with whom he established the best relation,—small farmers and tradesmen, shepherds, fishermen, gypsies, peasant-girls, crones,—and came with these into real ties of mutual help and good will. From these originals he drew so genially his Jeanie Deans, his Dinmonts and Edie Ochiltrees, Caleb Balderstones and Fairservices, Cuddie Headriggs, Dominies, Meg Merrilies, and Jenny Rintherouts, full of life and reality; making these, too, the pivots on which the plots of his stories turn; and meantime without one word of brag of this discernment,—nay, this extreme sympathy reaching down to every beggar and beggar's dog, and horse and cow. In the number and variety of his characters he approaches Shakspeare. Other painters in verse or prose have thrown into literature a few type-figures, as Cervantes, De Foe, Richardson,

Goldsmith, Sterne and Fielding;[82] but Scott portrayed with equal strength and success every figure in his crowded company.

His strong good sense saved him from the faults and foibles incident to poets,—from nervous egotism, sham modesty or jealousy. He played ever a manly part. With such a fortune and such a genius, we should look to see what heavy toll the Fates took of him, as of Rousseau or Voltaire, of Swift or Byron. But no: he had no insanity, or vice, or blemish. He was a thoroughly upright, wise and great-hearted man, equal to whatever event or fortune should try him. Disasters only drove him to immense exertion. What an ornament and safeguard is humor! Far better than wit for a poet and writer. It is a genius itself, and so defends from the insanities.

Under what rare conjunction of stars was this man born, that, wherever he lived, he found superior men, passed all his life in the best company, and still found himself the best of the best! He was apprenticed at Edinburgh to a Writer to the Signet,[83] and became a Writer to the Signet, and found himself in his youth and manhood and age in the society of Mackintosh, Horner, Jeffrey, Playfair, Dugald Stewart, Sydney Smith, Leslie, Sir William Hamilton, Wilson, Hogg, De Quincey,[84]—to name only some of his literary neighbors, and, as soon as he died, all this brilliant circle was broken up.

Excerpted from "Modern Aspects of Letters," EL 1:375–76, lecture (1836). "Walter Scott," *Miscellanies*, W 11:461–67; speech (1871).

Margaret Fuller

From 1836 to 1846 Emerson came to know Margaret—seven years his junior—as a close friend, a person of deep feeling and good sense, a courageous thinker, a somewhat florid letter-writer, and a brilliant conversationalist, witty and entertaining, with a voice of "silver eloquence." At the time of her death in 1850, he composed a tribute to the talents and character of this "brave, eloquent, subtle, accomplished, devoted, constant soul!" (J 8:115–19; JMN 11:256–

60). The two chapters that he contributed to the Memoirs of Margaret Fuller Ossoli *(1852) again sympathetically described her character and intellect,
her correspondence and conversations, but neglected her major writings. As a
nature essayist she seemed deficient in observation and style. And, by modern standards, both Emerson and she underestimated her achievement in literary and
social criticism, especially her essays for the New York* Daily Tribune. *Her
writing did not seem to justify research into its consequences: "All that can be said,
is, that she represents an interesting hour and group in American cultivation; then,
that she was herself a fine, generous, inspiring, vinous, eloquent talker, who did
not outlive her influence"* (JMN *11:431–32). In contrast to Hawthorne's
intense dislike for Margaret Fuller, however, Emerson praised her as a guest (at
Brook Farm) whose "joyful conversation and large sympathy" and "rich and
brilliant genius" contrasted greatly with "the dismal mask which the public
fancied was meant for her in that disagreeable story"* (The Blithedale Romance), *which was "quite unworthy of his [Hawthorne's] genius"* (W *10:362,
364). The selection that follows represents Emerson at his best as a portrait
painter of the mind and character of an artist in temperament, tone, and language.*

1843

Margaret. A pure and purifying mind, self-purifying also, full of
faith in men, and inspiring it. Unable to find any companion great
enough to receive the rich effusions of her thought, so that her riches
are still unknown and seem unknowable. It is a great joy to find that
we have underrated our friend, that he or she is far more excellent
than we had thought. All natures seem poor beside one so rich, which
pours a stream of amber over all objects, clean and unclean, that lie
in its path, and makes that comely and presentable which was mean
in itself. We are taught by her plenty how lifeless and outward we
were, what poor Laplanders burrowing under the snows of prudence
and pedantry. Beside her friendship, other friendships seem trade,
and by the firmness with which she treads her upward path, all
mortals are convinced that another road exists than that which their
feet know. The wonderful generosity of her sentiments pours a contempt on books and writing at the very time when one asks how shall
this fiery picture be kept in its glow and variety for other eyes. She
excels other intellectual persons in this, that her sentiments are more
blended with her life; so the expression of them has greater steadi-

ness and greater clearness. I have never known any example of such steady progress from stage to stage of thought and of character. An inspirer of courage, the secret friend of all nobleness, the patient waiter for the realization of character, forgiver of injuries, gracefully waving aside folly, and elevating lowness,—in her presence all were apprised of their fettered estate and longed for liberation, of ugliness and longed for their beauty; of meanness and panted for grandeur.

Her growth is visible. All the persons whom we know have reached their height, or else their growth is so nearly at the same rate with ours, that it is imperceptible, but this child inspires always more faith in her. She rose before me at times into heroical and godlike regions, and I could remember no superior women, but thought of Ceres, Minerva, Proserpine, and the august ideal forms of the foreworld. She said that no man gave such invitation to her mind as to tempt her to full expression; that she felt a power to enrich her thought with such wealth and variety of embellishment as would, no doubt, be tedious to such as she conversed with. And there is no form that does not seem to wait her beck,—dramatic, lyric, epic, passionate, pictorial, humorous.

She has great sincerity, force, and fluency as a writer, yet her powers of speech throw her writing into the shade. What method, what exquisite judgment, as well as energy, in the selection of her words; what character and wisdom they convey! You cannot predict her opinion. She sympathizes so fast with all forms of life, that she talks never narrowly or hostilely, nor betrays, like all the rest, under a thin garb of new words, the old droning cast-iron opinions or notions of many years' standing. What richness of experience, what newness of dress, and fast as Olympus to her principle. And a silver eloquence, which inmost Polymnia[85] taught. Meantime, all this pathos of sentiment and riches of literature, and of invention, and this march of character threatening to arrive presently at the shores and plunge into the sea of Buddhism and mystic trances, consists with a boundless fun and drollery, with light satire, and the most entertaining conversation in America.

Her experience contains, I know, golden moments, which, if they could be fitly narrated, would stand equally beside any histories of magnanimity which the world contains; and whilst Dante's *Nuova Vita* is almost unique in the literature of Sentiment, I have called the imperfect record she gave me of two of her days, "Nuovissima Vita."

J 6:363–66 (cf. *JMN* 8:368–69).

Hawthorne

Emerson frequently refers to Hawthorne in his letters and journals, but more often to Hawthorne the man than the writer. As a friend, neighbor, and fellow writer, Hawthorne existed mainly as a personality and a companion, about whom, as Emerson remarked in 1843, he "never had a moment's regret or uneasiness" (L 3:198). In his journal description of Hawthorne's funeral, however, Emerson expressed his disappointment over Hawthorne's writings: "I thought him a greater man than any of his works betray, that there was still a great deal of work in him, and that he might one day show a purer power." That description, reprinted here, is Emerson's only extended commentary on Hawthorne, his life, and work. All other references to Hawthorne's writing are disappointingly brief and mainly negative. Hawthorne's "Footprints on the Seashore" (1838) has "no inside to it" (J 4:479; JMN 7:21). Hawthorne, along with Cooper, Sterling, and Dickens, cannot write dialogue (J 5:257; JMN 7:242). The most unqualified rejection came in 1842, when only Twice-Told Tales *had been published: "Nathaniel Hawthorne's reputation as a writer is a very pleasing fact, because his writing is not good for anything, and this is a tribute to the man" (J 6:240; JMN 7:465). On 27–28 September of the same year, Emerson and Hawthorne walked from Concord to the town of Harvard and back, twenty miles each way, to see the Shaker community. In his lengthy journal account (J 6:258–63; JMN 8:271–75) Emerson noted that "we were in excellent spirits, had much conversation." Yet neither he nor Hawthorne, whose entry is very brief (10 October 1842 in* American Notebooks*), hints at any exchange of views on literature. In this regard, the record of their relationship remains surprisingly fragmentary. In 1843 Emerson wrote that "friend and neighbour Mr. Hawthorne . . . is a better*

critic than he is a writer" (L 3:199). In "The Old Manse" (1846) Hawthorne
included two paragraphs on the queer visionaries and theorists who came to see
Emerson, "a great original thinker," adding that though he "admired Emerson as
a poet of deep beauty and austere tenderness, he sought nothing from him as a
philosopher." Many years later, in Emerson's "Life and Letters in New Eng-
land" (probably written in 1867), there are only the passing references to
Hawthorne's "cold yet gentle genius" and to The Blithedale Romance:
"Hawthorne drew some sketches, not happily, as I think; I should rather say,
quite unworthy of his genius. No friend who knew Margaret Fuller could
recognize her rich and brilliant genius under the dismal mask which the public
fancied was meant for her in that disagreeable story" (W 10:363-64). In his
address at the opening of the Concord Library (1873), Emerson merely mentioned
Hawthorne's "careful studies of Concord life and history." Years later still, Wil-
liam Dean Howells reported that The Marble Faun, *then being criticized for*
its indefinite ending, was pronounced "a mere mush" by Emerson. Although
Emerson is said to have liked "The Celestial Railroad," one must conclude that,
however incomplete the record of his responses to Hawthorne's works, apparently
he so disliked Hawthorne's dark view of human nature and tragic sense of
experience that he found almost nothing to praise, not even the art in Hawthorne's
fiction. But Hawthorne the man he did value unreservedly.

May 24, 1864

Yesterday, May 23, we buried Hawthorne in Sleepy Hollow, in a
pomp of sunshine and verdure, and gentle winds. James Freeman
Clarke read the service in the church and at the grave. Longfellow,
Lowell, Holmes, Agassiz, Hoar, Dwight, Whipple, Norton, Alcott,
Hillard, Fields, Judge Thomas, and I attended the hearse as pall-
bearers. Franklin Pierce was with the family. The church was co-
piously decorated with white flowers delicately arranged. The corpse
was unwillingly shown,—only a few moments to this company of his
friends. But it was noble and serene in its aspect,—nothing amiss,—a
calm and powerful head. A large company filled the church and the
grounds of the cemetery. All was so bright and quiet that pain or
mourning was hardly suggested, and Holmes said to me that it looked
like a happy meeting.

Clarke in the church said that Hawthorne had done more justice than any other to the shades of life, shown a sympathy with the crime in our nature, and, like Jesus, was the friend of sinners.

I thought there was a tragic element in the event, that might be more fully rendered,—in the painful solitude of the man, which, I suppose, could not longer be endured, and he died of it.

I have found in his death a surprise and disappointment. I thought him a greater man than any of his works betray, that there was still a great deal of work in him, and that he might one day show a purer power. Moreover, I have felt sure of him in his neighbourhood, and in his necessities of sympathy and intelligence,—that I could well wait his time,—his unwillingness and caprice,—and might one day conquer a friendship. It would have been a happiness, doubtless to both of us, to have come into habits of unreserved intercourse. It was easy to talk with him,—there were no barriers,—only, he said so little, that I talked too much, and stopped only because, as he gave no indications, I feared to exceed. He showed no egotism or self-assertion, rather a humility, and, at one time, a fear that he had written himself out. One day, when I found him on the top of his hill, in the woods, he paced back the path to his house, and said, *"This path is the only remembrance of me that will remain."* Now it appears that I waited too long.

Lately he had removed himself the more by the indignation his perverse politics and unfortunate friendship for that paltry Franklin Pierce awakened, though it rather moved pity for Hawthorne, and the assured belief that he would outlive it, and come right at last.

I have forgotten in what year [Sept. 27, 1842], but it was whilst he lived in the Manse, soon after his marriage, that I said to him, "I shall never see you in this hazardous way; we must take a long walk together. Will you go Harvard and visit the Shakers?"

He agreed, and we took a June day, and walked the twelve miles, got our dinner from the Brethren, slept at the Harvard Inn, and returned home by another road, the next day. It was a satisfactory tramp, and we had good talk on the way, of which I set down some record in my journal.

J 10:39–41.

Thoreau

In 1862, at the death of Thoreau, his early discovery and protégé, Emerson was called upon to give the funeral address. Widely available, this evaluation of Thoreau's life is represented here only by the pages on Thoreau's poetry, symbolic thinking, realistic use of paradox, and insight-sentences. Emerson's earlier mixed view of Thoreau's poetry (J 6:304–5; JMN 8:257) is restated more fully in this eulogy: despite their technical defects, the poems have a fine "spiritual perception," illustrated by two examples of hymning "the Cause of causes" (the organic Universal Spirit). In the poem "Sympathy" Emerson found the theme of tenderness under "that triple steel of stoicism" which characterized Thoreau's indirection, his mythic language. Also noteworthy was Thoreau's controlled use of paradox of statement. The address ends with a long series of mostly insight-sentences from Thoreau's then unpublished manuscripts. By 1844 Thoreau appeared to be one of "the other grand promisers" who failed to realize their potential,—for executive leadership, in Thoreau's case. The silence of Emerson in his journals and letters on Thoreau's long stay at Walden implies a lack of approval, although Thoreau wrote that Emerson "looked in upon me from time to time." Otherwise, Emerson was constant in his loyalty and support, as in his efforts to obtain a publisher for A Week, which in 1847 he praised as "admirable" and as "a book of extraordinary merit," in fact, of "many merits. It will be as attractive to lovers of nature, in every sense, that is, to naturalists, and to poets, as Isaak Walton. It will be attractive to scholars for its excellent literature, & to all thoughtful persons for its originality & profoundness. . . . It is really a book of the results of the studies of years" (L 3:377, 384). In a letter to Richard Bentley of London on 20 March 1854 Emerson recommended Walden for publication in England. And on 28 August, shortly after the first American edition appeared, he reported:

> *All American kind are delighted with 'Walden' as far as they have dared say. The little pond sinks in these very days as tremulous at its human fame. I do not know if the book has come to you yet;—but it is cheerful, sparkling, readable, with all kinds of merits, & rising sometimes to very great heights. We account Henry the undoubted King of all American lions" (L 4:459–60).*

In 1863, Emerson compared the vigor and concreteness of Thoreau's journal style with his own dependence on "a sleepy generality." In sum, if Thoreau failed to fulfill his promise of executive leadership, as a writer he earned Emerson's high praise for power of style and transcendental insight.

*   *   *

His poetry might be bad or good; he no doubt wanted a lyric facility and technical skill, but he had the source of poetry in his spiritual perception. He was a good reader and critic, and his judgment on poetry was to the ground of it. He could not be deceived as to the presence or absence of the poetic element in any composition, and his thirst for this made him negligent and perhaps scornful of superficial graces. He would pass by many delicate rhythms, but he would have detected every live stanza or lines in a volume and knew very well where to find an equal poetic charm in prose. He was so enamoured of the spiritual beauty that he held all actual written poems in very light esteem in the comparison. He admired Aeschylus and Pindar; but when some one was commending them, he said that Aeschylus and the Greeks, in describing Apollo and Orpheus, had given no song, or no good one. "They ought not to have moved trees, but to have chanted to the gods such a hymn as would have sung all their old ideas out of their heads, and new ones in." His own verses are often rude and defective. The gold does not yet run pure, is drossy and crude. The thyme and marjoram are not yet honey. But if he want lyric fineness and technical merits, if he have not the poetic temperament, he never lacks the causal thought, showing that his genius was better than his talent. He knew the worth of the Imagination for the uplifting and consolation of human life, and liked to throw every thought into a symbol. The fact you tell is of no value, but only the impression. For this reason his presence was poetic, always piqued the curiosity to know more deeply the secrets of his mind. He had many reserves, an unwillingness to exhibit to profane eyes what was still sacred in his own, and knew well how to throw a poetic veil over his experience. All readers of Walden will remember his mythical record of his disappointments:—

"I long ago lost a hound, a bay horse and a turtle-dove, and am still

on their trail. Many are the travellers I have spoken concerning them,
describing their tracks, and what calls they answered to. I have met
one or two who have heard the hound, and the tramp of the horse,
and even seen the dove disappear behind a cloud; and they seemed as
anxious to recover them as if they had lost them themselves."

His riddles were worth the reading, and I confide that if at any time
I do not understand the expression, it is yet just. Such was the wealth
of his truth that it was not worth his while to use words in vain. His
poem entitled "Sympathy" reveals the tenderness under that triple
steel of stoicism, and the intellectual subtility it could animate. His
classic poem on "Smoke" suggests Simonides,[86] but is better than any
poem of Simonides. His biography is in his verses. His habitual
thought makes all his poetry a hymn to the Cause of causes, the Spirit
which vivifies and controls his own:—

> "I hearing get, who had but ears,
>   And sight, who had but eyes before;
>   I moments live, who lived but years,
>   And truth discern, who knew but learning's lore."

And still more in these religious lines:—

> "Now chiefly is my natal hour,
>   And only now my prime of life;
>   I will not doubt the love untold,
>   Which not my worth nor want have bought,
>   Which wooed me young, and wooes me old,
>   And to this evening hath me brought."[87]

*   *   *

The habit of a realist to find things the reverse of their appearance
inclined him to put every statement in a paradox. A certain habit of
antagonism defaced his earlier writings,—a trick of rhetoric not quite
outgrown in his later, of substituting for the obvious word and
thought its diametrical opposite. He praised wild mountains and
winter forests for their domestic air, in snow and ice he would find
sultriness, and commended the wilderness for resembling Rome and
Paris. "It was so dry, that you might call it wet."

*   *   *

The axe was always destroying his forest. "Thank God," he said, "they cannot cut down the clouds!" "All kinds of figures are drawn on the blue ground with this fibrous white paint."

I subjoin a few sentences taken from his unpublished manuscripts, not only as records of his thought and feeling, but for their power of description and literary excellence—

"Some circumstantial evidence is very strong, as when you find a trout in the milk."

"The chub is a soft fish, and tastes like boiled brown paper salted."

"The youth gets together his materials to build a bridge to the moon, or, perchance, a palace or temple on the earth, and, at length the middle-aged man concludes to build a wood-shed with them."

"The locust z-ing."

"Devil's-needles zigzagging along the Nut-Meadow brook."

"Sugar is not so sweet to the palate as sound to the healthy ear."

"I put on some hemlock-boughs, and the rich salt crackling of their leaves was like mustard to the ear, the crackling of uncountable regiments. Dead trees love the fire."

"The bluebird carries the sky on his back."

"The tanager flies through the green foliage as if it would ignite the leaves."

"If I wish for a horse-hair for my compass-sight I must go to the stable; but the hair-bird, with her sharp eyes, goes to the road."

"Immortal water, alive even to the superficies."

"Fire is the most tolerable third party."

"Nature made ferns for pure leaves, to show what she could do in that line."

"No tree has so fair a bole and so handsome an instep as the beech."

"How did these beautiful rainbow-tints get into the shell of the fresh-water clam, buried in the mud at the bottom of our dark river?"

"Only he can be trusted with gifts who can present a face of bronze to expectations."

"I ask to be melted. You can only ask of the metals that they be tender to the fire that melts them. To nought else can they be tender."

"Hard are the times when the infant's shoes are second-foot."

"We are strictly confined to our men to whom we give liberty."

"Nothing is so much to be feared as fear. Atheism may comparatively be popular with God himself."

"Of what significance the things you can forget? A little thought is sexton to all the world."

"How can we expect a harvest of thought who have not had a seed-time of character?"

*   *   *

1863

In reading Henry Thoreau's journal, I am very sensible of the vigour of his constitution. That oaken strength which I noted whenever he walked, or worked, or surveyed wood-lots, the same unhesitating hand with which a field-labourer accosts a piece of work, which I should shun as a waste of strength, Henry shows in his literary task. He has muscle, and ventures on and performs feats which I am forced to decline. In reading him, I find the same thought, the same spirit that is in me, but he takes a step beyond, and illustrates by excellent images that which I should have conveyed in a sleepy generality. 'T is as if I went into a gymnasium, and saw youths leap, climb, and swing with a force unapproachable,—though their feats are only continuations of my initial grapplings and jumps.

Lectures and Biographical Sketches, W 10:474–77, 479, 482–84; first published in the *Atlantic Monthly*, August 1862; from funeral speech (1862). *J* 9:522.

Whitman

Like Thoreau, Whitman was one of Emerson's authentic discoveries. Considering the bold unconventionality of the 1855 Leaves of Grass, *Emerson's famous letter hailing that achievement is all the more remarkable. Astonished when Whitman printed his letter without permission, and questioned by friends for its unqualified approval of the* Leaves, *Emerson thereafter confined most of his comments on Whitman to his journals and letters. Yet, chiefly through Emerson's initiative, their friendship lasted until Emerson's death. The openness, intelligence, and magnanimity of this relationship has been documented by Carlos Baker and Alvin Rosenfeld.[88] In 1887 Whitman recalled that over the years there had been some dozen or twenty "meetings, talks, walks, etc." and that during the long discussion with Emerson on the Boston Common in 1861 Emerson's objections to certain passages in the "Children of Adam" poems were based solely on expediency, not morality—"He offered absolutely no spiritual argument against the book exactly as it stood." If Emerson had been uncomfortable with the form or content of the 1855* Leaves, *he would hardly have written his unqualified praise of its "wit and wisdom," "the courage of the treatment," and the "solid sense of the book." Two months later, however, he asked James Cabot whether he had seen "the American Poem," "the strange Whitman's poems . . . . He seems a Mirabeau of a man, with such insight & equal expression, but hurt by hard life & too animal experience" (L 4:530–31). These qualities—the Americanness, the power, and the seeming grossness—are to be emphasized also in his letter to Carlyle describing the 1855* Leaves *as "a nondescript monster which yet has terrible eyes & buffalo strength, & was indisputably American. . . . and wanted good morals."[89] In October 1857 these qualities are again implied in "Our wild Whitman, with real inspiration but choked by Titanic abdomen" (L 5:87). In 1859, "Whitman is our American master" of the vernacular ("Art and Criticism," W 12:285; see above, Part III). His 1863 journal recognized Whitman's epic achievement: "And one must thank Walt Whitman for service to American literature in the Appalachian enlargement of his outline and treatment," undoubtedly with reference to the third edition. In the same year, at Whitman's urgent request, Emerson addressed*

*almost identical letters of recommendation to William Henry Seward, secretary of
state, and to Salmon P. Chase, secretary of the treasury. With only the slightest
qualification, these letters strongly praise Whitman as poet, person, and patriot.
Here is no evidence that Emerson recanted his "greeting" of 1855. In the early
1870s Emerson is said to have complained of Whitman's "inventories" and the
lack of order and restraint in the poems. But, except for Whitman's article in the
Boston* Literary World *in 1880, their relationship was marked by mutual
respect and friendship, culminating in Whitman's visit with Emerson at Concord
in September 1881.*

Concord, Massachusetts
Jan. 10, 1863

Dear Sir,

Mr Walt Whitman, of New York, writes me, that he wishes to
obtain employment in the public service in Washington, & has made,
or is about making some application to yourself.

Permit me to say that he is known to me as a man of strong original
genius, combining, with marked eccentricities, great powers & valuable traits of character: a self-relying, large-hearted man, much
beloved by his friends; entirely patriotic & benevolent in his theory,
tastes, & practice.

If his writings are in certain points open to criticism, they yet show
extraordinary power, & are more deeply American, democratic, & in
the interest of political liberty, than those of any other poet. He is
indeed a child of the people, & their champion.[90]

A man of his talents & dispositions will quickly make himself
useful. And if the Government has work that he can do, I think it may
easily find, that it has called to its side more valuable aid than it
bargained for.

With great respect,
Your obedient servant,

R. W. EMERSON

Hon. William H. Seward.
Secretary of State.

Concord, Massachusetts

21 July 1855

Dear Sir,

I am not blind to the worth of the wonderful gift of "Leaves of Grass." I find it the most extraordinary piece of wit & wisdom that America has yet contributed. I am very happy in reading it, as great power makes us happy. It meets the demand I am always making of what seemed the sterile & stingy Nature, as if too much handiwork or too much lymph in the temperament were making our western wits fat & mean.

I give you joy of your free & brave thought. I have great joy in it. I find incomparable things said incomparably well, as they must be. I find the courage of *treatment*, which so delights us, & which large perception only can inspire.

I greet you at the beginning of a great career, which yet must have had a long foreground somewhere, for such a start. I rubbed my eyes a little to see if this sunbeam were no illusion; but the solid sense of the book is a sober certainty. It has the best merits, namely, of fortifying & encouraging.

I did not know until I, last night, saw the book advertised in a newspaper, that I could trust the name as real & available for a Post-office. I wish to see my benefactor, & have felt much like striking my tasks, & visiting New York to pay you my respects.

R. W. EMERSON

Mr Walter Whitman.

Concord

6 May 1856

Dear Carlyle,

*   *   *

One book, last summer, came out in New York, a nondescript monster which yet has terrible eyes & buffalo strength, & was indisputably American,—which I thought to send you; but the book throve so badly with the few to whom I showed it, & wanted good morals so much, that I never did. Yet I believe now again, I shall. It is called "Leaves of Grass,"—was written & printed by a journeyman printer in Brooklyn, N. Y. named Walter Whitman; and after you have looked into it, if you think, as you may, that it is only an auctioneer's inventory of a warehouse, you can light your pipe with it.

* * *

1863

Good out of evil. One must thank the genius of Brigham Young for the creation of Salt Lake City,—an inestimable hospitality to the Overland Emigrants, and an efficient example to all men in the vast desert, teaching how to subdue and turn it to a habitable garden. And one must thank Walt Whitman for service to American literature in the Appalachian enlargement of his outline and treatment.

Kenneth Walter Cameron, "Emerson's Recommendation of Whitman in 1863: The Remainder of the Evidence," *ESQ* 3 (Q2, 1956): 14. Horace Traubel, *With Walt Whitman in Camden*, vol. 4, ed. Sculley Bradley (Philadelphia: University of Pennsylvania Press, 1953), pp. 152–53. *CEC*, p. 509. *J* 9:540.

NOTES

1. Sir Henry Taylor (1800–1886), English poet and dramatist.

2. Thomas Wakeley (1795–1862), English surgeon, coroner, and medical reformer.

3. Thomas Moore (1779–1852), Irish poet and wit, author of *Lalla Rookh.*

4. Jane Porter (1776–1850), English novelist, author of *Thaddeus of Warsaw* and *The Scottish Chiefs*, et al.; Maria Edgeworth (1767–1849), British novelist, author of *Castle Rackrent* (see note 23 below).

5. Novel by Goethe, also discussed in Emerson's "Goethe."

6. Catherine Grace Frances Gore, née Moody (1799–1861), English novelist and dramatist; Robert P. Ward (1765–1846), author of *De Clifford; or, The Constant Man*, about which Emerson comments in *JMN* 8:92; *J* 6:69–70.

7. Novel by Benjamin Disraeli.

8. Mark Van Doren, ed., *The Portable Emerson* (New York: Viking Press, 1946), p. 14; Howard Mumford Jones, ed., *English Traits* (Cambridge, Mass.: Harvard University Press, 1966), pp. ix, xxiv.

9. In Mr. Emerson's notebook of 1878, appears this comment: "40 *per cent.* of the English people cannot write their names. One half of one *per cent.* of the Massachusetts people cannot, and these are probably Britons born. It is certain that more people speak English correctly in the United States than in Britain." [*W*]

10. The Scottish form of *kale*, a very hardy member of the cabbage family.

11. Scottish physicist (1781–1868) and biographer of Sir Isaac Newton. Brewster was himself a successful investigator in the field of optics, and a writer of distinction. [*W*]

12. Robert Hooke (1635–1703), the eminent mathematician and physicist who disputed with Newton the honor of the discovery of the law of gravitation; Robert Boyle (1626–91), the physical experimenter and learned writer sometimes called "the Christian philosopher"; Edmund Halley (1656–1742), the distinguished astronomer and mathematician, the friend of Newton, whose *Principia* he published at his own expense. [*W*]

13. Cf. Goldsmith's "Retaliation" (1774), describing Edmund Burke.

14. Robert Anderson (1750–1830), Scottish editor and biographer, who edited *The Works of the British Poets: With Prefaces, Biographical and Critical*, (13 vols., Edinburgh, 1792–95; vol. 14, 1807); Alexander Chalmers (1759–1834), who according to the *DNB* was the foremost anthologist of his time. Among the many volumes of literature he edited was a twenty-one-volume edition of English poets.

15. Robert Chester's *Loves Martyr; or, Rosalins Complaint* (1601) with its supplement, *Diverse Poeticall Essaies on . . . the "Turtle" and the "Phoenix,"* by Shakespeare, Jonson, et al.

16. *Willson*: Byron Forceythe Willson (1837–67), whose pro-Federal Civil War poems, in the *Louisville* (Ky.) *Journal*, were very popular, particularly "The Old Sargeant" (January 1863). A volume of his poems was published during his two-year stay in Cambridge, between 1864 and 1866. They were characterized by a "remarkable . . . tenderness of . . . sentiment." (*The National Cyclopaedia of American Biography*, v. 7). *H.H.*: Helen Hunt Jackson (1830–85), author of *Verses* (1870) and *Sonnets and Lyrics* (1886). *Another hand:* Sara H. Palfrey (1823–1914), under pseudonym of E. Foxton, author of fiction, including *Herman; or, Young Knighthood*, and verse. "Sir Pavon and St. Pavon" (1867) is a long eight-part ballad on a religious theme.

17. "The Nun's Priest's Tale," ll. B 4565–91 (VII 3375–4001). Six lines are omitted by Emerson.

18. *Specimens of Table Talk* (London, 1835), 2:101. [*EL*]

19. *The influence of Chaucer I have remarked. . . . French poetess.* See *W* 4: 197–98. Based on Thomas Warton, *The History of English Poetry*, ed. Richard Price (London, 1834), 1:128–31. Cf. Warton, 2:179–80, 292–304. [*EL*]

20. Hugo Grotius, or Huig de Groot, (1583–1645), Dutch statesman and jurist, author of *De Veritate Religionis Christianae* (1627).

21. Quoted in Vivian Hopkins, "Emerson and Bacon," *American Literature* 29 (1958): 418.

22. In modern French: *Que sais-je?*: What do I know?

23. Miss Edgeworth's stories for children are so little read in this generation that it may be well to say that Old Poz was a character who bore this nickname because he was positive of his knowledge on all topics. [*W*]

24. See the journal passage on Montaigne above under "Diction and Style."

25. *Brut:* first major poem in Middle English, ca. 1205, by Layamon.

26. Edmund Malone (1741–1812), celebrated Irish Shakespearean scholar.

27. *Lydgate and Caxton:* as pointed out in the *Works*, Emerson has confused his dates. John Lydgate (ca. 1370–ca. 1450) was a poet much younger than Chaucer, whose poems (as well as Chaucer's) were printed by William Caxton (ca. 1421–91), the first English printer.

Ovid and Statius are not main sources for Chaucer's *Troilus*; Statius is not mentioned as historian of the Trojan War in *The House of Fame*. Guido delle Colonne's Latin romance, *Historia Troiana* (ca. 1285), is actually a Latin translation of Benoît de Sainte-Maure's *Roman de Troie* (ca. 1165). Chaucer's *Troilus* is based principally on Boccaccio's *Il Filostrato*, which derives from Benoît de Sainte-Maure and Guido delle Colonne. Benoît in turn derives from Dares Phrygius and Dictys Cretensis.

Petrarch and Boccaccio were Italian writers of the fourteenth century, from whom Chaucer not only derived inspiration but also borrowed much material; the Provençal poets were troubadours who flourished from the eleventh century to the end of the thirteenth century in southern France and northern Italy. Guillaume de Lorris and Jean de Meun were the authors of the *Romaunt of the Rose*, written between 1236 and 1280. Lollius "of Urbine," Chaucer acknowledges as his Latin source for *Troilus and Criseyde*. Chaucer thought of Lollius as one of the chief authors of the Trojan War, but he apparently based this impression on a mistranslation of an ode of Horace. *The Lais of Marie* is a collection of short romances by Marie de France (late twelfth century). The source for the *Nun's Priest's Tale* is in the Renard cycle and possibly also in the *Fables* of Marie. John Gower (1330?–1408) was a poet friend of Chaucer's to whom *Troilus* was dedicated.

28. See note 20, above.

29. *Ferrex and Porrex:* Characters in *Gorboduc*, a tragedy written about 1561 by Norton and Sackville. *Gammer Gurton's Needle:* a comedy of the same period of uncertain authorship.

30. A few of the lesser-known persons in this passage are: Theodore Beza (1519–1605), French religious reformer; Isaac Casaubon (1599–1614), French theologian and scholar; Sir Henry Vane (1616–62), English Puritan statesman; Robert Francis Romulus, Saint Bellarmine (1542–1621), Jesuit cardinal and theologian, chief defender of Roman Catholicism in the sixteenth century; Charles Cotton (1630–87), English author and translator; John Pym (1584–1643), English politician; John Hales (1584–1656), English divine, the "Ever-Memorable"; Franciscus Vieta (1540–1603), French mathematician and privy councillor to Henry VI; Alberico Gentili (1552–1608), Italian writer on international law and politics, exiled as a heretic in 1580; Pietro Sarpi, or Fra Paolo, (1552–1623), Venetian professor of philosophy at the Servite monastery, excommunicated for his unorthodox views; Jacob Arminius (1560–1609), Dutch theologian.

31. A private theater in London purchased in 1608 by a group called The King's Men, which included Shakespeare. It eventually became the principal stage for their performances, along with the Globe Theatre at Southwark. Shakespeare shared the ownership of the Globe for seventeen years and the "housekeeping" of the Blackfriars for eight years.

32. That is, Plutarch considered as being "modern."

33. Nineteenth-century British editors and Shakespearean scholars.

34. All famous Shakespearean actors.

35. The room off-stage where Shakespearean actors awaited their next appearance on the stage.

36. *Cyclopaean:* cyclopean, mighty, awesome, having immortal proportions. *Phidian:* of the classical sculptor Phidias (fifth century B.C.), whose statue of Zeus was considered one of the seven wonders of the ancient world. *Ministers:* Cathedrals.

37. The priestess of Apollo's oracle at Delphi sat on a tripod above a fissure, from which arose gases which supposedly caused her to commune with the god; Emerson is thus referring to a conception of the artist as seer.

38. Alexander Dyce (1798–1869), Scottish critic who edited Shakespeare in 1857, and John Payne Collier (1789–1883), English journalist and Shakespearean author.

39. John Aubrey (1626–97) and Nicholas Rowe (1674–1718), antiquaries who collected anecdotes on Shakespeare's life.

40. Characters from Shakespeare's *Timon of Athens*, *Henry VI*, and *The Merchant of Venice*, respectively.

41. Francois Joseph Talma (1763–1826), French tragic actor.

42. Louis Jacques Mandé Daguerre (1789–1851), a painter who invented the daguerreotype, an early photographic process.

43. One of Emerson's short poems in "The Poet" in *Poems, W* 9:330.

44. *Defensio pro Populo Anglicano* (1651), Milton's reply to *Defensio Regia pro Carolo Primo* (1649) by Salmasius, or Claude de Saumaise, (1588–1653), a Dutch scholar.

45. William Robertson, author of *The History of Scotland* (1757); Henry Hallam, author of *Constitutional History of England* (1827).

46. Philip Melancthon (1497–1560), German scholar and important figure in the Reformation.

47. Pope, "The First Epistle of the Second Book of Horace Imitated," l. 102.

48. "Of Education," *The Prose Works of John Milton*, ed. Charles Symmons (London, 1806), 1:277; "An Apology for Smectymnuus," Symmons, 1:224. [*EL*]

49. Symmons, 1:268 [*EL*]

50. *Paradise Regained*, 4:361–62. [*EL*]

51. *The Advancement of Learning*, Book 2, *Works* (London, 1834), 1:90. [*EL*]

52. From "Burns," ll. 53–56, 109–12, by Fitz-Greene Halleck (1790–1867), American poet.

53. Cf. *J* 3:98–99 (*JMN* 4:165), 20 April 1833: "I have paid a last visit to the Capitoline Museum and Gallery. One visit is not enough, no, nor two, to learn the lesson. The Dying Gladiator is a most expressive statue, but it will always be indebted to the muse of Byron for fixing upon it forever his pathetic thought. Indeed Italy is Byron's debtor, and I think no one knows how fine a poet he is who has not seen the subjects of his verse, and so learned to appreciate the justness of his thought and at the same time their great superiority to other men's. I know well the great defects of *Childe Harold*."

54. James Hutchinson Stirling's *Jerrold, Tennyson and Macaulay with Other Critical Essays* (Edinburgh, 1868). The essay on Tennyson contains high praise of Shelley and Keats, who, Stirling says, form, with Tennyson, the richest of poetic triads—The Three Graces of English Literature (p. 53). [*L*]

55. "The Lotos-Eaters," ll. 3–4, first published in *Poems* in 1832.

56. Presumably "The Death of the Old Year."

57. "Forgetful of his promise to the king" is the first of five successive lines beginning with "Forgetful" in "The Marriage of Geraint" (ll. 50–54). Warwick's dying soliloquy is in *3 Henry VI*, (5.2.5–28). *JMN* 14:288 also includes the lines omitted from the *J* version (after "alive"): "And such a line occurs sometimes, as, 'You hardly know me yet' ["Merlin and Vivien," l. 353] Again C. objects, that he has taken this old legend, instead of a theme of today."

58. Presumably "The Holy Grail," one book of *The Idylls of the King* (1869). An editorial note in *J* states that "the date January 1, 1870, follows this paragraph, but it does not appear how much was the later writing." Because

"The Holy Grail" was not published until 1869, however, the 1870 date seems correct for the entire paragraph, although it appears in the journal for 1868.

59. Frank T. Thompson, "Emerson's Theory and Practice of Poetry," *PMLA* 43 (1928): 1174, 1184.

60. Edward Young, *The Complaint; or, Night Thoughts . . .*, 8:334–35.

61. Jean Louis De Lolme (1740?–1807), author of *The Constitution of England* (1771; English eds., 1793, 1807).

62. William Ellery Channing (1780–1842), American Unitarian divine and writer.

63. Victor Cousin (1792–1867), French philosopher.

64. The legendary cave on the island of Staffa, the Inner Hebrides, Scotland, where bands of professional soldiers, half hunters, half warriors, led by Finn MacCool, are said to have lived.

65. The two poems are "Indignation of a High-Minded Spaniard" (1810), and "Thought of a Briton on the Subjugation of Switzerland" (1807), which begins "Two Voices . . . ."

66. *Yarrow Revisited, and Other Poems* (1835).

67. *Uncollected Writings*, pp. 26–27.

68. The first draft has here "I love a Man." [*CEC*]

69. *Twelfth Night*, 2.3.125. [*CEC*]

70. Emerson had been reading Clarendon in August (see *J* 4:264). [*CEC*]

71. Richard Bentley (1662–1742), English critic and classical scholar.

72. Jakob Böhme (or Boehme) (1575–1624), German mystic; Paul de Rapin-Thoyras (1661–1725), French-born English historian.

73. *Biographia Literaria* (New York and Boston, 1834), pp. 86–89; *The Friend* (London, 1818), 3:81–83, 70–77. [*EL*]

74. Cf. *J* 3:529. See *Phaedrus*, 266. [*EL*]

75. The two items before the last refer to *Biographia Literaria*, the rest mainly to *The Friend*, though the last alludes also to *Church and State*. Reason and Understanding are much discussed in *Aids to Reflection*, but this volume, though Emerson certainly knew it, figures curiously little in these lectures. [*EL*]

76. Wordsworth, "The Recluse," quoted in the Preface to "The Excursion," ll. 46–47. [*EL*]

77. Cf. *J* 3:327. [*EL*]

78. Coleridge, *The Friend*, 3:265. [*EL*]

79. From a lecture, "Being and Seeming" [*sic*] (1838), *EL* 2:307.

80. *Lord of the Isles* (1815), *Marmion* (1808), *The Lay of the Last Minstrel* (1805), narrative poems by Scott.

81. *Waverley* (1814), Scott's first novel; *The Bride of Lammermoor* (1819).

82. Cervantes developed the Quixotic hero; Defoe, the resourceful man (Robinson Crusoe); Richardson, the virtuous but endangered maid (Pamela); Goldsmith, the ideal Christian pastoral vicar (the Vicar of Wakefield); Sterne, a man lacking moral vigor (Tristram Shandy); Fielding, the picaresque hero (Tom Jones).

83. A member of the principal class of solicitors in Scotland.

84. A group of distinguished, mostly Scottish, men of letters, philosophers, etc.

85. Polyhymnia, the Muse of the sacred lyric.

86. Simonides of Keos (556–468 B.C.), Greek lyric poet.

87. The lines quoted here are all from the poem "Inspiration" by Thoreau. *Journal, 1839.* "August 1. Last night came to me a beautiful poem from Henry Thoreau, 'Sympathy,'—the purest strain and the loftiest, I think, that has yet pealed from this unpoetic American forest. I hear his verses with as much triumph as I point to my Guido when they praise half poets and half painters." [*W*]

88. Carlos Baker, "The Road to Concord: Another Milestone in the Whitman–Emerson Friendship," *Princeton University Library Chronicle* 7 (1946): 100–117; Alvin Rosenfeld, "Emerson and Whitman" (Ph.D. diss., Brown University, 1967).

89. *CEC*, p. 509.

90. This sentence does not appear in the letter to Chase. Otherwise, the two letters differ only in minor respects—the phrasing of paragraph 1, the opening words of paragraph 2, and the complimentary close. There are also minor discrepancies in punctuation and paragraph indentation between the manuscripts and the texts printed by Baker and Cameron. The letter to Chase, now in the National Archives, was first published in the Washington *Daily News*, 9 May 1931.

Bibliography

Abel, Darrel, ed. *Critical Theory in the American Renaissance*. Hartford, Conn.: Transcendental Books, 1969.

Abrams, M. H. *The Mirror and the Lamp: Romantic Theory and the Critical Tradition*. New York: W. W. Norton & Company, 1958.

Adams, Richard P. "Emerson and the Organic Metaphor." *PMLA* 69 (1954): 117–30.

Adkins, Nelson F. "Emerson and the Bardic Tradition." *PMLA* 63 (1948): 662–77.

Anderson, John Q. *The Liberating Gods: Emerson on Poets and Poetry*. Coral Gables, Fla.: University of Miami Press, 1971.

Barton, William B. "Emerson's Method as a Philosopher." In *Emerson's Relevance Today*, edited by Eric W. Carlson and J. Lasley Dameron, pp. 20–28. Hartford, Conn.: Transcendental Books, 1971.

Beach, Joseph Warren "Emerson and Evolution." *University of Toronto Quarterly* 3 (1934): 474–97.

Benoit, Ray. "Emerson on Plato: The Fire's Center." *American Literature* 34 (1963): 487–98.

Bercovitch, Sacvan. *The Puritan Origins of the American Self*. New Haven, Conn., Yale University Press, 1975.

Berry, Edmund G. *Emerson's Plutarch*. Cambridge, Mass.: Harvard University Press, 1961.

Bishop, Jonathan. *Emerson on the Soul*. Cambridge, Mass.: Harvard University Press, 1964.

Blair, Walter, and Clarence Faust. "'Emerson's Literary Method." *Modern Philology* 42 (1944): 79–95.

Bloom, Harold. "The Central Man: Emerson, Whitman, Wallace Stevens." *Massachusetts Review* 7 (1966): 23–42.

_____. "Emerson: The Glory and the Sorrows of American Romanticism." *Virginia Quarterly Review* 47 (1971): 546–63. Reprinted as "Emerson: The Self-Reliance of American Romanticism," in *Figures of Capable Imagination*, pp. 46–64.

_____. *Figures of Capable Imagination*. New York: The Seabury Press, 1976. See pp. 46–64, 67–88, 123–49.

_____. "The Freshness of Transformation: Emerson's Dialectics of Influence." In *Emerson: Prophecy, Metamorphosis, and Influence: Selected Papers from the English Institute*, edited by David Levin, pp. 129–48. New York: Columbia University Press, 1975. Reprinted as "Emerson and Influence" in *A Map of Misreading*, pp. 160–76.

_____. *A Map of Misreading*. New York: Oxford University Press, 1975.

_____. *Poetry and Repression: Revisionism from Blake to Stevens*. New Haven, Conn.: Yale University Press, 1976.

_____. *The Ringers in the Tower: Studies in Romantic Tradition*. Chicago: University of Chicago Press, 1971. See pp. 291–321.

_____. *Wallace Stevens: The Poems of Our Climate*. Ithaca, N.Y.: Cornell University Press, 1977.

Buell, Lawrence. *Literary Transcendentalism: Style and Vision in the American Renaissance*. Ithaca, N.Y.: Cornell University Press, 1973.

Cameron, Kenneth Walter. "Emerson's Recommendation of Whitman in 1863: The Remainder of the Evidence." *ESQ* 3 (Q2, 1956): 14–20.

_____. *Emerson the Essayist: An Outline of His Philosophical Development through 1836*. 2 vols. Hartford, Conn.: Transcendental Books, 1945.

_____. *Young Emerson's Transcendental Vision: An Exposition of His World View with an Analysis of the Structure, Backgrounds, and Meaning of Nature (1836)*. *ESQ* 64, 65 (1971): 1–584. Issued as a separate volume. Hartford, Conn.: Transcendental Books, 1971.

Campbell, Harry M. "Emerson and Whitehead." *PMLA* 75 (1960): 577–82.

Carpenter, Frederick Ives. *Emerson and Asia*. Cambridge, Mass.: Harvard University Press, 1930.

_____. *Emerson Handbook*. New York: Hendricks House, 1953.

_____. "Points of Comparison between Emerson and William James." *New England Quarterly* 2 (1929): 458–74.

_____. "William James and Emerson." *American Literature* 11 (1939): 39–57.

Charvat, William. *The Origins of American Critical Thought, 1810–1835*. Philadelphia: University of Pennsylvania Press, 1936. Reprint. New York: Russell & Russell, 1968.

Christy, Arthur. *The Orient in American Transcendentalism: A Study of Emerson, Thoreau, and Alcott*. New York: Columbia University Press, 1932, 1960. Reprint. New York: Octagon Books, 1963.

Clark, Harry Hayden. "Changing Attitudes in Early American Literary Criticism: 1800–1840." In *The Development of American Literary Criticism*, edited by Floyd Stovall, pp. 15–73. Chapel Hill, N.C.: University of North Carolina Press (1955).

_____. "Emerson and Science." *Philological Quarterly* 10 (1931): 225–60.

Conner, Frederick W. *Cosmic Optimism: A Study of the Interpretation of Evolution by*

American Poets from Emerson to Robinson. Gainesville, Fla.: University of Florida Press, 1949. Reprint. New York: Octagon Books, 1973. See pages on "Emerson."

Dewey, John. "Ralph Waldo Emerson." In *Characters and Events*. Edited by Joseph Ratner. Vol. 1, pp. 69–77. New York: Henry Holt & Co., 1929.

Duncan, Jeffrey L. *The Power and Form of Emerson's Thought*. Charlottesville: University Press of Virginia, 1973.

Falk, Robert. "Emerson and Shakespeare." *PMLA* 56 (1941): 532–43.

Feidelson, Charles, Jr. *Symbolism and American Literature*. Chicago: University of Chicago Press, 1953. See chap. 4.

Flanagan, John T. "Emerson as a Critic of Fiction." *Philological Quarterly* 15 (1936): 30–45.

Foerster, Norman. *American Criticism*. Boston: Houghton Mifflin Co., 1928. See pp. 52–110.

Fogle, Richard H. "Organic Form in American Criticism: 1840–1870." In *The Development of American Literary Criticism*, edited by Floyd Stovall, pp. 75–111. Chapel Hill, N.C.: University of North Carolina Press, 1955.

Foster, Charles H. *Emerson's Theory of Poetry*. Iowa City, Iowa: Midland House, 1939.

Friedrich, Gerhard. "A Note on Emerson's *Parnassus*." *New England Quarterly* 27 (1954): 397–99.

Gelpi, Albert. "Emerson: The Paradox of Organic Form." In *Emerson: Prophecy, Metamorphosis, and Influence: Selected Papers from the English Institute*, edited by David Levin, pp. 149–70. New York: Columbia University Press, 1975.

―――――. *The Tenth Muse: The Psyche of the American Poet*. Cambridge, Mass.: Harvard University Press, 1975. See pp. 57–111.

Glick, Wendell. "The Moral and Ethical Dimensions of Emerson's Aesthetics." *ESQ* 55 (1969): 11–18.

Gohdes, Clarence L. "Whitman and Emerson." *Sewanee Review* 37 (1929): 79–93.

Greenleaf, Richard. "Emerson and Wordsworth." *Science and Society* 22 (1958): 218–30.

Hagboldt, Peter. "Emerson's Goethe." *Open Court* 46 (1932): 234–44.

Harding, Walter. *Emerson's Library*. Charlottesville: University Press of Virginia, 1967.

Harrison, John S. *The Teachers of Emerson*. New York: Sturgis & Walton Co., 1910.

Hopkins, Vivian C. "Emerson and Bacon." *American Literature* 29 (1958): 408–30.

―――――. "Emerson and Cudworth: Plastic Nature and Transcendental Art."

American Literature 23 (1951): 80–98.

—————. "The Influence of Goethe on Emerson's Aesthetic Theory." *Philological Quarterly* 27 (1948): 325–44.

—————. *Spires of Form: A Study of Emerson's Aesthetic Theory.* Cambridge, Mass.: Harvard University Press, 1951.

James, William. *Memories and Studies.* New York: Longmans, Green, & Co., 1911. See pp. 18–34.

Johnson, Ellwood. "Emerson's Psychology of Power." *Rendezvous* 5 (1970): 13–25.

Jordan, Elizabeth Leach. "The Fundamentals of Emerson's Literary Criticism." Ph.D. dissertation, University of Pennsylvania, 1945.

LaRosa, Ralph C. "Bacon and the 'Organic Method' of Emerson's Early Lectures." *ELN* 8 (1970): 107–14.

Liebman, Sheldon W. "The Development of Emerson's Theory of Rhetoric, 1821–1836." *American Literature* 41 (1969): 178–206.

—————. "Emerson's Discovery of the English Romantics, 1818–1836." *American Transcendental Quarterly* 21 (1974): 36–44.

MacRae, Donald. "Emerson and the Arts." *Art Bulletin* 20 (1938): 78–95.

Magat, Joan A. "Emerson's Aesthetics of Fiction." *ESQ* 23 (1977): 139–53.

Martin, Terence. *The Instructed Vision: Scottish Common Sense Philosophy and the Origins of American Fiction.* Bloomington: Indiana University Press, 1961.

Matthiessen, F. O. *American Renaissance: Art and Expression in the Age of Emerson and Whitman.* New York: Oxford University Press, 1941.

Metzger, Charles R. *Emerson and Greenough: Transcendental Pioneers of an American Esthetic.* Berkeley: University of California Press, 1954.

—————. "Emerson's Religious Conception of Beauty." *Journal of Aesthetics and Art Criticism* 11 (1952): 67–74.

Michaud, Régis, *L'Esthétique d'Emerson: l'art, la nature, l'histoire.* Paris: Félix Alcare, 1927.

Moore, John B. "The Master of Whitman." *Studies in Philology* 23 (1926): 77–89.

Morton, Doris. "Ralph Waldo Emerson and *The Dial*: A Study in Literary Criticism." *Emporia State Research Studies* 18, no. 2 (1969): 5–49.

Neufeldt, Leonard. "The Vital Mind: Emerson's Epistemology." *Philological Quarterly* 50 (1971): 253–70.

Obuchowski, Peter A. "Emerson's Science: An Analysis." *Philological Quarterly* 54 (1975): 624–32.

O'Daniel, Therman B. "Emerson as a Literary Critic." *College Language Association Journal* 8 (1964–65): 21–43; 157–89; 246–76.

Paris, Bernard J. "Emerson's 'Bacchus.'" *Modern Language Quarterly* 23 (1962): 150–59.

Paul, Sherman. *Emerson's Angle of Vision: Man and Nature in American Experience.* Cambridge, Mass.: Harvard University Press, 1952.

Pettigrew, Richard C. "Emerson and Milton." *American Literature* 3 (1931): 45–59.

Pochmann, Henry A. *German Culture in America: Philosophical and Literary Influences, 1600–1900.* Madison: University of Wisconsin Press, 1957. See pp. 153–207; 586–617.

Pollock, Robert C. "A Reappraisal of Emerson." *Thought* 32 (1957): 86–132.

Pritchard, John P. *Criticism in America.* Norman: University of Oklahoma Press, 1956. See pp. 43–56.

Reaver, J. Russell. *Emerson as Mythmaker.* Gainesville: University of Florida Press, 1954.

———. "Mythology in Emerson's Poems." *ESQ* 39 (1965): 56–63.

Roberts, J. Russell. "Emerson's Debt to the Seventeenth Century." *American Literature* 21 (1949): 305–8.

Quinn, Patrick F. "Emerson and Mysticism." *American Literature* 21 (1950): 397–414.

Scheick, William. *The Slender Human Word: Emerson's Artistry in Prose.* Knoxville: University of Tennessee Press, 1978.

Shaffer, Robert B. "Emerson and His Circle: Advocates of Functionalism." *Journal of Society of Architectural Historians* 7, no. 3-4 (1948): 17–20.

Steinbrink, Jeffrey. "Novels of Circumstance and Novels of Character: Emerson's View of Fiction." *ESQ* 20 (1974): 101–10.

Strauch, Carl Ferdinand. "Emerson's Adaptation of Myth in 'The Initial Love.'" *American Transcendental Quarterly* 25 (1975): 51–65.

———. "Emerson's Sacred Science," *PMLA* 73 (1958): 237–50.

———. "Emerson's Use of the Organic Method." In *Critical Theory in the American Renaissance*, edited by Darrel Abel, pp. 18–24. Hartford, Conn.: Transcendental Books, 1969.

Sutcliffe, Emerson Grant. *Emerson's Theories of Literary Expressions.* University of Illinois Studies in Language and Literature 8 (1923): 9–152.

Thompson, Frank T. "Emerson's Indebtedness to Coleridge." *Studies in Philology* 23 (1926): 55–76.

———. "Emerson's Theory and Practice of Poetry." *PMLA* 43 (1928): 1170–84.

Wagenknecht, Edward. *Ralph Waldo Emerson: Portrait of a Balanced Soul.* New York: Oxford University Press, 1974. See pp. 66–106, 260–67.

Waggoner, Hyatt H. *American Poets: From the Puritans to the Present.* New York: Dell Publishing Co., 1968.

———. *Emerson as Poet.* Princeton, N.J.: Princeton University Press, 1974.

Wellek, René. *A History of Modern Criticism, 1750–1950.* Vol. 3, *The Age of*

Transition. New Haven, Conn.: Yale University Press, 1965.

Whicher, Stephen Emerson. *Freedom and Fate: An Inner Life of Ralph Waldo Emerson.* Philadelphia: University of Pennsylvania Press, 1953.

Wynkoop, William M. *Three Children of the Universe: Emerson's View of Shakespeare, Bacon, and Milton.* The Hague: Mouton Publishing Co., 1966.

Young, Charles L. *Emerson's Montaigne.* New York: Macmillan Co., 1941.

Acknowledgments

I owe much to the expert assistance, technical and clerical, of several students—Esther Iwanga, Michael Dembrow, Sheila Gee, Alice Jacquemin, and Cynthia McGowan—in the preparation of the notes, although responsibility for them is, of course, mine. The staff of the Reference Department at the Wilbur Cross Library of the University of Connecticut has been of unfailing assistance. To my wife, Doris, I am greatly indebted for the typing of the final draft. In underwriting the costs of duplication and student labor, the University of Connecticut Research Foundation has been most generous over a longer period than anticipated. Finally, I wish to express my gratitude to Paul Olson, general editor of the Regents Critics Series for suggestions based on his close reading of the manuscript through the several stages to completion.

A number of publishers and persons have kindly granted permission for the use of copyrighted material. The following excerpts are reprinted by permission of the publishers from *The Early Lectures of Ralph Waldo Emerson*, vols. 1 and 3, edited by Stephen E. Whicher, Robert E. Spiller, and Wallace E. Williams, Cambridge, Mass.: The Belknap Press of Harvard University Press, © 1959 and 1972 by the President and Fellows of Harvard College: "Chaucer," 1:272–73, 274–76, 278, 283–85, 286, and notes 4, 7–9, 17, 28–29; "Lord Bacon," 1:333–35; "Modern Aspects of Letters," 1:372–74, 375–76, 377–80, and notes 1–3, 6–7, 8–11; "The Poet," 3:358–59 and notes 1–2. The Trustees of the Ralph Waldo Emerson Association and Columbia University Press permitted the reprinting of the excerpts from the letters to Carlyle from *The Correspondence of Emerson and Carlyle*, edited by Joseph Slater (New York: Columbia University Press, 1964), pp. 166–68, 509, and from the letter to J. H. Stirling from *The Letters of Ralph Waldo Emerson*, vol. 6, edited by Ralph L. Rusk (New York: Columbia University Press, 1939), p. 19 and note 71. The letter from

Emerson to Secretary of State Seward of 10 January 1863 is reprinted by permission of the Houghton Library, Harvard University; the Ralph Waldo Emerson Memorial Association; Charles E. Feinberg of Detroit; and Kenneth W. Cameron, who first reproduced this letter in manuscript and type in *ESQ* 3 (Q2, 1956), 14–20.

Index

Novum Organon (Bacon), 158

Ode on Immortality (Wordsworth), 149, 197, 198, 203
Ode to Duty (Wordsworth), 197, 199
Oliver Twist (Dickens), 210–11
Organic form. *See* Form, organic
Organic nature of creative thought, xxii, 62
"Oriental largeness," 141–42
Oriental writings, influence of, xvi–xvii
Originality, 163, 168, 169
Orphism, American, xi, xv
Othello (Shakespeare), 63

Palfrey, Sarah H., 50, 231 n. 16
Paradise Lost (Milton), xxxviii, 147, 182, 185, 186
Paradise Regained (Milton), 185
Parnassus (Emerson), 143
Perception, xxi
Perspective: individuated, xxiv–xxv, 111; modern critical, xxviii
Plato, xiv–xvi, xlvii n. 10, 51
Poems (1832) (Tennyson), 194
Poet(s), 26, 148, 163; American, xli, 143–44; as children of the fire, 25, 52 n. 25; dream power of, 43; as language-maker, 34; as liberating gods, 38–39; and nature, 44–45; in *Parnassus*, 143–44; as poet-priest, 179; as the Sayer, 26–27
Poetry, 38, 96–99; anthologies, 144; bardic, 73–74; craft of, 28, 96; epic, 98, 119; and experience, 176; form in, xxvii, 96–99; inspiration in, 70–76; music of, 98; nature and function of, 119; as perception, xxi; Persian, 78 n. 8; sound and sense in, 96–97; stock,

99; tone in, 97, 150. *See also* Form(s)
Polarity, xxiii, 73–77
Pope, Alexander, 140
Pragmatism, xiii–xiv
Prisci theologi, xv. *See also* Trismegisti
Process: beauty in, 48; philosophy and theology of, xiv–xvi, xlvii n. 8; reality as, 8, 9, 71
Proclus, quoted, 49, 53 n. 34
Prose. *See* Diction; Rhetoric; Style; Vernacular

Quentin Durward (Scott), 212

Raphael, *The Transfiguration* of, 21
Reason, 10, 71–72, 207. *See also* Soul
Reed, Sampson, xxiv
Reiser, Oliver, xv
Rhetoric, xxvi–xxviii, 83–84, 93–95. *See also* Diction; Style
Rhyme, 97–99
Rhythm, 96–98
Romantic, the, xxxii
Romantics, the English, xxxviii

Saadi, 45–46, 54 n. 61, quoted, 177
Samson Agonistes (Milton), 147, 185
Sand, George, 122
Sayer, the, xxxvii, 26–27
Scheick, William J., xlviii n. 18
Science, xvii, xix–xx, 12
Scott, Sir Walter, xli, 212–16
Seward, William Henry, 227–28
Seyd. *See* Saadi
Shakespeare, William, xxxvi–xxxvii, 146, 177; biographical facts on, 148, 172–74; influence of, 91, 170–171; as poet, 137, 146; 178; and popular tradition, 166–67; vernacular, use of, 90–91;